Crossing the Threshold

Etheric Imagination in the
Post-Kantian Process Philosophy
of Schelling and Whitehead

Crossing the Threshold

*Etheric Imagination in the
Post-Kantian Process
Philosophy
of
Schelling and Whitehead*

Matthew David Segall

Integral Imprint
Olympia, WA
2023

© 2023 Matthew David Segall

All rights reserved. No part of this publication may be reproduced or utilized in any form or by any means, electronic or mechanical, including photocopying, recording, or by any information storage and retrieval system, without permission in writing from the Publishers.

Publisher's Cataloging-in-Publication
(Provided by Cassidy Cataloguing Services, Inc.).
Names: Segall, Matthew David, author.
Title: Crossing the threshold : etheric imagination in the post-Kantian process philosophy of Schelling and Whitehead / Matthew David Segall.
Description: Olympia, WA : Integral Imprint, 2023. | Includes bibliographical references and index.
Identifiers: ISBN: 978-1-947544-48-2 (paperback) | 978-1-947544-49-9 (ebook)
Subjects: LCSH: Process philosophy. | Imagination (Philosophy) | Kant, Immanuel, 1724-1804. | Schelling, Friedrich Wilhelm Joseph von, 1775-1854. | Whitehead, Alfred North, 1861-1947. | Cosmogony--Philosophy. | Aesthetics. | Transcendentalism.
Classification: LCC: BD372 .S44 2023 | DDC: 146.7--dc23

Book and cover design by Jenn Zahrt.
Cover image by Nathan Anderson via Unsplash.
Printed globally on demand through IngramSpark

First printed in 2023 by INTEGRAL IMPRINT,
a REVELORE® imprint.

Integral Imprint/
Revelore Press
1910 4th Ave E PMB#141
Olympia, WA 98506

www.integralimprint.com
www.revelore.press

*To all the creatures who have been and who are yet to become.
May we continue to co-create eternally.*

Table of Contents

Preface • 11

*Prologue
Imagining Cosmos, Theos, and Anthropos in
Post-Kantian Process Philosophy • 13*

Chapter 1
Kant as Guardian of the Threshold of Imagination • 23
    1.1 Whitehead, Schelling, and the Aftermath
    of Kant • 30
    1.2 The Kantian Mode of Thought • 37
          1.2.1 Thinking • 39
          1.2.2 Desiring • 49
          1.2.3 Feeling • 53

Chapter 2
Inverting Kant:
From a Mechanistic to an Organic Cosmology • 63
    2.1 The Transmutation of Kant's "Refutation of
    Idealism": From Subject-Substance Correlation to
    Process-Relational Creativity • 80
    2.2 From Geometric Conditions of Possibility to
    Genetic Conditions of Actuality • 95

Chiasmus
Descendental Aesthetic in Schelling and Whitehead:
Crossing the Kantian Threshold • 104

Chapter 3
Descendental Philosophy and Aesthetic Ontology:
Reimagining the Kantian Mode of Thought • 125
    3.1 Aesthetic Ontology and Nietzsche's
    Encounter with Nihilism • 139

3.2 Aesthetic Ontology in Sallis'
Elemental Phenomenology • 162
3.3 Aesthetic Ontology in Deleuze's
Transcendental Empiricism • 165

Chapter 4
Etheric Imagination in Naturphilosophie:
Physics of the World-Soul • 177
    4.1 Traces of the Ether in Kant's
    Opus Postumum • 181
    4.2 Etheric Imagination in Schelling
    and Whitehead • 191
    4.3 Nature Philosophy as "Spiritual Sensation" • 200
    4.4 Etheric Imagination and Vegetal Metaphysics • 207

Epilogue
Incarnational Process Philosophy in the Worldly
Religion of Schelling, Whitehead, and Deleuze • 225

References • 248
Index • 259

All flesh is grass.

> —Isaiah 40:6

A child said *What is the grass?* fetching it to me with full hands;
How could I answer the child? I do not know what it is any more than he.

I guess it must be the flag of my disposition, out of hopeful green stuff woven.

Or I guess it is the handkerchief of the Lord,
A scented gift and remembrancer designedly dropt,
Bearing the owner's name someway in the corners, that we may see and remark, and say Whose?

Or I guess the grass is itself a child, the produced babe of the vegetation.

Or I guess it is a uniform hieroglyphic,
And it means, Sprouting alike in broad zones and narrow zones,
Growing among black as among white,
Kanuck, Tuckahoe, Congressman, Cuff, I give them the same, I receive them the same.

And now it seems to me the beautiful uncut hair of graves.
Tenderly will I use you, curling grass,
It may be you transpire from the breasts of young men,
It may be if I had known them I would have loved them,
It may be you are from old people, or from offspring taken soon out of their mothers' laps.
And here you are the mothers' laps.

This grass is very dark to be from the white heads of old mothers,
Darker than the colorless beards of old men,
Dark to come from under the faint red roofs of mouths.

O I perceive after all so many uttering tongues,
And I perceive they do not come from the roofs of mouths for nothing.

I wish I could translate the hints about the dead young men and women,
And the hints about old men and mothers, and the offspring taken soon out of their laps.

What do you think has become of the young and old men?
And what do you think has become of the women and
    children?

They are alive and well somewhere,
The smallest sprout shows there is really no death,
And if ever there was it led forward life, and does not wait at the
    end to arrest it,
And ceas'd the moment life appear'd.

All goes onward and outward, nothing collapses,
And to die is different from what any one supposed, and luckier.

 —Walt Whitman, "Song of Myself"[1]

But who are the grown-ups?

Don't ask me, she answered. That's a question for a neurotheologian.

Meaning what? he asked.

Meaning precisely what it says. Somebody who thinks about people in terms, simultaneously, of the Clear Light of the Void and the vegetative nervous system. The grown-ups are a mixture of Mind and physiology.

 —Aldous Huxley, *Island*[2]

The Gods of the earth and sea
Sought thro' Nature to find this tree;
But their search was all in vain:
There grows one in the Human brain.

 —William Blake, "Songs of Experience"[3]

---

1. Whitman, Leaves of Grass, 195–96.
2. Huxley, Island, 112.
3. Blake, The Portable William Blake, 113.

Preface

> Whitehead, like Schelling, believed...that reality is neither undiscoverable, nor discoverable by the intellect alone, but by the whole embodied being, senses, feeling, intellect and imagination.
> —Iain McGilchrist[1]

THIS BOOK RECORDS AN EXPERIMENT in thinking, feeling, and willing beyond the transcendental threshold of Immanuel Kant's critical philosophy, drawing inspiration from the organic process philosophies of F. W. J. Schelling and A. N. Whitehead. While much work remains to be done, the pages to follow at least initiate the effort to articulate a *descendental aesthetic ontology* that would show the way across the epistemological chasm that Kant's critiques hewed between knowledge and reality. While Kant's problematic scission between the phenomenal world and the thing-in-itself represents an important phase in the maturation of modern human consciousness, the present project presupposes that such a split does not represent the full realization of mind's potential in relation to Nature. I interpret Schelling and Whitehead's philosophy as a descendental inversion of Kantian transcendentalism that bridges the chasm—not by resolving the structure of reality into clear and distinct concepts—but by replanting cognition in the aesthetic processes that power it. Hidden at the generative root of the seemingly separate human capacities for theoretical reflection, corporeal sensation, and practical action is a universally distributed imaginal ether whose creative power expresses itself in star formation and blooming flowers no less than in human consciousness. Experiments presuppose theoretical abduction: the philosophical experiment to follow is engendered by the hermetic idea that the

---

1. McGilchrist, *The Matter With Things*, 576.

human mind is a microcosmic participant in the Life of the Whole, rather than a transcendental onlooker cut off from the world-process. Humanity is a development of what has always been enveloped in the Earth and wider cosmos, as natural as leaves on a tree.[2]

Through a creative appropriation of their imaginative methods, I outline how Schelling and Whitehead's process-relational philosophy can grant genuine experiential insight into *Cosmos*, *Theos*, and *Anthropos* in the aftermath of the Kantian revolution. The two—*Anthropos* and *Cosmos*—are perceived as one by a *common sense* described herein as *etheric imagination*. This etheric organ of perception puts us in touch with the divine life of Nature, a life the ancients personified as the ψυχὴ του κόσμου or *anima mundi*. The pages to follow do not lay out a linear argument attempting to prove the existence of a world-soul or the possibility of supersensory knowledge. Rather, they invite the reader into a series of self-amplifying metaphysical experiments seeking to produce intensified experience of this etheric intuition.

Without the intellectual mentorship of Jake Sherman, Sean Kelly, Frederick Amrine, Brian Swimme, Robert McDermott, Eric Weiss, Steven Goodman, Elizabeth Allison, and Rick Tarnas, this book, originally my dissertation thesis, could not have been written. Thanks to each of them, and also to the entire community of graduate students and alumni of the Philosophy, Cosmology, and Consciousness Program at California Institute of Integral Studies for the conversations that helped spark many of the ideas expressed herein.

---

2. See Alan Watts, *The Book*, 9:
The feeling of being lonely and very temporary visitors in the universe is in flat contradiction to everything known about man (and all other living organisms) in the sciences. We do not "come into" this world; we come *out* of it, as leaves from a tree. As the ocean "waves," the universe "peoples." Every individual is an expression of the whole realm of nature, a unique action of the total universe.

Prologue
Imagining Cosmos, Theos, and Anthropos in
Post-Kantian Process Philosophy

The Cosmotheandric vision is the most obvious human experience, so obvious that it becomes an obstacle to see it once we begin to specialize in our knowledge and forget the whole. ... The vision of primordial Man, and I suspect our first vision as children as well, is an undiscriminated view of the whole. To see parts as parts presupposes already the view of a certain totality of which the parts are parts. One of the most common data of which humanity is aware is not the notion of Being but the experience of Life. We experience ourselves as living, and we see life everywhere. Reality is not a dead thing.

—Raimon Panikkar[1]

Whenever the light of that revelation faded and humans knew things not from the All, but from other things, not from their unity but from their separation, and in the same fashion wanted to conceive themselves in isolation and segregation from the All, you see science desolated amid broad spaces. With great effort, a small amount of progress is made, grain of sand by grain of sand, in constructing the universe. You see at the same time the beauty of life disappear, and the diffusion of a wild war of opinions about the primary and most important things, as everything falls apart into isolated details.

—Friedrich Wilhelm Joseph von Schelling[2]

There is a unity in the universe, enjoying value and (by its immanence) sharing value. For example, take the subtle beauty of a flower in some isolated glade of a primeval forest. No animal has ever had the subtlety of experience to enjoy its full beauty. And yet this beauty is a grand fact in the universe. When we survey nature and think however flitting and superficial has been the animal enjoyment of its wonders, and when we realize how incapable the separate cells and pulsations of each flower are of enjoying the total effect—then our sense of the value of the details for the totality dawns upon our consciousness. That is the intuition of holiness, the intuition of the sacred, which is at the foundation of all religion.

—Alfred North Whitehead[3]

---

1. Panikkar, *The Rhythm of Being*, 267.
2. Schelling, *Werke*, 1/7, 140; excerpted and translated by Wirth, *Schelling's Practice of the Wild*, 149.
3. Whitehead, *Modes of Thought*, 119–20.

THIS BOOK IS INSPIRED BY PANIKKAR'S *cosmotheanthropic vision*, the mysterious intuition that, hidden in the trinitarian entanglement of the human, the universe, and the divine lies an "open secret" giving integral meaning to the experience of all Life. While Pannikar tends to use the term "cosmotheandric," I have chosen a gender-neutral version (replacing *aner* with *anthropos*).[4]

In his Gifford Lectures, published as *The Rhythm of Being* (2010), Panikkar employs the term Life in the widest and deepest possible sense, such that it is understood to belong not only to plants and animals, but to living Nature, to *physis*, as a whole.[5] He then connects the cosmotheanthropic experience pervading the Life of all beings to the common ancient belief in the *anima mundi*, or soul of the world. Panikkar laments the rise of technocratic civilization's anemic view of Nature as merely the sum total of mechanically interacting material surfaces, a view that snuffs out all intuitions of the deeper Life animating the whole.[6] As Schelling describes it, all modern philosophy, beginning with the mechanistic nature philosophy of Descartes, "has the common defect that nature is not available for it and that it lacks a living ground."[7] Like

---

4. Thanks to Richard Tarnas, in conversation with whom I decided to borrow his alternative neologism, as well as the phrase "cosmotheanthropic imagination" itself (personal communications, May 4, 2015 and March 5, 2016). I later discovered, with Tarnas' assistance, that other scholars independently arrived at this neologism. See for example *Rhythms of Life* (2008) by Frédérique Apffel-Marglin, where she chooses "cosmotheanthropic" over Panikkar's original word for the same reason (28). See also James Kelley's *Anatomyzing Divinity* (2011), wherein he suggests that the "cosmo-theanthropic" analogy is the core of all Western esotericism and refers to the "dynamic glue which holds world, [hu]man, and God together through its common motion." He speculates further that, according to this trinitarian analogy, "*there is not a single thing in the world or above it that stands outside of the grand mystico-temporal process that yokes God, [hu]man, and cosmos together in the common quest for cosmo-theanthropic self-realization*" (71, italics in original).
5. Panikkar, *The Rhythm of Being*, 271.
6. Panikkar, *The Rhythm of Being*, 269.
7. Schelling, *Human Freedom*, 26.

Panikkar, Schelling and Whitehead see God as intrinsically bound up with the life of Nature and of humanity. All of Schelling's work records his struggle to articulate the conceptual consequences of the experiential fact that "God is not a God of the dead, but of the living."[8] He rejects in kind the modern beliefs in a mechanistic universe, a lonely, accidental, and peripheral human species, and a non-existent God (or at best a belief in God as "a transcendent engineer on sabbatical leave," as Panikkar puts it).[9] For Schelling, human consciousness is the seed-form or latent power of divine imagination otherwise unconsciously active throughout cosmogenesis. It is our human calling, says Schelling, to make this imagination conscious so that, through us, God can freely love Creation.[10] In Panikkar's triadic vision of the whole, these three experiential principles (Creation, Creator, and Creature) are affirmed as mutually entwined realities, independent and interdependent at once.[11] As for Whitehead, his process theology resonates profoundly with Panikkar's cosmotheanthropic vision in that both insist upon the incarnational and cosmically-indwelling nature of divine reality. God is not, in Whitehead's vision, the transcendent architect of all things human and cosmic, but a co-creator subject to Creativity like every other creature.

Instead of approaching Schelling and Whitehead's ideas as a museum curator or historian of philosophy, the chapters to follow record my attempt to *think with* them in the present, as though we were friends engaged in dialogue. As Whitehead put it in the preface to his historical and metaphysical study *Science and the Modern World*, I am attempting "a sympathetic study of [their] main ideas as seen from the inside."[12] In the course of the dialogue, I draw upon the speculative resources

---

8. Schelling, *Human Freedom*, 18.
9. Panikkar, *Christophany*, 162.
10. Schelling, *Human Freedom*, 32.
11. Panikkar, *The Rhythm of Being*, 278.
12. Whitehead, *Science and the Modern World*, viii.

of the process-relational imagination to all but alloy their already resonant metaphysical intuitions into a post-Kantian cosmotheanthropic process philosophy. I make the case that, when imaginatively integrated, the process philosophies of Schelling and Whitehead provide a viable path forward for cosmology, theology, and anthropology in the aftermath of Kant's critical philosophy. Kant argued that the origin of the cosmos, the immortality of the soul, and the reality of a divine being were ideas beyond the reach of our merely discursive type of understanding.[13] I aim to show that genuine knowledge of such ideas—or better, experiential participation in their reality—is possible if only contemporary philosophy is willing to reignite the power of imagination lying dormant at its heart.

Imagination has always possessed a somewhat ambiguous and liminal status within the corpus of Western philosophy. Alexander Schlutz summarizes the situation well:

> From the beginning of its philosophical conceptualization, imagination is situated at—or rather constitutes itself as—the decisive interface between the "outer" and "inner" world, the realm of objects and sense-perceptions on the one hand, and the realm of (self)consciousness and intellect on the other.... Due to this position, assessments of imagination's values and merits, promises and threats, vary considerably.... Oscillating between mind and body, self and world, the ideal and the real, the human and the divine, imagination is a highly ambiguous term with considerable discursive charge that consistently leads directly to the heart of an ongoing philosophical debate.[14]

The pages to follow record my explicit engagement, despite the risks, with precisely this imaginal interface between our

---

13. As Panikkar describes them, "the 'World, the Soul, and God' are the three 'realities' off-limits to the kantian 'pure reason'" (*The Rhythm of Being*, 34).
14. Schlutz, *Mind's World*, 5–6.

inner and outer aesthesis of reality. For many philosophers in the Western tradition, imagination's ineffable, unruly, and erotic powers are considered deeply suspect both for epistemological and for ethical reasons. This is the case even when imagination plays a central part in a philosopher's own system. For example, while Descartes explicitly denies imagination any involvement in the intellect's construction of the Cogito, he implicitly admits that *doubt*, the foundation of his new rational epistemology, is ultimately an act of imagination.[15] Kant is similarly forced to ambiguously acknowledge that imagination is a "blind though indispensable function of the human soul"—blind because we are rarely if ever conscious of the bulk of its activity, and yet indispensable because *we could not be conscious without it*.[16]

This book records my attempt to cross the threshold of the Kantian transcendental imagination by descending into the depths of the sensible. I descend with the help of Schelling and Whitehead's process-oriented categories, ultimately arguing that their descendental philosophy is rooted in the cultivation of a new organ of cognitive perception (or intellectual intuition) called *etheric imagination*. I claim that this new organ can bring philosophy into epistemic resonance with an aesthetic ontology of organism (something Kant explicitly denied). Once this etheric organ of perceptual cognition has flowered, the material world of isolated objects in empty space apprehended by the reflective ego is revealed to be merely the outer layer or dead husk (*Natura naturata*) of a living process that creatively produces and reproduces itself from the inside out (*Natura naturans*).

The aesthetic ontology I distill from Schelling and Whitehead is neither a continuation of Kant's transcendentalism, nor a simple empiricist reaction against it. As Deleuze reminds us, theirs is a deeper and more radical empiricism, which

---

15. Descartes, *Discourse on Method*, 32, 167. See also Schlutz, *Mind's World*, 4, 77.
16. Kant, *Critique of Pure Reason*, 211.

is by no means a reaction against concepts, nor a simple appeal to lived experience . . . . On the contrary, it undertakes the most insane creation of concepts ever seen or heard. Empiricism is a mysticism and a mathematicism of concepts, but precisely one which treats the concept as an object of encounter . . . . Only an empiricist could say concepts are indeed things, but things in their free and wild state beyond "anthropological predicates."[17]

Deleuze plays a special role in this book. He both presents a post-structuralist challenge to the cosmotheanthropic vision of Schelling and Whitehead, and at the same time he is one of the most powerful inheritors of many of their deepest insights. I follow Deleuze in construing the work of philosophical writing as part detective novel, part science fiction.

As detective novel, this book investigates imagination as perhaps the most profound mystery in the history of philosophy. Imagination's pro-fundity, or groundlessness, unsettled even the Western tradition's most sober philosophers. Orthodox modern philosophers have tended to restrain the otherwise unruly force of imagination so as to prevent it from clouding their measured pursuit of clear and distinct truths. This book treats the history of modern philosophy as a crime scene. In effect, modern philosophy since Descartes is guilty of *imagicide*. The philosophical murder of imagination has left modern philosophy in an impossible situation: if mind is entirely separate from Nature,[18] if I am absolutely independent of what is not-I, how can the philosopher pretend to love Wisdom? "Wisdom, of which philosophy professes to be the love," Iain Mcgilchrist reminds us, "cannot exist without the capacity to feel one's way *into* what one wishes to understand." Further, how can natural philosophers understand the Life

---

17. Deleuze, *Difference and Repetition*, xx.
18. I capitalize Nature throughout this book to signal that it is not simply the dead "nature" or abstract object thought to be studied by natural scientists. Nature is alive, as much subject as object.

animating things themselves? If no synthesis can be woven between the ideal web of concepts "in here" and our percepts of real things "out there"—if the blood clot preventing the concrescence of thought and sense cannot be dissolved—then there is no Love, no Wisdom, and no Life to be had. "Imagination," Mcgilchrist continues,

> far from deceiving us, is the only means whereby we experience reality: it is the place where our individual creative consciousness meets the creative cosmos as a whole. ... It is not a means of placing something else between us and the world, but of removing the accretions that prevent us from that world's fuller realization. To see is not just to register sense-data, but to see "into" the life of what is seen; and "through" it to the greater picture that lies beyond it, is implicit in it, and makes sense of it in terms of the totality of experience.[19]

As science fiction, this book involves an investigation into the metaphysical significance of the *etheric* character of Nature. Framing my investigation are Rudolf Steiner's esoteric ether of formative forces, Schelling's polarized ether of universal organization, and Whitehead's topological ether of creative events. These ether theories are not "scientific" in the standard sense of being rooted in some experimental protocol. Fortunately, making concepts scientifically operational is not the philosopher's role. The philosopher, according to Whitehead, is the "critic of cosmologies." Philosophy's business, he continues, "is to render explicit, and—so as may be—efficient, a process which otherwise is unconsciously performed without rational test."[20] The ether theory that is developed herein with help from Schelling, Steiner, and Whitehead is not meant to compete with the evidence of natural science, but to philosophically re-interpret the scientific evidence already

---

19. McGilchrist, *The Matter With Things*, 773–74.
20. Whitehead, *Science and the Modern World*, vii.

available. The concept of an etheric life in Nature is not a hypothesis concerning a supposedly mind-independent material world that might be experimentally falsified. It is, rather, the *descendental condition for any scientific knowledge of Nature at all*—a condition of *actual*, not merely possible experience.[21]

A chapter-by-chapter map of the metaphysical experiments to follow: In the first chapter, I unpack Kant's transcendental philosophy, examining in particular his critiques of our human capacities for thinking, desiring, and feeling. This chapter thus dwells upon the anthropological dimension of Panikkar's threefold vision of reality. I argue that Kant artificially divides these capacities and show how each is necessarily implicated in the activity of the others. Chapter 2 engages with Kant's attempted refutation of idealism and lays the metaphysical groundwork for an organic, non-metrical, and etheric alternative to his still basically Newtonian-Euclidian vision of Nature. In the pivotal chiasmatic section, I delve into our aesthetic encounter with the depths of cosmogenesis and argue that a descendental revisioning of Kant's Transcendental Aesthetic allows philosophy to step through the Kantian threshold so as to resurrect the ancient notion of a world-soul in a contemporary naturalistic context. The third chapter brings Schelling and Whitehead into conversation with several streams of post-Kantian and post-modern philosophy, including Friedrich Nietzsche, John Sallis, and Deleuze, in an effort to show how a descendental approach avoids many of the usual criticisms of traditional metaphysics. The fourth chapter begins by tracing the tentative emergence of an ether theory in an aging Kant's *Opus Postumum*. I then amplify the

---

21. Here I follow Deleuze's reversal of Kant in *Difference and Repetition* (285). It should be noted, however, that in his *Opus Postumum* Kant sketched his own ether theory to account for the supposedly supersensible ground unifying thought and sense, a ground he had first speculated upon a decade earlier in the *Critique of Judgment*. This underdeveloped aspect of Kant's late work is unpacked in the first section of Chapter 4.

ether's cosmotheanthropic potential by turning to Schelling and Whitehead's more developed scientific and religious elaborations on the same theme. Rather than viewing Nature as either a lifeless machine or a full-blooded animal, an etheric cosmology allows us to imagine the universe as a plant. I thus draw the fourth chapter to a close by making the case that Schelling and Whitehead's etheric reimagination of Nature finds its conceptual roots in a *vegetal* ontology. Finally, in the epilogue, I attempt to liturgize Schelling and Whitehead's etheric conception of Nature by comparing their philosophical religion to Deleuze's call for an immanent form of spiritual practice motivated by worldly renewal rather than escape to a personal afterlife. Whereas Kant ties the possibility of meaningful human life to the immortality of the individual soul, I seek out new sources of meaning in the co-creativity of a divinely inhabited world.

To bring this introduction to a close, I invite the reader to engage the chapters that follow with Panikkar's words in your heart and mind:

> The destiny of the universe passes in and through us—once the us, of course, has been purified of all that is "our" private property. We are not isolated beings. Man [*sic*] bears the burden, the responsibility, but also the joy and the beauty of the universe.

We human beings, like all beings, are bound up with the eternally verdant divine imagination that gives dynamic form both to the whole and to the microcosmic parts of reality. The task of becoming a conscious participant in the work of this divine creative power is not only an intellectual or theoretical one. It has moral and aesthetic dimensions, as well. "This implies," continues Panikkar,

> that thinking is much more than just concocting thoughts. Thinking discovers the real, and by this uncovering we shape reality by participation in its rhythm, by "listening"

to it, and by being obedient (ob-audire) to it. Creative thinking is a genuine creation, a contribution to cosmogony, but in order that our contemplation have this resonance and power, we need to be free from both preconceived ideas (inertia of the mind) and egoistic will. A traditional name for this is sanctity; a more academic name, wisdom. The strongest formulation is perhaps that of the Beatitudes: the pure in heart shall see God,[22] that is, the entire reality.[23]

---

22. Matthew, 5:8.
23. Panikkar, *The Rhythm of Being*, 35–36.

1

Kant as Guardian of the Threshold of Imagination

> For the hurt eye an instant cure you find;
> Then why neglect, for years, the sickening mind?
> Dare to be wise; begin; for, once begun,
> Your task is easy; half the work is done:
> And sure the man, who has it in his power
> To practice virtue, and protracts the hour,
> Waits, like the rustic, till the river dried;
> Still glides the river, and will ever glide.
> —Horace[1]

> "When all criticisms have been made, it seems to me that Kant's failures are more important than most men's successes."
> —C. D. Broad[2]

THIS CHAPTER SKETCHES THE MAIN TENETS of Kant's transcendental philosophy. I do so in the context of the wider thesis of this book, that upon close inspection a conceptual harmony between Whitehead's and Schelling's at first glance dissonant philosophical commitments is detectable, and that their process-relational and "aesthetically-oriented cosmology"[3] provides a realistic response to Kant's transcendental critiques. My aim is to show that an integration of Whitehead's and Schelling's approaches allows for the imaginative reconstruction of speculative philosophy as

---

1. Horace, *The Epistles*, 15 (lines 55–62). Kant excerpts these lines in the preface of his *Prolegomena to Any Future Metaphysics*.
2. Broad, *Ethical Theory*, 11.
3. Lucas, *Whitehead*, 87.

a source of genuine insight into cosmos, theos, and anthropos in the aftermath of the Kantian revolution.

In the context of my thesis on the role of imagination in process philosophy, Kant serves as the guardian of the threshold: his philosophy pushes the human mind to the outer and inner edges of its incarnate experience. I borrow the phrase "guardian of the threshold" from Rudolf Steiner, who describes the experience of encountering the experiential edges of our incarnation as a complete melting away of the habitual threads binding together our thinking, feeling, and willing capacities. "Step not across my Threshold," Steiner has the guardian say,

> until thou dost clearly realize that thou wilt thyself illumine the darkness ahead of thee; take not a single step forward until thou art positive that thou hast sufficient oil in thine own lamp. The lamps of the guides whom thou hast hitherto followed will now no longer be available to thee.[4]

Kant stands along the pathway of wisdom, straddling the unstable bridge separating the shoreline of the sensible (i.e., the physical) from the intelligible (i.e., the metaphysical) realm. "These two territories," Kant tells us,

> do not immediately come into contact; and hence, one cannot cross from one to the other simply by putting one foot in front of the other. Rather, there exists a gulf between the two, over which philosophy must build a bridge in order to reach the opposite bank.[5]

The bridge is unstable because the design for its construction remains a matter of unending controversy. Ever since Plato drew his famous line in the sand dividing empirically based

---

4. Steiner, *Higher Worlds*, ix.
5. Kant, *Opus Postumum*, 39.

Chapter 1: Kant as Guardian of the Threshold of Imagination

opinion from true knowledge,[6] this bridge has doubled as a metaphysical battlefield upon which numerous philosophical architects have vied for the rights to its proper plan. Kant warns all who would dare to complete the bridge and venture across the abyssal gulf beneath it of the metaphysical dangers that await. Despite the perils of crossing the threshold, Kant also denies us the comfort of maintaining our present footing.[7] His transcendental philosophy calls the very ground of our understanding of the world into question. Kant captures his readers in this catch-22 with the first sentence of the Preface to his *Critique of Pure Reason*:

> Human reason has the peculiar fate . . . that it is burdened with questions which it cannot dismiss, since they are given to it as problems by the nature of reason itself, but which it also cannot answer, since they transcend every capacity of human reason.[8]

There can be no turning back from this nadir of the philosophic quest: once the threshold of sense-bound understanding has been encountered and defined as such, the mind turns back upon itself, there glimpsing a light and feeling a warmth whose source remains obscure. Turning to face the world again, the mind's certainty of things sensory is henceforth shattered. A metanoia occurs: the mind becomes a hopeless heliotrope, a desperate wanderer, dizzily spiraling around an inner Sun whose brightness veils its being. But here the ancient love of wisdom grew too fast for its means, as though through the fog bank hovering over the darkness of the gulf it thought it could dimly apprehend divine ideas waiting to be seized at will. It is like the "ancient legend" Schelling refers to

---

6. *Republic*, 509d–511e. All references to Plato are from *Complete Works*, edited by Cooper.
7. Kant, *Prolegomena*, 5.
8. Kant, *Critique of Pure Reason*, 99.

in Homer's epic poem *The Odyssey*, wherein "the irresistible song of the sirens reverberates from the depths in order to drag the passing sailor into the maelstrom."[9] Kant mocks the ancient philosophers who proudly ventured out upon "the broad and stormy ocean" of metaphysics only to find themselves "ceaselessly [deceived]" and "[entwined] in adventures from which [they could] never escape and yet also never bring to an end."[10] Kant accepts that metaphysical speculation is as necessary to a philosophic life as the physiological activities of breathing and eating are for the life of the body. But he demands of us that we become enlightened moderns, that we give up the easy ideas thought by ancient schoolmen and dare instead to *think for ourselves*. He commands us to think freely, but also reminds us that, should our thinking venture beyond itself in an attempt to produce knowledge of the world, the human soul, or God, it will soon find itself entangled in contradictions, perplexed by unceasing questions, and frustrated by its inability to discover the logical errors that have led it astray. We leap for the other side as the bridge sways wildly and crumbles beneath our feet. Even as our eyes remain transfixed by the hint of numinous glories hidden just out of sight, our body falls into the abyss, and with it our claim to higher knowledge is dissolved in an ocean of ignorance. If we avoid drowning on our first go, human nature demands of us that we try again.

It is sometimes suggested that Kant sought to put an end to metaphysics, that he understood his critical project as an effort to lay bare the futility of building a bridge toward real theological, cosmological, and psychological knowledge. It is true that in his *Critiques* he denied outright the possibility of what can be variously described as supersensible knowledge, intellectual intuition, or intuitive understanding of things-in-themselves. As Deleuze writes:

9. Schelling, *Human Freedom*, 47.
10. Kant, *Critique of Pure Reason*, 339.

Chapter 1: Kant as Guardian of the Threshold of Imagination

> Kant exposes the speculative illusions of Reason, the false problems into which it leads us concerning the soul, the world and God.... These illusions are said to be inevitable.... All Critique can do is to exorcise the effects of illusion on knowledge itself, but it cannot prevent its formation in the faculty of knowledge.[11]

Indeed, because Kant felt firsthand the human mind's intense desire, even *need*, for such knowledge, rather than reject metaphysics outright, he heralded *and himself helped to initiate* the rebirth of a new kind of metaphysics, this time from the womb of a mother more conscious of her own creative capacity.[12] Unbeknownst to Kant, however, the philosophical child he helped to father would take a form somewhat removed from what he had intended. According to Schelling, Kant's new transcendental method unfolded like the growth of a plant which begins its formation without knowledge of the end it will eventually realize, but that has at first at least a sure *feeling* for that end: "Precisely this feeling, this drive, which came into philosophy with Kant, distinguished [his] epoch from all earlier ones."[13] Schelling, himself infected by the Kantian feeling, was driven by it to articulate ideas Kant himself only just began to imagine at the end of his life (as we will see in Chapter 4). Schelling admits in no uncertain terms that he could not have constructed a bridge across the threshold *without* Kant. Befitting his ever-restless mind, Schelling boldly claims that "Kant's contribution is diminished by those who contribute nothing to going beyond Kant."[14]

On the first page of the preface to his essay on cosmology, *Process and Reality*, Whitehead expresses his surprise that, after endeavoring upon a careful investigation of the

---

11. Deleuze, *Kant's Critical Philosophy*, 25.
12. Kant, *Prolegomena*, 7.
13. Schelling, *Modern Philosophy*, 95.
14. Schelling, *Modern Philosophy*, 94.

exact statements of the main philosophers and scientists of the early modern period (including, in particular Descartes, Spinoza, Leibniz, Newton, Berkeley, Locke, Hume, and Kant), he realized that his own "philosophy of organism" required "a recurrence to pre-Kantian modes of thought."[15] Does this imply that Whitehead encountered Kant at the threshold only to attempt an about face, to return to the pre-critical speculative methods of the likes of Spinoza and Leibniz, rather than venturing ahead, as Schelling did? I do not believe the matter is so simple.

On George Lucas, Jr.'s reading, Whitehead's recurrence to pre-Kantian modes of thought may expose his philosophy of organism to the charge that it is nothing more than regressive pre-critical dogmatism.[16] But rather than overplaying the polemic between Whitehead and Kant, Lucas instead seeks to obviate the necessity of Whitehead's pre-Kantian recursion by pointing out the way Whitehead's admittedly more radical panexperientialism[17] in effect generalizes to *all* actual occasions of experience many of Kant's insights regarding the supposedly special structure of *human* experience. A further convergence is that both sought to protect moral and aesthetic experience from the erroneous overextension of Cartesian-Newtonian mechanism into metaphysics. Lucas acknowledges that there are also plenty of areas where the two thinkers clearly part ways, chief among them being the extent and genetic origins of experience itself. Kant, for example, was no panexperientialist and explicitly rejects the similar doctrine of hylozoism, which suggests that matter is enliv-

---

15. Whitehead, *Process and Reality*, xi.
16. Lucas, *Whitehead*, 75–80.
17. The term *panexperientialism* was coined by the Whiteheadian philosopher David Ray Griffin, for whom affirming it means "attributing the two basic features that we associate with mind—experience and spontaneity—to all units of nature," thereby "[carrying] through the regulative principle" of so much contemporary philosophy "that mind should be naturalized" (*Unsnarling the World-Knot*, 78).

ened by an all-inhabiting world-soul.[18]

Another set of recent commentators, Randall E. Auxier and Gary L. Herstein, argue that interpreting Whitehead's cosmological scheme as though it "belongs to the post-Kantian discussion in philosophy" is itself "erroneous" and potentially crippling for Whitehead scholarship.[19] They characterize Whitehead's work as a "counter-revolution" that undoes the wrong turn initiated by Kant's so-called Copernican revolution, pointing in particular to Kant's construal of spatial experience in terms of the "transcendental conditions governing the space of *presentation*,"[20] an account Whitehead indeed regards as disastrous for any realistic cosmological scheme. I return to these issues later in the book. My position is somewhat softer than Auxier and Herstein's in that while I acknowledge and even stress important divergences from Kant, I also highlight areas where Kant's revolutionary new mode of thought stimulated Whitehead in crucial ways. Based on Whitehead's own account, I do not think it is simply an error to place Whitehead's thought within the conversational lineage originating in Kant's critiques. One of the premises of this book is that many of Whitehead's key conceptual innovations are brought into sharper relief when read as responses, both critical and constructive, to Kant. By further supplementing Whitehead's cosmological scheme with the more transcendentally-attuned Schelling's *Naturphilosophie*, I hope to avoid proceeding in the blindly uncritical fashion that Lucas worries some Whiteheadians do.[21]

---

18. Kant, *Critique of Judgment*, 178.
19. Auxier and Herstein, "The Quantum of Explanation," 155.
20. Auxier and Herstein, "The Quantum of Explanation," 156.
21. Lucas, *Whitehead*, 75.

1.1 Whitehead, Schelling, and the Aftermath of Kant

On the face of it, Schelling and Whitehead would seem to be representatives of disparate schools of philosophy: the former is normally considered an idealist inheritor of Kant, while the latter (at least in his philosophical phase) is known mostly as Bertrand Russell's collaborator on the *Principia Mathematica,* though his later work as a philosophical systematizer of William James' radical empiricism is gaining admirers. The labels "absolute idealist" and "radical empiricist" obscure a deeper convergence of thought. Schelling is commonly made historically relevant only as the stepping stone between Fichte's "subjective" and Hegel's "absolute" idealism. Indeed, this common account stems from Hegel's own influential version of the history of philosophy, which has it that the whole Western tradition culminates in himself.[22] Heidegger famously argues, however, that Schelling "drives German idealism from within right past its own fundamental position."[23] As Terry Pinkard put it, Schelling argues forcefully "that the earlier systems of post-Kantian idealism had gone too far in their attempt to create a form of idealism that was fully self-contained."[24] The rational mind cannot account for its own nor for the world's existence purely in terms of conceptual abstractions. Schelling was convinced that something deeper and darker was at play beneath the blinding light of Reason. Pinkard follows many historians of philosophy in dividing Schelling's work into seemingly discontinuous phases, including his youthful allegiance to *Naturphilosophie,* his mid-life flirtation with Neoplatonism, and his mature fascination with mythology and revelation.[25] This common perception of the winding course of Schell-

---

22. Beiser, *After Hegel,* 9.
23. Heidegger, *Schelling's Treatise,* 4.
24. Pinkard, *German Philosophy,* 324.
25. Pinkard, *German Philosophy,* 325.

ing's admittedly experimental approach to philosophizing probably stems from Hegel's comment during his lectures on the history of philosophy that his old friend Schelling "carried out his education in public."[26] Some, like Pinkard and D. C. Schindler, dampen Hegel's reading of Schelling as "the proteus of philosophy" by insisting that, underlying all the twists and turns of his thinking, it was always the question of "*a properly ontological notion* of freedom" that lured him onward.[27] Other scholars, including Dalia Nassar,[28] Iain Hamilton Grant,[29] Bruce Matthews,[30] and Jason Wirth[31] have contended that, despite the shifting foci of his lifelong philosophical output, Schelling remains, in Wirth's words, "first and foremost a thinker of the question of Nature."[32] In that Schelling's quest for an adequate philosophical expression of freedom drove him "beyond the strictly human sphere all the way into the deepest crevices . . . of the world,"[33] these two perspectives on his work are not necessarily contradictory. "Only one who has tasted freedom," Schelling writes, "can feel the longing to make everything analogous to it, to spread it throughout the whole universe."[34]

As for Whitehead, Grant mentions him alongside Schelling as one of the most promising examples of speculative

---

26. As quoted in Schindler, *The Perfection of Freedom*, 114.
27. Schindler, *The Perfection of Freedom*, 171; Pinkard, *German Philosophy*, 325.
28. Nassar, "From a Philosophy of Self to a Philosophy of Nature." Nassar suggests that Schelling broke with Fichte largely as a result of Johann Wolfgang von Goethe's influence.
29. Grant, *Philosophies of Nature After Schelling*. Grant complains that contemporary scholarship on Schelling's philosophy pays "scant attention . . . to the deep vein of naturephilosophy running through it" (3).
30. Matthews, *Schelling's Organic Form of Philosophy*.
31. Wirth, "Schelling's Contemporary Resurgence," in *Philosophy Compass*. See also *The Conspiracy of Life* and *Schelling's Practice of the Wild*.
32. Wirth, "Schelling's Contemporary Resurgence," 594n6.
33. Schindler, *The Perfection of Freedom*, 172.
34. Schelling, *Human Freedom*, 22.

cosmologizing "beyond the epistemological concerns of the philosophy of science."[35] Whitehead shared with Schelling a desire to break free of the epistemic shackles Kant had placed around philosophical speculation. Lucas confirms their philosophical affinity by reading Schelling's *Naturphilosophie* as a historical precursor to Whitehead's philosophy of organism.[36] Arran Gare goes even further, labeling Whitehead a "[Schellingian] of some stripe."[37] Whitehead remarks on the "great achievements of German philosophy" in several of his books, calling on future philosophers to integrate German idealism's insights into aesthetics and ethics with the deliverances of contemporary science.[38] Even though Whitehead evidently read little of Schelling's writing, Gare's label is defensible in light of Whitehead's use of an excerpt from an essay of Schelling's in *The Concept of Nature*.[39] Whitehead leans on Schelling's conception of Nature as a self-constructing "subject–object" to support his move beyond modern science's bifurcated mode of thought, wherein reality is said to be divided in two, with the experiential dream of the mind on one side and its conjectured physical cause on the other. As will be explicated in more detail as this book unfolds, Schelling and Whitehead alike sought to conceive of Nature not merely as a dead object or collection of objects, but as a living and dynamically evolving community of subjects.

William Hamrick and Jan Van Der Veken show how Schelling and Whitehead's cosmotheanthropic process

---

35. Grant, *After Schelling*, vii, ix.
36. Lucas, *Whitehead*, 25–26.
37. Gare, "The Roots of Postmodernism," 36.
38. Whitehead, *Science and the Modern World*, 157. Whitehead's opinion earlier in the same chapter that, "the whole of the great German idealistic movement... [was] out of effective touch with its contemporary science" betrays his lack of familiarity with Schelling's *Naturphilosophie*, which engaged deeply with the new scientific paradigms emerging in Schelling's day (139).
39. Whitehead, *The Concept of Nature*, 47.

philosophy happily converged with, and reemerged from, the imagination of Maurice Merleau-Ponty during his lectures on Nature at the Collège de France in the late 1950s.[40] Merleau-Ponty approves of Schelling and Whitehead's shared cosmotheanthropic intuitions that, (1) rather than an anomalous accident, "the human being [is] a species of the recreation of the world," and, (2) rather than being merely an idea of Reason reflected upon by the understanding, "God [is] an empirical fact . . . at the base of all experience."[41] Hamerik and Van Der Veken argue that Whitehead "incorporated important Schellingian insights" into his philosophy.[42] In support of this claim they point to Antoon Braeckman's work linking Whitehead's philosophical scheme to Schelling's through the intermediary of the Schellingian philosopher-poet Samuel Taylor Coleridge.[43] Coleridge's role in the formation of William Wordsworth's aesthetic vision of Nature is well known. Though he was quite familiar with Coleridge,[44] the deepest impact on Whitehead came through the poetry of Wordsworth, which he studied throughout his life. According to his daughter's testimony, he would read *The Prelude* almost daily "as if it were the Bible, poring over the meaning of various passages."[45] Along with the impact of Schelling through Coleridge and Wordsworth, Whitehead was deeply influenced by the British idealists John McTaggart and F. H. Bradley. In light of his idealistic inheritances,

---

40. Hamrick and Van Der Veken, *Nature and Logos*; Merleau-Ponty, *Nature*.
41. Merleau-Ponty as quoted in Hamrick and Van Den Veken, *Nature and Logos*, 140; Merleau-Ponty, *Nature*, 47.
42. Hamrick and Van Den Veken, *Nature and Logos*, 228.
43. Braeckman, "Whitehead and German Idealism" in *Process Studies*, 265–86. Schelling mentions the "talented Brit" in a footnote to his lectures on the philosophy of mythology, forgiving him for plagiarism and thanking him for his neologism "tautegorical," which Schelling gladly appropriates to distinguish the meaning of mythic imagery from allegory (*Philosophy of Mythology*, 136, 187e).
44. Whitehead, *Science and the Modern World*, 79.
45. Wyman, "Whitehead's Philosophy," in *Philosophy of Science*, 283.

Whitehead admitted that in the final analysis his own cosmology might be considered "a transformation of some main doctrines of Absolute Idealism onto a realistic basis."[46]

The philosophies of Schelling and Whitehead can evidently be understood to orbit around a common intuition, namely that the conceptual division opposing objective reality to subjective ideality can be healed only through an aesthetic act of creative imagination. Whitehead and Schelling are both system-builders seeking comprehensive conceptual insight into the formation of actual processes in Nature. But neither of them conceived of systematic philosophy as a finite task with a definite end. No system of philosophy can ever claim completion because reality is not simply a rational system. The creative natality of Nature always slips through the net rationality tries to cast upon the world. Reality is not a mummified corpse but a living *creality*. Philosophy attains its deepest insights into creality not just through the theoretical interpretation of facts, but through interpreting both facts and theories in light of moral and aesthetic acts of imagination. Even from Kant's critical perspective, imagination is the most indispensable of the soul's cognitive powers, mysteriously generating both sensibility and understanding.[47] But for him the power of imagination works its magic at a depth unreachable by the light of conscious will. Though he helped to bring them to the attention of philosophers in his *Critique of Judgment*, Kant tended to downplay the concrete aesthetic ideas that emerge from the creative imagination, while giving greater importance to universal moral ideals of Reason and determinate concepts of the merely reflective (i.e., unproductive) understanding.[48] A speculative philosophy that leans too heavily on such ideal concepts in its pursuit of the real can lead only to "those insoluble contradictions which Kant set forth under

---

46. Whitehead, *Process and Reality*, xiii.
47. Kant, *Critique of Pure Reason*, 152.
48. Kant, *Critique of Judgment*, 59, 142.

the name of the antinomies."[49] These antinomies forbid the philosopher real knowledge concerning God, the universe, and the human soul, since in each case, critical reflection alone leads only to the aporias inherent to sense-bound understanding. The understanding, says Kant, "stretches its wings in vain, if it tries to soar beyond the world of sense by the mere power of speculation."[50]

If we take him at his word and follow the rhythm of his thought through to the end, it is clear that Schelling understood Kant's critical method as well as anyone, including even Kant himself. But Schelling felt that Kant had only begun the process of "the transfiguration of philosophy."[51] It was up to Fichte, Hegel, and Schelling himself to bring the project further toward its full potential. Schelling did not rush to leap *beyond* Kant's transcendental expositions, but patiently went *through* them to discover deeper presuppositions missed even by Kant. Schelling was only able to peer further into the creative abyss of imagination than Kant because he started his philosophical endeavors with the increased lucidity provided him by Kant's critical method. There can be no doubt, however, that from the very beginning of his philosophical career the precocious Schelling felt the Kantian categorical scheme (especially as laid out in the first two critiques) to be uncomfortably cramped and lopsided.

The cosmological scope of Whitehead's "free and wild creation of concepts"[52] makes him one of the twentieth century's most important inheritors of the spirit (if not the letter) of German Idealism. Although he aligns himself more with the empiricist tradition, Whitehead's "recursion" is not a retreat from the Kantian threshold. He apparently read and re-read

---

49. Schelling, *Transcendental Idealism*, 176.
50. Kant, *Critique of Pure Reason*, 287.
51. Schelling, *Modern Philosophy*, 95.
52. Deleuze and Guattari, *What Is Philosophy?*, 105. Deleuze and Guattari describe "English philosophy" as such.

the *Critique of Pure Reason* enough to commit crucial sections of it to memory.[53] His philosophy of organism, though it diverges from Kant at crucial junctures, is an attempt at constructing precisely the sort of systematic, self-correcting, and experimental metaphysics that Kant had hoped to initiate. Whitehead may have had aspects of Kant's philosophy in mind when he wrote the following:

> A new idea introduces a new alternative; and we are not less indebted to a thinker when we adopt the alternative which he discarded. Philosophy never reverts to its old position after the shock of a great philosopher.[54]

Whitehead not only constructs an entirely novel set of categories, his understanding of the metaphysical status of these categories represents a reformed version of the Lockean alternative—the so-called "physiology of Reason"—that Kant discarded.[55] Only if we have already accepted Kant's ontological bifurcation between appearance and reality (or the phenomenal and noumenal realms) does Whitehead's "recursion" imply that he is a pre-Kantian thinker. Whitehead and Schelling's aesthetically-oriented philosophy reaches deeper into reality than Kant's transcendentalism precisely because it questions the basis of this bifurcation. But before examining Schelling and Whitehead's novel categoreal[56] schemes we must first come to terms with Kant's revolutionary mode of thought.

---

53. Lucas, *Whitehead*, xx; Hartshorne and Peden, *Whitehead's View*, 33.

54. Whitehead, *Process and Reality*, 11.

55. Whitehead, *Process and Reality*, xi. Whitehead says that Locke "most fully anticipated the main positions of the philosophy of organism" in the later sections of *An Essay Concerning Human Understanding*.

56. Whitehead corrected galleys of *Process and Reality* to render the adjectival form of "category" as "categoreal" instead of "categorical" (*Process and Reality*, vii). While his precise reasons for doing so remain obscure to me, I employ the term here to indicate that both Schelling and Whitehead aim to articulate categories of *reality*, rather than merely to explicate categories of our mind.

1.2 The Kantian Mode of Thought

This book approaches Kant not as a fundamentally misguided thinker, but rather as guardian of the threshold of metaphysical knowledge, an epistemic gatekeeper and destroyer of dogmatic modes of speculation. Schelling and Whitehead end up in a very different universe from Kant, but they arrived in that universe only after seriously grappling with his ideas. Kant's three critiques—of theoretical reason, practical reason, and judgment—forever changed the way philosophers conceive of the relationship of human consciousness to itself (the soul), to God, and to the universe. Whitehead and Schelling imaginatively engage these speculative ideas in light of the transfiguration of philosophy that Kant initiated. To appreciate the novelty of their cosmotheanthropic process philosophy, it is necessary to first unpack Kant's transcendental critique of all prior metaphysics.

In his *Critique of Pure Reason*, Kant set himself the task of determining "how much we can hope to achieve by reason, when all the material and assistance of experience are taken away."[57] In other words, he hoped to determine what the mind was capable of discovering about its own cognitive powers independent of what it receives from outside itself. He would go on to articulate the conditions of the possibility of all knowledge in terms of our formal intuitions of space and time and the categories of our understanding. He argued that these forms and categories provide *a priori* logical and aesthetic structure to all experience, whether of appearances within the soul or in external Nature.

Kant lists three powers, or "capacities of the soul...which cannot be any further derived from one common ground: the faculty of knowledge, the feeling of pleasure and pain, and the faculty of desire."[58] These powers can be summarized

---

57. Kant, *Critique of Pure Reason*, 11.
58. Kant, *Critique of Judgment*, 10.

as thinking, feeling, and desiring, respectively. They, along with the forms of intuition of space and time underlying all their content, configure the whole of our phenomenal experience. In the *Critique of Pure Reason*, Kant lists three different faculties, but claims, as he does above, that "they are original sources . . . and cannot themselves be derived from any [others]": they are sense, imagination, and apperception.[59] What is to be made of this apparent diversity in what Kant claims are the most basic of the soul's powers? One possible answer is that there is a correspondence between the pairs of three, an answer which will be explored in the three subsections below. Another possibility is that, while the soul can be divided abstractly into different faculties, in truth each is merely a moment within a deeper, unifying movement. Despite Kant's usual insistence upon the distinction between sensibility and understanding, he writes elsewhere in the *Critique of Pure Reason* that, while "there are two stems of human knowledge, namely, sensibility and understanding," they "perhaps spring from a common, but to us unknown root."[60] Once the fallacy of bifurcation has been seen through, it does not require much imagination to infer that this common root is, in fact, imagination itself. The inner image-making force (the literal translation of the German *Einbildungskraft*) is the source of the mediating and unifying tensile movement that continually weaves the soul's otherwise disjointed conceptual and sensory faculties into concrete, living wholeness. As I argue later in this chapter, imagination remains unknown only to the extent that the soul is unable to participate consciously in its activities. While still operating entirely unconsciously, the imagination synthetically constructs for the understanding a unified picture of the sensory world. Without what Kant refers to as the schematizing activity of the transcendental imagination, the abstract universal categories of the understanding could

59. Kant, *Critique of Pure Reason*, 127.
60. Kant, *Critique of Pure Reason*, 61.

never find their application to the concrete particulars of the perceptual world. When consciously activated, imagination becomes not just the servant of the understanding, synthesizing its concepts with percepts, but Reason's way of giving the philosopher's otherwise unrealizable ideas concrete expression. Kant lists three principle ideas of Reason: psyche (or the soul), cosmos (or the universe), and theos (or God). My argument throughout this book is that it is only through the power of imagination that we may concretely experience the freedom of the soul, the love of the divine, and the beauty of the cosmos. An activated and philosophically cultivated imagination grants human beings the ability to actualize what would otherwise remain mere logical possibilities.

Because Kant stopped short of fully affirming the central importance of imagination, he ends up artificially separating the three faculties of knowing, feeling, and desiring. While the clear distinction of these capacities is an essential step along the way of his initiatory philosophy, the cosmotheanthropic process philosopher cannot remain content with their dissociation. I hope to show that, once across the Kantian threshold, our philosophizing can become conscious of the way these faculties interpenetrate and work upon one another to form the human being, the universe, and the divine into a dynamic living whole.

1.2.1 Thinking

Kant introduces his transcendental analysis of theoretical knowledge through an extended analogy with the sixteenth-century astronomer Nicholas Copernicus' heliocentric hypothesis. Copernicus' hypothesis called into question what had been the taken for granted perception of ancient people for thousands of years: that the physical earth stood still at the center of a nested series of revolving heavenly spheres ascending stepwise toward God, who was thought to be the transcendent cause of their perfect circular motion. As Kant tells the story, while many astronomers continued to complicate Ptolemy's increasingly epicyclic model of planetary motions based on the assumption that "the entire celestial host revolves around the observer," Copernicus, following a Platonic intuition (and the ancient theory of Aristarchus),[61] decided to simplify his model by inverting the classical perspective. Instead of interpreting his sensory experience of the heavenly bodies as though *they* were in motion around him, he imagined that *he himself*, as an earthly observer, was the true source of their apparent movements.[62] By proceeding at first "in a manner contradictory to the senses,"[63] Copernicus initiated the scientific revolution by becoming conscious of the effect of his own motion as an observer on the observed motion of the heavens. In Fernand Hallyn's terms, Copernicus "thus . . . considered man as the 'source' of the apparent motion of the planets and the Sun." Astronomical movement, in other words, "can only be approached within an investigation that includes the subject as the origin of possible error and truth."[64] In the same way, Kant initiated his "Copernican revolution" in philosophy by becoming conscious of the until then unacknowledged contribution of the mind's conceptual activity to the formation of the phenomenal world. Just as Copernicus inverted the traditional image of the relationship between earth and sky, Kant inverted the traditional image of the relationship between the thinking mind and objective Nature (an image that rationalists and empiricists alike had been assuming). Copernicus' heliocentric revolution in astronomy is thus analogous to Kant's epistemic revolution in philosophy.

The traditional image of the relationship between the subjective knower and the objects known assumed that some

---

61. Steiner, *The Relation of the Diverse Branches of Natural Science to Astronomy* (CW 323), Lecture 14, 1. Translated as *Interdisciplinary Astronomy* (2020).
62. Kant, *Critique of Pure Reason*, 110.
63. Kant, *Critique of Pure Reason*, 113n.
64. Hallyn, *Poetic Structure*, 72.

divinely decreed harmony existed between the order of ideas in the mind and the order of things in Nature. This is the theological origin of the so-called correspondence theory of truth.[65] Descartes, a supposedly modern rationalist philosopher, still attempted to ground the universality and necessity of human knowledge—that is, the ability of our mind to conceptually grasp the lawfully ordered objects of Nature—on the goodness of a transcendent God. God, whose goodness prevents him from deceiving us, created a rational world and stamped the blueprint of it in our souls in the form of innate ideas. Even atheistic empiricists like Hume still assumed that the mind was in the business of internally mirroring the external sense world, though his skepticism forced him to limit the degree to which we could ever be certain of the universality and necessity of such knowledge. The revolutionary aim of Kant's new method of philosophy arose largely in response to Descartes, Hume, and other modern philosophers of both the rationalist and empiricist schools. He sought to provide an *immanent* critique of rational knowledge—a critique that makes reason the sole judge of itself—rather than subordinating its self-revealing reflections either to the divine revelations of a transcendent God, or to the sensory impressions of ordinary experience. Kant proposed his transcendental hypothesis as nothing short of a "transformation in our way of thinking" about the ontological status of "our representations of space and time" and the object determining "concepts of the understanding."[66]

How did Kant accomplish this revolutionary break from the traditional correspondence theory of knowledge? He is willing to grant the traditional definition of truth: "the agreement of cognition with its object."[67] But in the new Kantian

---

65. While the traditional understanding of such correspondence is challenged not only by Kant, but also by Whitehead, both retain reformulated versions of the doctrine (see below and Whitehead, *Process and Reality*, 190).
66. Kant, *Critique of Pure Reason*, 113n.
67. Kant, *Critique of Pure Reason*, 197.

framework, "objects" take on an entirely new status. Once again, Kant's revolutionary innovation was accomplished by reversing the assumed relationship between the subjective knower and the objects known. Assuming that cognition conforms to objects (either due to a theological miracle, as rationalists assumed, or due to some natural habit or social custom, as empiricists assumed) led traditional philosophers down a blind alley. Kant hypothetically assumes the reverse, that *objects must conform to our cognition*. As he put it: "the order and regularity in appearances, which we entitle nature, we ourselves introduce."[68] This hypothesis allowed him, so he argued, to apodictically prove that the world around us arises through the practical and theoretical activity of the mind. It was as if the centrality of the physical Sun was replaced by an invisible transcendental star, or *noumenon*, hidden within the human soul whose light radiated out to give phenomenal form to all the extended bodies revolving around it. "Objects" are no longer given to us ready-made through the senses, but actively constructed by the powers of our own intuition and understanding.

Kant's reversal also rests upon a new conception of subjectivity. For Hume nothing could be known with any certainty, whether it be the nature of the human subject or of the natural objects to which it relates. Hume understood the self to be nothing but a bundle of impressions with no special significance or transcendental ground. Kant famously credits Hume's deconstruction of the concept of causality for awakening him from his "dogmatic slumber" and leading him, eventually, to articulate his transcendental reconstruction of knowledge.[69] Whitehead also felt compelled to respond to Hume's analysis of causality, but as I discuss later, his response is very different from Kant's. For Kant, while Hume's *empirical* examination of the self was true enough as

68. Kant, *Critique of Pure Reason*, 147.
69. Kant, *Prolegomena*, 10.

an account of experience, a *transcendental* analysis reveals that the faculty of knowledge depends *a priori* upon what he called the unity of apperception,

> the abiding and unchanging "I" [forming] the correlate of all our representations in so far as it is to be at all possible that we should become conscious of them.[70]

The Kantian "I" is a more critically explicated version of Descartes' Cogito, meaning that for Kant, although thinking does imply a thing that thinks, this thing need not be an actually existing substance. Descartes argues that the mind has an *immediate* intuition of itself as such a substance, while Kant argues that our immediate inner intuition of temporal succession can only be determined as a substance through the *mediation* of a concept. Kant's is a transcendental ego, while Descartes' remains an empirical ego mistaken for something transcendent.

Kant's synthetically abiding "I" allows diverse experiences to be unified by and judged according to the same categories of the understanding, categories that apply universally because they constitute the very possibility of our having any experience of objects at all. But the "I" cannot unify experience on its own: in order for the understanding to judge the manifold of sensory experience according to its categories, it depends upon the synthetic activity of imagination, which draws together outer intuitions into a *communis sensus*,[71] a holistic view of the world no longer divided into the various modalities of the individual sensory organs. The thinking "I" also depends upon imagination to unify its inner intuitions of itself as it unfolds through time.

---

70. Kant, *Critique of Pure Reason*, 146.
71. In Greek, *koinē aísthēsis*. This theory dates back to Aristotle's *De Anima* (Book 3, Chapter 2). I continually revisit and expand upon this concept in the pages to follow.

In Kant's scheme, the synthesizing activity of imagination is responsible for unconsciously drawing together the chaos of raw sensory experience so that the world appears to us as always already ordered and coherent. Only once sensation has been so ordered does it become amenable to conceptual determination by the understanding. This claim is significant because, as I discuss later, Whitehead diverges from Kant's usual characterization of the material of sensory experience before it is formally reconstructed by the conceptual structures of the human mind. Kant denies that sensory impressions "provide experience with any objective content."[72] From Whitehead's perspective, denying that embodied experience puts us in touch with a real world inevitably leads to solipsism. Whitehead credits Kant with being the first philosopher to explicitly introduce the idea of "an act of experience as a constructive functioning," but whereas Kant understood the construction as beginning with the subjective activity of the mind and issuing in apparent objectivity, Whitehead's philosophy of organism reverses the process: the creation of each moment of experience begins with the prehension of environing objects and issues in subjectivity.[73] But before jumping ahead to unpack Whitehead's alternative processual account of perception, wherein the problems of knowledge and of causality receive a common explanation, and wherein "no thinker thinks twice,"[74] I must continue to introduce Kant's transcendental treatment of the soul's cognitive powers.

For Kant, the "I"—the "pure, original, unchanging consciousness" at the helm of our soul-powers—is a function of what he terms "transcendental apperception."[75] This faculty grants us consciousness of ourselves as subjects together with the world of objects as elements necessarily involved in

---

72. Whitehead, *Process and Reality*, 152.
73. Whitehead, *Process and Reality*, 156.
74. Whitehead, *Process and Reality*, 29.
75. Kant, *Critique of Pure Reason*, 232.

"one and the same universal experience." Were it not for this synthesizing activity, "a swarm of appearances [would] fill up our soul without [conscious] experience ever being able to arise from it."[76] Out of manifold perceptions, transcendental apperception constructs the systematic unity of Nature for our understanding. This unity depends also on the synthetic power of the creative imagination, which by an *a priori* "affinity of all appearances" draws the manifold together into an intelligible unity of experience.[77]

> Thus we ourselves bring into the appearances that order and regularity in them that we call nature, and moreover we would not be able to find it there if we, or the nature of our mind, had not originally put it there.[78]

For Kant, the soul's reliance upon the transcendental activity of imagination to bring unity not only to Nature's manifoldness, but to itself as an unchanging thinker, did not call the autonomy of the "I" into question. The practical freedom of the "I" remained the precondition for both the mind's capacity for knowledge of Nature as well as its capacity for moral action in a kingdom of ends (where others would be treated as ends in themselves, and never as means). But to preview an argument made later, if moral action is rooted in the free decision to love one another, rather than in a duty to abstract law (as it was for Kant), then true knowledge of Nature can be shown to depend upon the possibility of descendental empathy, or moral intersubjectivity. Without the moral activity of imagination, the thinker, in her attempt to know herself, can only divide and reify herself, becoming a dead thought, which is precisely not-"I," not the active thinker originally sought. Self-consciousness cannot establish itself without coming into

---

76. Kant, *Critique of Pure Reason*, 234.
77. Kant, *Critique of Pure Reason*, 240.
78. Kant, *Critique of Pure Reason*, 241.

loving relation with and being mutually recognized and appreciated by a thinker, an "I," other than itself. Contrary to classical liberal theory, *I do not belong only to myself*. My own coming to self-consciousness is at least partially the result of a feeling of responsibility placed on me by others. I am obligated by the existence of other self-consciousnesses to become conscious of myself.[79] In the words of Martin Luther King, Jr. (who was influenced by Whitehead and the process theologian Henry Nelson Wieman),[80] due to "the interrelated structure of reality,"

> "I can never be what I ought to be until you are what you ought to be. And you can never be what you ought to be until I am what I ought to be."[81]

Just as the power of imagination works to make theoretical knowledge of Nature possible by synthesizing the sensory manifold into systematically conceived objects, it also works to make moral action in relation to other existing selves possible by at least potentially synthesizing the freedom of my will with that of every other will. While imagination in both cases performs acts of transcendental *synthesis*, the latter is also an act of *sympathy*. In other words, imaginatively synthesizing two or more free wills means as much as each one imaginatively *sympathizing* or *feeling-with* the other. The freedom to will the Good and the feeling of sympathy with others are thus inextricably wed. Practical reason thus depends as much on communal feeling as it does on autonomous freedom. To the extent that seeing myself reflected in the faces of others and learning to speak a shared language supports the formation of my own identity and capacity for thinking, I am always already an *inter-subject*. Because my "I" is noumenal,

---

79. Schelling, *Transcendental Idealism*, 163.
80. King, *Papers*, 17, 19. Thanks to the poet-activist Drew Dellinger for drawing my attention to this influence.
81. King, "Remaining Awake," par. 9.

it cannot be known through inward self-reflection alone—its light at first shines only outward. I come to imagine myself in the sympathetic image of other selves. As Keller argues, "a primal empathy . . . founds reality," such that "I cannot exist without in some sense taking part in you."[82] Others are therefore always a constitutive ingredient in the formation of my own identity. My desire for self-identity is correlated with my desire to recognize and be recognized, to love and be loved, by others. Thus knowing and willing, or the theoretical and practical branches of philosophy, dependently co-arise. As Schelling put it, "a rational being in isolation could not only not arrive at a consciousness of freedom, but would be equally unable to attain consciousness of the objective world."[83] Schelling also repeatedly emphasizes that the completion of his *Naturphilosophie* must be taken up as a "common labor" pursued by all "the thinking heads of the age."[84] As Iain Hamilton Grant elaborates, *Naturphilosophie* thus "not only theoretically exceeds the transcendental, but also practically exceeds the isolated 'thinking head,' the *Ich* [or "I"], of the transcendental philosopher."[85] Simply put, in Whitehead's terms, "every actual entity is present in every other actual entity."[86]

Although for different reasons, Kant also affirms that knowing the True depends upon willing the Good. He also emphasizes practical over theoretical reason, a preference with an ancient pedigree. In the *Republic*, Plato suggests that the Good is to the True in the intelligible realm what the Sun is to sight in the visible. One cannot see without the Sun, just as one cannot know Truth without first being Good. Truth and knowledge are like the Good, but not the Good itself, "for the Good is yet more prized." Plato continues: "What gives truth

---

82. Keller, *From a Broken Web*, 184.
83. Schelling, *Transcendental Idealism*, 174.
84. Schelling, *First Outline*, 232.
85. Grant, *After Schelling*, 159.
86. Whitehead, *Process and Reality*, 50.

to the things known and the power to know to the knower is the form of the Good."[87] Though Kant is not always consistent on this point, much like its synthetic function in perception to bind the various outward senses by affinity with one another into one inward common sense (a function discussed in more depth later in this chapter), imagination also functions to form an affective moral bond between apperceiving selves, granting them participation as inter-subjects in what Whitehead calls a "democracy of fellow creatures."[88] "Pure" theoretical reason is thus not actually separable from practical reason. Theoretical knowledge based on the *a priori* categories of the understanding already presupposes a sympathetic relation to others, as I cannot conceive of my own apperceiving "I" but by way of an imaginatively generated sense of community. Taking a step beyond Kant's kingdom of ends, we can say that as members of a democracy of fellow creatures, our human community extends also into the cosmos. In Panikkar's words:

> Although humans become so in community, the human community is not limited to its fellow human creatures. The human community is also cosmic, since the human being is an integral and, even, constitutive part of the cosmos.[89]

Kant would almost certainly reject my reading of the imaginal, intersubjective, and indeed cosmic grounds of the transcendental unity of apperception, but I am certainly not the first to push his thought in this direction.[90] Fichte and Hegel in the nineteenth, and Husserl and Levinas in the twentieth century attempted similar interpretative interventions (though perhaps not as cosmological). Deleuze articulates similar complaints that Kant's critique of practical reason fails to give

---

87. Plato, *Republic*, 508e.
88. Whitehead, *Process and Reality*, 50.
89. Panikkar, *The Experience of God*, 127.
90. Kant would insist upon moral law over intersubjective empathy, and a merely human kingdom of ends over a democracy of fellow creatures.

feeling and imagination an important enough role. Because for Kant "free beings and free causality are not the object of any intuition," he is ultimately forced to separate the "suprasensible Nature" of freedom from the "sensible nature" of bodily life "by an abyss."[91]

This necessary link between the Good and the True raises the question of how human freedom can be possible given that, according to Kant, the natural world we are embedded within is knowable only according to the lawfully determined categories of our understanding. It may be that theoretically knowing the True presupposes practically willing the Good, but this still leaves unanswered how our theoretical knowledge of the True can be harmonized with Reason's practical demand for freedom. As I unpack in the subsections to follow, Kant confronts this problem in his final *Critique of Judgment*, a work wherein he argues that the Beauty of an apparently purposefully organized natural world provides for the possibility of a "point of union between theoretical and practical philosophy," as Schelling describes it.[92] The mediating role of Beauty would prove invaluable for Schelling's and Whitehead's efforts to build a speculative bridge across the gulf Kant defended between physics and metaphysics.

1.2.2 Desiring

Desire is defined by Kant as "a being's faculty of becoming by means of its representations the cause of the actuality of the objects of these representations."[93] Desire depends upon the power of imagination to conjure feeling-toned pictures of objects within the subject that are distant in (or as yet absent from) time and space, thereby providing the will with a motivating lure. Desire and imagination are integral to Kant's

---

91. Deleuze, *Kant's Critical Philosophy*, 39.
92. Schelling, *Transcendental Idealism*, 12.
93. Kant, *Critique of Judgment*, 10.

account of morality as developed in the *Critique of Practical Reason*.

> Two things fill the mind with ever-renewing wonder and awe, the more often and the more intensely the mind is drawn to think of them: *the starry heavens above me and the moral law within me*.[94]

This sentence, adorning his tombstone, is among Kant's most iconic. It summarizes the driving force of his life's work. Kant's entire philosophical project, more than anything else, was designed to reconcile the scientific world of Newtonian mechanics (i.e., "the starry heavens above") with the religious world of immortal souls (i.e., "the moral law within").[95] To accomplish this reconciliation, he is forced to divide our experience of sensory phenomena, upon which scientific knowledge is based, from supersensible noumena, of which nothing can be known save our moral confrontation with the command of conscience that, paradoxically, we *must* be *free*. Kant found the phenomenal/noumenal divide necessary because the category of mechanical causality applying to Nature flatly contradicts the moral principle of free will. His philosophy is in part constructed in order to save the dignity of the human soul from reduction to the determinisms of a mechanical Nature. Kant tries to accomplish this by limiting science's theoretical knowledge of Nature in order to leave room for religion's practical faith in freedom. He admits that the actuality of freedom cannot be *proven* theoretically, but argues that it remains nonetheless *possible* in theory and indeed *must* be lived in practice. Though we cannot know how freedom is possible, we also cannot act morally without presupposing it. Even the mere thought

---

94. Kant, *Critique of Practical Reason*, 161.
95. Many commentators have suggested as much. See Kauffman, *Discovering the Mind*, 118, 122, and, more recently, Naragon, "Kant's Career in German Idealism," 23.

that freedom is impossible presupposes the freedom to think otherwise.

But desire is capable of willing freely, according to Kant, only so long as it aligns itself with the dictates of disembodied rational principles over and against the pleasures of the bodily senses. If our will merely responds to feeling-toned pictures conjured in the soul by the power of imagination, Kant argues that it is acting out of self-interest instead of disinterested moral duty.[96] However, without the power of imagination to tailor the universal ideal of freedom to the specific situations in which it is summoned to serve, the moral agent can reason only abstractly. Furthermore, if as was argued above, the ipseity of the self is reciprocally bound up with the sympathetic activity of imagination and intrinsically linked to the desire to be recognized by others, then independent of the feelings arising from its relational bonds the will remains entirely impotent. Unconditional love[97] rather than disinterested duty is the *descendental* (rather than transcendental) condition of moral action.

Kant's categorical imperative, because it remains at the level of abstract universal law, is ineffectual in the real world of interpersonal life, where every encounter places complex and unique demands upon the individual conscience. Moral imagination is required to transform universal laws of Reason into particular acts of good will. Imagination thus translates the universal ideal of freedom into the unique acts of actual life. Without imagination's creative capacity to reveal the universal in the particular by forming motivating representations for the will, freedom remains a mere abstract possibility incapable of embodied expression. As Hegel would argue in his *Philosophy of Right*, unless it descends into and communicates with (even if sometimes violently) the emotionality of

---

96. Kant, *Groundwork*, 13–14.
97. That is, love which precedes even my own consciousness of myself, as I argued earlier.

family relations and the customs of society, the will "wanders aimlessly around without being able to find a way of escape from the mere abstract imperative."[98] As we will see, Schelling and Whitehead go even further than Hegel by insisting that the human will concretizes abstract freedom by remembering its roots in the creativity of cosmogenesis itself. They put the human being into ethical relationship not only with other humans but with the entire community of creatures composing the cosmos.

Though Kant recognized the power of imagination as the most mysterious of the soul's faculties, he finally assigned it a merely epistemological, rather than an ontological, cosmological, or ethical role as that which synthesizes the sensory manifold and schematically connects percepts with their appropriate concepts. His morality was without imagination, built upon an individual's freedom to will that which Reason dictates. Only if the source of my actions transcends the images of my soul and the feelings of my body, be they loving or hateful, pleasurable or painful, are they to be considered moral. An action is moral only if I am able, in good conscience, to generalize it as a universal law applicable to everyone, everywhere, every time. The subjective stake my embodied soul has in the world must be bracketed entirely, since disinterested duty based in abstract universalizability is the sole basis of Kant's moral philosophy. This follows directly from the chasm his transcendentalism constructs between phenomena and things-in-themselves. The Good is considered by Kant to be an idea of Reason existing beyond all sensory perception and imaginal production, and so no feeling rooted in the passions of the body or image generated by the creativity of the soul, even if they be genuinely compassionate and love-imbued, can provide the conscience with moral guidance. Emotion-laded imagery, Kant believed,

---

98. Hegel, *Hegel's Philosophy of Right*, 129.

could only lead the soul astray from its divinely decreed duty.

So long as Kant's thoughts define the limits of thought, I cannot fully love another person because I cannot truly know them (or better, because I cannot truly know *with* them) by way of imagination, our common sense. Moral theory and practice must draw their sap from this root or risk continuing the spiral into relativistic nihilism typical of so much modern and postmodern philosophy. The most philosophy can provide in regard to the good life without the spirited cultivation of imagination is but a system of consistent maxims or a series of laudable sentiments. Without full participation, body and soul, in the *communis sensus*, moral thought and action are uprooted from relationship and thus dissolve into the suffocating thin air of solipsism.

1.2.3 Feeling

With the "Copernican revolution" brought about by his first two critiques of theoretical and practical philosophy, Kant believed he had successfully deflected the attempt by skeptical empiricists like Hume to remove the keystone from the conceptual bridge supporting all prior metaphysics. The keystone is the idea of causality, or necessary connection. It could also be described in epistemic terms as the principle of sufficient reason. Whatever we call it, Hume called its metaphysical necessity into question. Kant responded that his new transcendental method had reestablished philosophy on a scientific footing. But Kant's critiques of theoretical and practical reason can only provide a sufficient foundation for a new scientific form of philosophy if we human beings are sufficiently describable as essentially thinking and willing creatures. It takes only a moment to notice, however, that we are more than reflecting and desiring beings. The human is also a *feeling* being, and as such, we are conscious not only of our bare existence as spirits (through transcendental apperception of the Cogito or "I think"), but of our well- or ill-being as organisms. We are embodied creatures, situated in the emotional currents of life, concerned to avoid pain and seek pleasure, and if we are lucky enough to have such basic needs met, to disinterestedly experience the beauty of Nature and of art. Disembodied spirits could have no sense of well- or ill-being. They could not get sick, they could not be lonely, they could not love or perceive beauty. They would exist in a merely intellectual way, relating to all physical things from behind a net of logically determined concepts without any hint of subjective feeling for them. The conscious thinking and willing of human beings, despite any pretense to *pure* theoretical or practical reason, always comes clothed in affect, for we are *incarnate* spirits. The disincarnate purity sought by Kant in his first two critiques was severely challenged by what he unwittingly uncovered in his third critique, the *Critique of Judgment*. Kant recognized after completing his first two critiques of pure and practical reason (which focused on thinking and willing respectively) that a gulf remained between the two, a gap preventing any transition from one to the other. This gap was the impetus behind his final critique of the faculty of judgment, wherein through reflections upon our perception of beauty and conception of organic life he sought the mediating principle that might bridge the two species of philosophy he had already critiqued. It is this final critique that set the stage for Fichte, Schelling, Goethe, and Hegel, each of whom would unfold the implications of Kant's Copernican revolution in a way Kant himself repeatedly expressed discomfort with toward the end of his life. This final critique also set the stage for Whitehead's philosophy of organism. Whitehead once remarked that Kant had written his critiques in the wrong order and should have started with the third.[99] Like all revolutionary inventions, Kant's

---

99. Lubbock, "Philosopher for the Muddleheaded."

transcendental method of philosophy was taken up, tinkered with, and developed further by subsequent generations of thinkers.

Kant thus set out to bridge the gulf in his philosophy through a critique of feeling. Kant says that, by way of feeling, "nothing in the object is signified," because what is felt as regards pleasure or pain refers only to a state within the subject "as it is affected by the representation" of the object.[100] It is important to note at this point that Kant's account of feeling differs starkly from Whitehead's view, wherein feelings are direct causal inheritances from superjective objects (i.e., perished subjects) streaming into our conscious and unconscious experience from the environing past.[101] Kant attempted to close the gap in his transcendentalism through a critique of feeling, that is, of our aesthetic encounter with the world, but as we will see in the chapters to follow, he was unable to find his footing. In the end, he retreats from the descent into the underworld of feeling and desire to return to the comfort and clarity of the understanding and Reason. Whereas Schelling and Whitehead's process philosophy sees physical motion and psychic emotion as two poles in a single process, Kant's transcendental philosophy severs them. Kant splits Spirit off from Nature, setting it free to become Nature's master and to conceive an unearthly destiny for itself apart from this world. Schelling rejects this transcendental surgical operation no less explicitly than Whitehead. Human beings are "not born to waste [their] mental power in conflict against the fantasy of an imaginary world," he argues,

> but to exert all [their] power upon a world which has influence upon [them], lets [them] feel its forces, and upon which [they] can react. Between [the human] and the

---

100. Kant, *Critique of Judgment*, 27.
101. Whitehead, *Process and Reality*, 231–33.

world, therefore, no rift must be established; contact and reciprocal action must be possible between the two.[102]

Despite the solipsism implied by his construal of feeling, Kant endeavors in his *Critique of Judgment* to articulate how it is that such subjective feelings also open us to experience of Beauty, and by analogy, to experience of the Good. Kant struggles to articulate how the mind can judge an object, whether natural or artificial, to be beautiful universally, rather than judging it based merely on the pleasure the object generates subjectively. It is in trying to formulate the faculty of feeling's capacity for universality that Kant comes closest to bridging the chasm between the physical/sensible and the mental/intelligible domains running throughout his system. The full unification of these dualities, however, would have to wait until Schelling and Whitehead's genius brought Kant's aesthetico-organic intimations to fruition, as is discussed in subsequent chapters.

In the *Critique of Judgment*, Kant suggests that feeling serves as an intermediary between the faculties of thinking and willing. Properly critiqued, feeling allows for at least a reflective (if not constitutive) judgment of Nature as purposeful, thereby opening a hypothetical economy between supersensible ideas of Reason and sense-bound concepts of the understanding. The feeling of pleasure associated with the beauty of certain natural forms, says Kant, provokes a sense of their purposefulness in us. The imagination senses this finality despite the understanding's lack of any such concept. For Kant, the understanding cannot know Nature as purposeful *a priori*—that is, through concepts alone—but Nature can nonetheless be judged purposeful through imagination's power of generalization: particular experiences of finality (elicited by feelings of pleasure) can become applicable as schematic rules for the judgment of Nature in general.

---

102. Schelling, *Ideas*, 10–11.

Chapter 1: Kant as Guardian of the Threshold of Imagination

Feeling undoubtedly provides the massive basis of human life. Without it, though I may have some *idea*, I would have no *sense* of myself as a unique and enduring being. Nor would I have either an idea or sense of Nature outside me. I would become, as it were, a mind without a body. Such a disembodied mind would also be stripped of most of its desires, except, Kant would argue, the desire to realize the ideas of Reason, especially that of freedom. But what sort of freedom is it that leaves me senseless and without a relation to Nature?

Feeling would seem to operate contrary to freedom, in that feelings are simply given: *they happen to me*. Freedom, in contrast, implies spontaneous self-determination: *I am responsible for my actions*. It is this distinction that Kant felt justified his epistemic dualism between the sensory world, of which the understanding provides *a priori* knowledge, and the supersensible world, with which conscience provides our only sure connection. Freedom and the moral duty determining it is for Kant the most important ideal of human life—more important even than scientific knowledge of an apparently mechanistic Nature. Nature can only be understood mechanistically *unless* we are willing to admit the testimony of our feelings as regards the body's and Nature's organic purposiveness. The finality of Nature as a systematic whole, and of the organisms composing it, is judged reflectively by Kant to be "self-organizing."[103] All of Nature, as well as each of its organisms, he considers to be at least relatively autonomous, being both cause and effect of their own organization.

A modicum of freedom here seeps into the constitution of a now living Nature, if only we are willing to feel it. Kant was ultimately not so willing, since for him feelings represent all that prevents the human soul from realizing the universal ideal of freedom (i.e., the categorical imperative) by leading the will astray into the pleasures of the flesh. So far as Kant is

---

103. Kant, *Critique of Judgment*, 164.

concerned, it would seem that embodied human life is therefore depraved: we are destined to remain at war with our own ideals and alienated from actual Nature, including our own impassioned bodies. As Nietzsche put it, Kant ends up sacrificing the feeling of freedom "to the Moloch of abstraction." Nietzsche continues:

> An action compelled by the instinct of life has in the joy of performing it the proof it is a *right* action.... What destroys more quickly than to work, to think, to feel without inner necessity, without a deep personal choice, without *joy*? as automaton of "duty"?[104]

But it would be premature to give up on Kant just yet. Elsewhere in the *Critique of Judgment*, Kant suggests that the beautiful can be read as a "symbol of the morally Good" because in recognizing a natural or artificial product as beautiful, we expect that other persons, through their common sense, will judge it in like manner.[105] Here Kant, whether directly influenced or not, echoes the ideas of the theosopher Friedrich Christoph Oetinger (1702–1782), an important influence on Schelling. Oetinger writes in his book *Die Wahrheit des Sensus Communis* (1753) that the *communis sensus* or common sense

> is concerned only with things that all men see before them, things that hold an entire society together, things that are concerned as much with truths and statements as with the arrangements and patterns comprised in statements.[106]

Oetinger adds that the *communis sensus* is what provides us with the "unmediated cognition" that overcomes the subject/object division and so establishes a deep bond between

---

104. Nietzsche, "The Anti-Christ," *The Nietzsche Reader*, 489.
105. Kant, *Critique of Judgment*, 149.
106. As quoted in Magee, *Hegel and the Hermetic Tradition*, 67.

human consciousness, the Universe, and God. Kant also comes close to affirming that our natural love of Beauty can guide our moral and cognitive activity. Feelings would thus be made intelligible and objective, providing us with more than merely subjective judgments of what is beautiful. Although Kant speculates that the apprehension of Beauty may be what awakens the ego to the common sense harmonizing its own aesthetic judgments with those of others, in the end he is unable to affirm the idea as anything more than a representation appearing before the reflective mind as a result of its own transcendental activity. Schelling and Whitehead seized upon Kant's half-hearted intimation and sought to intensify it. They articulated a philosophical vision in which Beauty points the soul to the profound erotic current hidden amidst the life of all things. They saw that imagination, the generative matrix and *communis sensus* of the animate universe, helps to remind the individual soul of the immanent divine Eros holding all things together in Goodness. The ancients knew this Eros as the lifeblood of the *anima mundi*, the world-soul. The practical imagination that grasps Beauty as an expression of the Good allows the self to place itself in the position—body and soul—of others, and indeed of *all* others, that is, of the *All*. A redeemed imagination can sympathetically identify with any ensouled part of the universe and also with the soul of the whole universe. It does so through the power of Love.

The faculty of feeling, according to Kant,

> both on account of this inner possibility in the subject [to judge an object as beautiful in common with others] and of the external possibility of a nature that agrees with it, finds itself to be referred to something which is neither nature nor freedom, but which yet is connected with the supersensible ground of the latter.[107]

---

107. Kant, *Critique of Judgment*, 150.

Kant goes on to suggest that, "in a way which though common is yet unknown," the supersensible ground of freedom binds the theoretical faculty of knowledge to the practical faculty of desire.[108] What would it mean to take seriously the insight provided by deep feelings shared in good will with others concerning the Beauty of organic processes? Perhaps it would be possible to understand Nature's beginnings in a nexus of more or less unconscious wills that over evolutionary time have been growing toward ever-greater differentiation-in-communion, finally striving to awaken to itself in the form of the spiritual animals we call human beings? Kant, though he lacked certainty, was nonetheless intrigued by the possibility of a similar notion, that the history of the human species could be understood as the gradual unfolding of a divine seed initially hidden in Nature.[109] Such judgment requires that we see Nature with eyes and heart aided by the highest potency of imagination, thereby being "enabled to understand the significance of the universe, to grasp its life and depth directly, as a felt experience," as Mary Warnock put it.[110]

Unfortunately, Kant's third critique culminates in his refusal to accept the testimony of his feelings as to Nature's genuine organic purposiveness. This purposiveness, he argues, is only projected onto Nature by the constitution of the human mind. He denies the possibility of real scientific insight into Nature's non-mechanical self-organization. Such insight would require *scientific genius*, but according to Kant, only artists and poets can be considered geniuses. For Kant, a genius is a person through whom Nature's creativity expresses itself in the form of art. A genius is someone who, without following explicit rules and so according to a method mysterious even to themselves, is able to give artistic expression to

---

108. Kant, *Critique of Judgment*, 150.
109. See Kant's 1784 essay, "Idea for a Universal History with a Cosmopolitan Purpose."
110. Warnock, *Imagination*, 119.

the formative forces of Nature. Without the slightest contrivance, as though they emerged merely from the free play of imagination, geniuses are able to produce beautiful works that, for those with cultivated taste at least, are suggestive of supersensible ideas and cosmic intelligences.[111]

A mind capable of knowing Nature and her products as self-organizing would amount to a *scientific* genius. Rather than sharply distinguishing between artistic and scientific forms of genius, Schelling intuited that

> the only difference between nature and the artist is that with nature the material is not outside the artist but rather one with it and inwardly growing together with it.[112]

For Kant, on the other hand, genius of the scientific kind was a contradiction in terms. Recall that according to Kant natural science presupposes the lawful system of categories imposed universally upon our experience of Nature by the understanding. Science thus produces conceptually determinant knowledge about Nature, principally in the form of synthetic *a priori* mathematical constructions. Those aspects of Nature that cannot be known *a priori* are sorted according to the sieve of experiment, which itself still presupposes the systematic conceptual order imposed by the understanding. From Kant's perspective, if a scientist cannot explain with logical or mathematical precision exactly how she came to know what she knows, then she does not know anything. Knowledge production is always such that anyone with sufficient training should be able to grasp and reproduce it. Though some technical and so teachable skill is always required, *artistic genius* cannot be taught. Its products remain forever beyond the reach of mere skill or algorithmic programming. Artistic geniuses gain aesthetic insight into Nature, but in so doing, according to Kant,

---

111. Kant, *Critique of Judgment*, 112–23.
112. Schelling, *The Ages of the World*, 56.

fail to provide any determinate scientific knowledge of Nature. Scientists, similarly, can catch no cognitive sight (i.e., they have no intellectual intuition) of the hidden causes of Nature's self-organizing processes. "It is quite certain," writes Kant,

> that we can never adequately come to know the organized beings and their internal possibility in accordance with merely mechanical principles of nature, let alone explain them; and indeed this is so certain that we can boldly say that it would be absurd for humans even to make such an attempt or to hope that there may yet arise a Newton who could make comprehensible even the generation of a blade of grass according to natural laws that no intention has ordered; rather, we must absolutely deny this insight to human beings.[113]

When it comes to our power to judge whether the apparently teleological or end-seeking strivings of Nature (in its products and as a whole) are real causes or merely illusory phantoms, Kant resolves what would otherwise remain an antinomy for Reason by denying natural science any knowledge one way or the other. Kant argues that we simply cannot know scientifically whether Nature is truly mechanical or whether purposeful processes are shaping its organic products. Science can neither affirm an intelligent cause behind Nature, nor deny that, at least for we as human knowers, such a cause may be necessary to explain the unity of Nature. The concept of unity is said to provide the very condition for the possibility of any natural science at all, and so for Kant, although we cannot know whether Nature is objectively purposive or organic, we are justified in our subjective assertions of its organic telos because our cognitive powers of imagination, understanding, and Reason cannot find internal harmony without operating as though this purposiveness is real.

---

113. Kant, *Critique of Judgment*, 185.

2

Inverting Kant: From a Mechanistic to an Organic Cosmology

> "When you understand all about the sun and all about the atmosphere and all about the rotation of the earth, you may still miss the radiance of the sunset."
> —Whitehead[1]

KANT, LIKE MANY MODERN PHILOSOPHERS writing in the wake of Galileo, Descartes, and Newton, "swallowed the scientific scheme in its entirety as being the only rendering of the facts of nature."[2] As we have seen, however, Kant had a unique way of digesting the mechanical image of the world: he rejected the scientific scheme's naive realism and reinterpreted its given facts as constructed appearances shaped *a priori* by the necessary and universal structure of the human mind. Schelling and Whitehead share with Kant a need to qualify the scientific view of the world so as not to do violence to the human values of freedom and beauty. But aside from lamenting the violence done by the early modern Cartesian-Newtonian scientific scheme to our concrete experience of Nature, Whitehead also sought to reconstruct natural science after the late modern breakdown of its Newtonian foundations due to the creation of non-Aristotelean logics and non-Euclidian geometries, as well as the discovery of evolutionary, relativity,

---

1. Whitehead, *Science and the Modern World*, 178.
2. Whitehead, *Science and the Modern World*, 63.

quantum, and complexity theories.[3] Whitehead's philosophy of organism is largely a response to the revolutionary implications of these new developments in mathematics, physics, and biology, implications that forced him decisively beyond the limited territory Kant had staked out for the speculative imagination. As Lucas suggests, "Whitehead read Kant as having enshrined in a peculiarly idiosyncratic way an epistemology grounded in Newtonian-Euclidian cosmology," and while Whitehead did not deny the importance of sound epistemological principles, "he recognized that epistemologies (including Kant's) entail cosmological assumptions."[4] As it turns out, objects in space and time—and the human subject who thinks about them—are not what they once appeared to be.

"In the year 1500," writes Whitehead, "Europe knew less than Archimedes who died in the year 212 BCE."[5] The commonsense assumption of a person living in 1500 was that Earth stood stationary at the center of a sacred series of eternally circling heavenly hosts. Below the moon, four elements composed everything; above it, something far subtler was thought to be at work. "Yet in the year 1700," continues Whitehead, "Newton's *Principia* had been written and the world was well started on the modern epoch."[6] Even before Kant, the new analytic methods of Descartes, Galileo, and Newton had succeeded in extinguishing the ancient bond between anthropos and cosmos by severing the numinous life of the soul from the mechanical motion of an insentient cosmos. The power of modern science was largely derived from its bifurcation of Nature into two distinct substances: the material, which could be analyzed objectively with

---

3. See Segall, *Physics of the World-Soul: Whitehead's Adventure in Cosmology* (SacraSage, 2021) for more on Whitehead's relevance to the new paradigm sciences.
4. Lucas, *Whitehead*, 78–79.
5. Whitehead, *Science and the Modern World*, 13.
6. Whitehead, *Science and the Modern World*, 13.

geometrical certainty, and the mental, which was subjective and so became increasingly unmoored from science.[7] Natural science made tremendous progress by bracketing metaphysical quandaries concerning the nature of the mental activity making it possible. From Whitehead's point of view, the questions of early modern science "[did] not enable [it] to formulate the problem of the 'mind' because these questions and their answers presuppose it."[8] Nature's subjectivity—her living agency, value, and qualitative spectra of colors, scents, and sounds—was ignored in favor of measurable quantities like mass and velocity. It was inevitable that some natural scientists would become carried away by the instrumental successes of their method and overreach their proper charter into metaphysics.

"If the living creature were removed," argues Galileo, the first to formalize the bifurcation of Nature in terms of primary physical and secondary psychical characteristics, "all these qualities would be wiped away and annihilated."[9] The warmth and hue of a sunset "are no more than mere names so far as the object in which we locate them are concerned."[10] They arise not from the real physicality of the cosmos but are projected upon matter by an epiphenomenal consciousness, a ghost in the machine. In Whitehead's words, early modern science's bifurcation of Nature inevitably left us with "two natures . . . one the conjecture and the other the dream."[11] Our subjective experience of Nature (the dream) was opposed to an abstract model of Nature theorized to be the objective cause of that experience (the conjecture).

---

7. This despite the fact that pre-Kantian rationalists like Descartes, Spinoza, and Leibniz attempted to explain the mind according to a no less certain "rational theology."
8. Stengers, *Thinking With Whitehead*, 35.
9. Galileo, "The Assayer," 274.
10. Galileo, "The Assayer," 274.
11. Whitehead, *The Concept of Nature*, 31.

Following upon Galileo's initial bifurcation of nature, Descartes brilliantly articulated the ontological and epistemological underpinnings of the modern scientific world view. The eclipse of Ptolemaic geocentric astronomy achieved by Copernicus' heliocentric model (as improved upon by Kepler and Newton) made it clear to Descartes that sensory perception could not be trusted for scientific purposes. Science was to become the study of the mechanisms of the extended things of Nature (*res extensa*), a study guided by the exact measurement and mathematical calculation of primary qualities including density, shape, and motion. Religion, on the other hand, was to retain responsibility for shaping the unearthly substance of the soul, providing moral guidance for existentially troubled thinking things like us (*res cogitans*).[12] Secondary qualities like color, sound, and taste were left to the free play of artists to be combined and recombined for the purpose of heightening the pleasure of appearances, rather than penetrating into the archetypal depths of reality.[13] While Kant eventually came to assign philosophical significance to our feelings of beauty, with minor epistemic qualifications he basically accepted Descartes' dualistic view of the extended and thinking substances.

As we have seen, Schelling and Whitehead's natural philosophy is something of an inversion of Kant's transcendental approach. Their cosmology is organized around a new concept of Nature and a novel way of framing the activity of science. Instead of construing the task of science to be that of overcoming subjective illusion in order to reach objective reality, Whitehead takes the speculative risk of defining Nature otherwise: Nature becomes, quite simply, "what we are aware

---

12. See Toulmin, *Cosmopolis*, 69–82.

13. Prior to the differentiation of art, science, and religion in the modern period, art served primarily a religious function as a sort of window from the earthly into the archetypal realm (Whitehead, *Science and the Modern World*, 20). Art also served science by mastering perspective, allowing for realistic representations of nature (ibid., 45).

of in perception."¹⁴ "Everything perceived is in nature," says Whitehead, "We may not pick and choose."¹⁵ Similarly, for Schelling,

> All quality in nature only has meaning insofar as it is itself originally sensation. The qualities of things cannot be explained mechanically and externally. They can only be explained by the original impressions that the being of nature itself obtains in creation.¹⁶

The validity of their reframing of the natural scientific method cannot be judged *a priori*. To judge it fairly, we must first trust it enough to take the "leap of the imagination"¹⁷ it requires, bridging the artificial chasm hewn by the founders of modern science and, once on the other side of their bifurcation, patiently considering the ways experience and knowledge are transformed. Helpful in this context is William James' notion of "precursive trust," a constructive, pragmatic alternative to the critical methods employed since Kant:

> We can and we may, as it were, jump with both feet off the ground into or towards a world of which we trust the other parts to meet our jump. ... Only through our precursive trust in it can it come into being. There is no inconstancy anywhere in this, and no "vicious circle" unless a circle of poles holding themselves upright by leaning on one another, or a circle of dancers revolving by holding each other's hands, be "vicious."¹⁸

Passing judgment on the veracity of Schelling and Whitehead's new concept of Nature thus requires first deploying it,

---

14. Whitehead, *The Concept of Nature*, 28.
15. Whitehead, *The Concept of Nature*, 29.
16. Schelling, *The Ages of the World*, 91, note ix (which is quoting Schelling's *Philosophy of Mythology*).
17. Whitehead, *Process and Reality*, 4.
18. James, *Some Problems of Philosophy*, 230–31.

experimenting with the ways it transfigures both our perception of the world and our conception of truth, establishing its relevance to the pragmatics of actual life. This is not simply an epistemological issue, but from a pragmatic point of view (and in James' words again), a matter of

> the difference between living against a background of foreignness and one of intimacy...between a general habit of wariness and one of trust. One might call it a social difference, for after all, the common *socius* of us all is the great universe whose children we are.[19]

Though writing specifically about materialism, James' distinctions between wariness and trust, foreignness and intimacy, hold equally well for any philosophy that severs the conscious knower from its place within Nature. These are attitudinal issues which inform the emotional background of modern philosophy without explicitly entering into its epistemological reflections.

Schelling and Whitehead's aesthetic orientation to cosmology follows from their invention and deployment of novel conceptions of space, time, causality, consciousness, and divinity. Their conceptual innovations pose new problems for natural philosophy, allowing it to become attentive to the relevance of both the quantitative patterns *and* the qualitative purposes ingredient in the passage of Nature. Natural philosophy is thus released from the irrational and polemical modern desire to replace concrete experience with inadequate abstract explanations. In one sense, Whitehead's philosophical method can be compared with Goethe's "gentle empiricism," which bracketed mechanico-mathematical explanations to pursue Nature's reasons by learning to participate more fully in the formative forces and archetypal powers incarnate in actual experience.[20]

---

19. James, *A Pluralistic Universe*, Lecture 1.
20. Zajonc, *Catching the Light*, 203.

Chapter 2: Inverting Kant: From a Mechanistic to an Organic Cosmology

"The divergence of the formulae about nature from the appearance of nature," argues Whitehead, "has robbed the formulae of any explanatory character."[21] In another sense, Whitehead was unlike Goethe and Schelling (and more like Plato and Leibniz) in that mathematics provided the original imaginative impetus for his adventure in cosmology.[22] For Whitehead, "nothing is more impressive" than the paradoxical fact that the increasing abstraction of mathematical thought has provided "the true weapons with which to control our thought of concrete fact."[23] But Whitehead does not seek to continue wielding mathematics like a weapon to dissect Nature into calculable geometric point-instants. As a radical empiricist, he employs mathematics only when and where it proves elucidatory of the passage of concrete fact. After all, it is from the passage of Nature itself that our mathematical understanding is derived. Whitehead provides the example of periodicity in Nature—the solar recurrence of days, lunar phases, seasons, planetary orbits, our own heartbeat and breath—as one important source of mathematical ideas.[24] Mathematics is essentially an abstraction from the various periodicities composing the concrete passage of Nature. As even the ur-idealist Plato suggested,

> our ability to see the periods of [the heavens] has led to the invention of number, and has given us the idea of time and opened the path to inquiry into the nature of the universe.[25]

---

21. Whitehead, *Modes of Thought*, 154.
22. For a more developed comparison between the participatory methodologies of Goethe and Whitehead, including the often unacknowledged mathematical aspects of Goethe's method, see Segall, "Goethe and Whitehead: Steps Toward a Science of Organism," in *Holistic Science Journal* (forthcoming 2022).
23. Whitehead, *Science and the Modern World*, 32.
24. Whitehead, *Science and the Modern World*, 31.
25. Plato, *Timaeus*, 47a.

Whitehead sought to disclose Nature to awareness as a community of evolving relationships among organisms. Organisms cannot be adequately characterized merely by the quantitative measures of mass, extension, and velocity. They are agents enjoying and expressing the aesthetic values of their own experience, values which are in part inherited from the feelings of others. Contrary to both the scientific metaphysics of Galileo, Descartes, and Newton, and to Kant's transcendental revolution, Schelling and Whitehead's vision of the cosmos is organic: the final real things are not point-instants or other geometrically determined categories but individual living creatures, each dependent on their ecological relationships with others in order to achieve and maintain enduring forms of value.

The scientistic presupposition that geometrically determined "matter in motion is the one concrete reality in nature," such that "aesthetic values form an . . . irrelevant addition," has proven itself to be an error of disastrous proportions.[26] Kant was awake to the danger of dismissing beauty as a mere illusion projected upon Nature by the mind, but the subject-centered orientation of his transcendental method ultimately left him ill-equipped to describe it otherwise. Instead of accepting the abstract categories of seventeenth century science, Whitehead climbed out of the rubble of the old mechanistic framework and set to work reconstructing metaphysics on an organic basis. He reimagined modern science's bifurcation of Nature, which had severed it into objective physical facts and subjective human values. With a conception of process-relational creativity rather than self-identical substance at the generative core of his system, Whitehead built a cosmology whose details elucidate, rather than eliminate, the common sense values of civilized life, such as moral freedom, aesthetic enjoyment, and veritable

---

26. Whitehead, *Science and the Modern World*, 182.

knowledge (or Goodness, Beauty, and Truth, respectively).

"If nature really is bifurcated," argues one of Whitehead's contemporary interpreters, Bruno Latour, "no living organism would be possible, since being an organism means being the sort of thing whose primary [physical] and secondary [psychical] qualities—if they exist—are endlessly blurred."[27] Whitehead's philosophy of organism rejects the bifurcation of such qualities, as well as any type of arbitrary ontological dualism. Nonetheless, it must be admitted that the widespread acceptance of dualism during the modern period implies that, as an abstract scheme, it can prove elucidatory of the texture of experience in some instances. Whitehead criticizes Descartes' dualism for its incoherence due to excessive abstraction, but adds that "[his] system obviously says something that is true."[28] Whitehead appropriates much from the modern tradition of natural philosophy, all the while keeping in mind that "the chief error in philosophy is overstatement."[29]

Before moving on to show the way beyond the Kantian threshold, a brief introduction to some of Whitehead's novel categories is in order. By way of his method of imaginative generalization, Whitehead is led to experimentally construct[30] an alternative cosmological scheme that is ultimately rooted in *creative process*, rather than *static substance*, and whose fundamental categories are *actual occasions*, *prehensions*, and *eternal objects*, rather than *minds*, *representations*, and *matter*. The dualistic Cartesian problematic is not thereby dismissed or explained away, but dissolved through a transformation

---

27. Latour, Foreword to *Thinking With Whitehead*, xiii.
28. Whitehead, *Process and Reality*, 6.
29. Whitehead, *Process and Reality*, 7.
30. His method is experimental in that it redesigns the philosophical instrument of language "in the same way that, in physical science, pre-existing appliances are redesigned" (Whitehead, *Process and Reality*, 11).

of its presuppositions.[31] The relationship between actual occasions and eternal objects is no longer one of substantial *duality*, where neither kind of entity requires the other in order to exist, but of vibrational *polarity*, such that the being of eternal objects cannot be grasped in abstraction from the becoming of actual occasions, or vice versa. Whitehead avoids the modern bifurcation of Nature by recognizing that every occasion of experience involves both a physical pole inheriting the feelings of realized actual facts and a mental pole anticipating realizable eternal possibilities.

Whitehead admits that the *conscious* mental pole of "high grade" organisms like human beings is so advanced in *degree* that it appears also to become different in *kind*. Instead of our special difference opening up an ontological rift between mind and Nature, Whitehead re-embeds the high abstractions achieved by our human kind of mind back into the nexus physical feelings out which it emerges. His philosophy of organism avoids making self-conscious human experience the hinge upon which all else turns by situating it as an admittedly rare and special example of a nonetheless cosmically pervasive capacity for experience.[32]

For Whitehead, to exist at all is already to partake in experience, and to experience is to value: "Realization is . . . in itself the attainment of value . . . . Aesthetic attainment is interwoven [with] the texture of realization."[33] While the mechanical natural philosophy begins by assuming the two independently existing substances, mind and matter—where material objects are modified by external relations of locomotion, and mental subjects are modified by internal private cogitations representative of external public objects—Whitehead's philosophy of organism begins with "the analysis of process as the realization of events disposed in an interlocked

---

31. Whitehead, *Process and Reality*, 108.
32. See Whitehead, *Process and Reality*, 108–9, 172.
33. Whitehead, *Science and the Modern World*, 89–90.

community."³⁴ Actual occasions, as the final realities of which the universe is composed, are self-creating buds of experience, each one uniquely itself even while it remains internally related to every antecedent occasion in the creative community of the universe. Occasions are interrelated by way of the pattern of eternal objects characterizing for each of them the quantitative and qualitative aspects of the other occasions in their community. Eternal objects "interpret [occasions], each to the other,"³⁵ such that they come to find themselves related to one another in an extended space-time continuum according to certain more or less stable geometric principles,³⁶ principles explored in the next section (2.2) examining Kant's view of the relations between Euclidian geometry and phenomenal space.

"The solidarity of the universe," writes Whitehead, "is based on the relational functioning of eternal objects."³⁷ As relational entities, eternal objects cannot themselves *cause* actual occasions, they can only characterize the *how* of prehension. "[Eternal objects] are adverbial, rather than substantive," according to Shaviro, in that "they determine and express *how* actual [occasions] relate to one another, take one another up, and 'enter into each others' constitutions.'"³⁸ Each actual occasion is, in this sense, nothing but the multiplicity of prehensions of other occasions (as characterized adverbially by eternal objects) which it unifies. But in another sense, as a self-unifying creature, an occasion not only prehends and reiterates the realized spatiotemporal pattern of the settled past, it adds a novel concretion of value—*itself*—to the ongoing evolution of the universe. Whitehead coined the term *concrescence* to refer to the "production of novel togetherness"

---

34. Whitehead, *Science and the Modern World*, 138.
35. Whitehead, *Science and the Modern World*, 137.
36. Whitehead, *Science and the Modern World*, 145.
37. Whitehead, *Science and the Modern World*, 137.
38. Shaviro, *Without Criteria*, 37; quoting Whitehead, *Process and Reality*, 148–49.

resulting from the completed satisfaction of each occasion of experience.[39] By way of concrescence, a particular actual occasion's many prehensions of past occasions becomes one, thereby adding another realized unity of experience to the ongoing creative advance of the cosmic community: "The many become one, and are increased by one."[40]

Whitehead's concept of prehension is meant to integrate both causal and perceptual relations. Whitehead invented the category of prehension in an attempt to subvert the modern bifurcation of Nature between mental images and mechanical impacts, between nature as it appears before us ("the dream") and nature as it is thought to be the cause of appearance ("the conjecture"). "Prehension" offers an aesthetic account of causation, an account that subverts the false dichotomy between appearance and reality that is typical of materialism, idealism, and dualism alike. In Whitehead's process-relational scheme, the power of imagination (as prehension) goes all the way down. Aesthetics becomes ontological.

Prehension should not be thought of as resulting in an actual occasion "having" experience of other occasions, as though an occasion were "the unchanging subject of change."[41] This would inevitably lead back to the classical bifurcated conception of substantial minds qualified by their private representations of supposedly public material objects. "If this be granted," argues Whitehead, "there is no escape from solipsism."[42] It was only the theological recourse to the goodness of an omnipotent God that allowed Descartes to re-establish a meaningful epistemic connection between ideas in the mind and facts in Nature. Kant tried to establish this link by transcendentally deducing the categorical presuppositions of synthetic *a priori* knowledge, but he did so

---

39. Whitehead, *Process and Reality*, 21.
40. Whitehead, *Process and Reality*, 21.
41. Whitehead, *Process and Reality*, 29.
42. Whitehead, *Science and the Modern World*, 137.

at the cost of reducing the reality of Nature to geometrically determined appearances in the mind. For the philosophy of organism, an actual occasion of experience is not a pre-existent subject qualified by its representations of ready-made objects. Instead, actual occasions are re-imagined as dipolar "subject-superjects."[43] The "subject" phase of a concrescing occasion emerges from the prehensions of aspects of antecedent occasions which it unifies, while in the "superject" phase the occasion, having attained satisfaction as a unified drop of decisively patterned experience, perishes into "objective immortality," thus making itself available for prehension by subsequently concrescing actual occasions. Whitehead expresses the perpetual perishing of subjective immediacy into objective immortality in terms of his "principle of relativity," such that "it belongs to the nature of a 'being' that it is a potential for every 'becoming.'"[44] Actual occasions are thus describable in two ways: as "being" and as "becoming." These ontological designations are not separable, since, according to Whitehead's correlative "principle of process," an occasion's "being" arises from its "becoming": "*how* an actual [occasion] *becomes* constitutes *what* that actual [occasion] *is*."[45] The description of an occasion according to its genetic "becoming" provides an account of the occasion's own subjective aim (i.e., its final cause), while the description according to its extensive "being" provides an account of its superjective effect as prehended by other occasions beyond itself (i.e., as efficient cause). Creative process is said to manifest in two ways, as the *concrescence* of each individual entity, and as the *transition* between one occasion and the next. Concrescence describes "the real internal constitution of a particular existent," while transition describes the perishing of a particular existent's process, thereby "constituting that existent as an original element in

---

43. Whitehead, *Process and Reality*, 29.
44. Whitehead, *Process and Reality*, 22.
45. Whitehead, *Process and Reality*, 23.

the constitutions of other particular existences elicited by repetitions of process."[46]

The continuity of the universe (its wholeness and unity) is preserved by the process of transition, while the individuality of actual occasions is preserved by the process of concrescence. Unlike the transitional process, concrescence is not simply prehensive, since each actual occasion defines the world from its unique perspective by ingressing novel eternal objects: "No two occasions can have identical actual worlds."[47] Concrescence is the process by which an actual occasion prehends the many occasions of its environment together with the ingression of relevant possibilities into some new definite form of unity, thereby achieving a subjective value to be added to the ongoing creative advance of Nature. The differentiation between concrescence and transition allows Whitehead's cosmological scheme, despite its generally processual orientation, to remain nonetheless atomic. Whitehead is led to conclude that "the ultimate metaphysical truth is atomism,"[48] but his atoms are dynamic events and not point-instants. The discoveries of quantum mechanics (that there can be no "nature at an instant") and relativity theory (that the universe has no single continuous time flow) forced him to give up the old idea of simply located material. Another crucial influence was Leibniz's monadic theory, with the important difference that Whitehead's atomic drops of experience are not windowless substances set in pre-established harmony but "an interlocked plurality" of creative events.[49] Whitehead's is not an idealistic atomism like Leibniz', nor is it a materialistic atomism like Newton's. His atoms, like Schelling's, are creatively emergent and internally related actual occasions of experience. On this point, Whitehead writes:

---

46. Whitehead, *Process and Reality*, 210.
47. Whitehead, *Process and Reality*, 210.
48. Whitehead, *Process and Reality*, 35.
49. Whitehead, *Science and the Modern World*, 70.

Chapter 2: Inverting Kant: From a Mechanistic to an Organic Cosmology

> There is a becoming of continuity, but no continuity of becoming. The actual occasions are the creatures which become, and they constitute a continuously extensive world. In other words, extensiveness becomes, but "becoming" is not itself extensive.[50]

Whitehead's atoms are not billiard balls falling in the void; they are not "in" space but grow into existence like cells cleaving into a developing embryo, achieving their aesthetic value and leaving metrical space-time in their wake. Whitehead's atomic occasions are "epochal" formations, each making their contribution to the emergence of a shared space-time morphology. The continuous extensive world with its specific spatiotemporal modes of relationality is considered a contingent fact of our cosmic epoch, a metaphysical accident rather than a necessity: "continuity is a special condition arising from the society of creatures which constitute our immediate epoch."[51] The creative advance of Nature involves an inheritance of rhythmic pattern from one concrescent occasion to the next. Between occasional beats, intervals are opened up, leaving room for improvisation. By conceiving the basic constituents of the world as dipolar processes of causal inheritance and conceptual innovation, rather than as static isolated substances qualified by accidental predicates and set within a block-like spatiotemporal manifold, Whitehead is able to preserve the unique identity of each individual organism without at the same time so exaggerating their separateness that continuity with the larger cosmic ecosystem is broken.

Having crowned Creativity "the universal of universals characterizing ultimate matter of fact," Whitehead still needed to account for the unique character of more mundane matters of fact (i.e., finite actual occasions). How is the infinite Creativity conditioning the universe to be canalized into the

---

50. Whitehead, *Process and Reality*, 35.
51. Whitehead, *Process and Reality*, 36.

relevant evaluations of possibility characterizing the concrescence of each of its unique finite creatures? To answer this question, Whitehead constructed a novel concept of divinity. Following his commitment to avoid ontologically exceptional entities, the only difference between God and every other actual occasion is that divine experience appears to occur in the reverse direction to that of finite experiences, such that God's mental pole is primary while God's physical pole is consequent. As we have seen, God's mental pole is described as the primordial creature of Creativity, the first act of unfettered conceptual valuation responsible for ordering the realm of eternal objects. This divine capacity for primordial envisagement may seem like an exceptional feature characterizing only God among all actual entities, but Whitehead is like Schelling in insisting that God's decision to order the chaos is a free act and not a determined necessity. In other words, God's primordial evaluation is "the ultimate irrationality," a contingently established fact and not a metaphysical necessity: "No reason can be given for the nature of God, because that nature is the ground of rationality."[52] God is thus simultaneously a creature of Creativity and, by God's persuasive influence on the decisions of finite actual occasions, a condition limiting the otherwise chaotic potency of Creativity. "By reason of this complete valuation," writes Whitehead,

> the objectification of God in each derivate actual [occasion] results in a graduation of the relevance of eternal objects to the concrescent occasion in question . . . . Apart from God, eternal objects unrealized in the actual world would be relatively non-existent for the concrescence in question.[53]

God, as the "primordial superject of creativity," is the first fact granting a definite face to the otherwise impersonal creative

---

52. Whitehead, *Science and the Modern World*, 178.
53. Whitehead, *Process and Reality*, 31.

advance. God's primordial nature assures that every finite occasion of experience, subsequent to God's initial act of envisagement, includes in its physical prehension of the actual world a conceptual prehension of the realm of possibilities *as relevant to it*. In this way, those abstract potentials remaining as yet unrealized in a particular occasion's actual world nonetheless find their definite relation to that occasion and its world without having to float into their situation from nowhere.[54] According to Whitehead's "ontological principle," "the general potentiality of the universe must be somewhere . . . this 'somewhere' is the non-temporal actual entity": God.[55]

God is a dipolar actual entity like every other, "finding [itself] in the double role of [agent] and [patient] in a common world."[56] God's primordial envisagement of the infinite hierarchy of eternal objects occurs in abstraction from finite actual occasions: it is accomplished by God alone. As such, the primordial aspect of God's nature remains unconscious and deficient in actuality. While the abstract order of the universe depends upon God's agential "adjustment of the togetherness of eternal objects," the concrete values of the universe are preserved by the "infinite patience" of God's consequent pole, God's "tender care that nothing be lost."[57] God experienced in full concreteness (i.e., as a conscious cosmic personality) is not the distant unmoved mover or all-powerful creator of traditional religious traditions, but the poet and lover of the world, "the fellow-sufferer who understands."[58] Whitehead's imaginative description of God has more in common with the intermediary World-Soul of Plato's *Timaeus* than it does with the "wholly transcendent"

---

54. Whitehead, *Process and Reality*, 32.
55. Whitehead, *Process and Reality*, 46.
56. Whitehead, *Process and Reality*, 315.
57. Whitehead, *Process and Reality*, 346.
58. Whitehead, *Process and Reality*, 346, 351.

Jehovah of Newton's *Scholium*, who "[creates] out of nothing an accidental universe."[59] Whitehead's dipolar imagination of God echoes in Schelling's pronouncement at the end of the third draft of his incomplete philosophical poem *The Ages of the World*:

> The whole spatially extended cosmos is ... the swelling heart of the Godhead that continues, retained by invisible forces, in a continuous pulsation or in an alternation of expansion and contraction.[60]

2.1 The Transmutation of Kant's "Refutation of Idealism": From Subject-Substance Correlation to Process-Relational Creativity

What I am essentially protesting against is the bifurcation of nature into two systems of reality, which, in so far as they are real, are real in different senses. One reality would be the entities such as electrons which are the study of speculative physics. This would be the reality which is there for knowledge; although on this theory it is never known. For what is known is the other sort of reality, which is the byplay of the mind. Thus there would be two natures, one is the conjecture and the other is the dream.

—Whitehead[61]

In this section, Kant's master categories of Subject and Substance as deployed in his "Refutation of Idealism" in the B edition of the *Critique of Pure Reason* are contrasted with Whitehead's most general categories of Process and Creativity. The latter are no longer "master" categories, because rather than lording over reality as the one exception to the rules determining everything else (e.g., Kant's transcendental Subject), Whitehead understood reality as a creative process potentially capable of generating its own conscious

---

59. Whitehead, *Process and Reality*, 95.
60. Schelling, *The Ages of the World*, 94.
61. Whitehead, *The Concept of Nature*, 31.

categoreal interpreters. His categories and concepts are thus exhibited as bubbling up from within, between, and as the things-themselves, as experiential mediators rather than transcendental masters.

Kant would almost certainly object to the accusation that his Transcendental Aesthetic is overly subjectivistic, that it lets mind so dominate over things that they evaporate into phantoms. He would probably defend his perspective for the same reasons he objected to the earliest reviews of the A edition of his *Critique of Pure Reason* by the empiricist *Popularphilosophen* Christian Garve and J. G. Feder.[62] These reviewers equated his transcendental idealism with the dogmatic idealism of Bishop Berkeley. Despite Kant's intentions, they argued that, consistently employed, the principles of his idealism lead unavoidably to subjectivism, or the reduction of all our knowledge of Nature to representations in the mind.[63] Berkeley's works, including his *Treatise Concerning the Principles of Human Knowledge*, had appeared in German translation in 1781.[64] This was the same year the first edition of the *Critique of Pure Reason* was published, making the comparison all too convenient. In 1783, Kant published a shorter introduction to his new method of philosophy titled *Prolegomena to Any Future Metaphysics* in an effort to clarify and defend his position against its initial reception. In the *Prolegomena*, Kant argues that his transcendental method provides the "proper antidote" for Berkeley's fantastical idealism, implying that the Bishop had been infected by mystical enthusiasm (*Schwärmerei*) and so had lost all use of his critical faculties.[65] Several years later, the B edition of the *Critique* was published, to which Kant added a short but important section titled "The Refutation of Idealism." In little

---

62. Beiser, *German Idealism*, 48.
63. Beiser, *German Idealism*, 49.
64. Kant, *Prolegomena*, 44n11. Originally published in Dublin in 1710.
65. Kant, *Prolegomena*, 44.

more than a page he devises a deceptively simple argument with a dual aim: 1) to distinguish his new form of idealism from what he called the dogmatic idealism of Berkeley (for whom the external world was merely imaginary but for its appearance before God), and 2) to distinguish it from the skeptical or problematic idealism of Descartes (for whom the reality of the external world could not be demonstrated by means of experience alone).[66] The success of Kant's refutation of idealism rests heavily on the claims of the Transcendental Aesthetic. My characterization of Kant's formalization of aesthesis in Chapter 1 does not directly address the arguments he articulates in his "Refutation." In responding to his arguments here, I hope to show the way across the threshold into a descendental inversion of his transcendental philosophy. Kant's attempt to defend himself from his empiricist critics ends up pushing him to make explicit a fundamental contradiction at the heart of his idealism.

Kant claims that his transcendental critique of our faculty of aesthesis "undercuts" Berkeley's argument that space together with the objects inhabiting it are merely imagined.[67] Rather than attacking Berkeley's argument head on, Kant changes the rules of the idealist game. He redefines space as a necessary form of our human kind of intuition, rather than assuming the common sense definition of it as a mind-independent reality. Kant thus concedes the ideality of space, but unlike Berkeley provides formal transcendental criteria for judging the real, non-imaginary status of objects in experience (i.e., for judging that they are not dreams or delusions), namely the *a priori* forms of spatial and temporal intuition and the necessary and universal categories of the understanding that make experience of objects possible in the first place. Experiences that do not obey the rules provided by these forms and categories must be dismissed as hallu-

66. Kant, *Critique of Pure Reason*, 326.
67. Kant, *Critique of Pure Reason*, 326.

cinatory, while experiences that do conform are objectively cognizable and thus real.[68]

Although he has no interest in affirming the results of Berkeley's overall scheme, Whitehead is not so quick to dismiss the Bishop's contributions to philosophy. He points out that, given Berkeley's important influence on Hume, and Hume's on Kant, it would be "absurd" to dismiss his philosophy as the ravings of a religious lunatic.[69] From Whitehead's perspective, Berkeley's importance stems from his concrete analysis of our intuitive experience, an analysis Whitehead deems more complete than the abstract mechanical scheme of seventeenth-century natural science. As for Schelling, because of the shortcomings he detects in Kant's merely *critical* idealism, he expresses, like Whitehead, a qualified support for aspects of Berkeley's *dogmatic* idealism. Schelling points out that Kant's critical version of philosophy begins with the assumption that an opposition exists between the free subjectivity of the mind and the deterministic objectivity of Nature. In contrast, the highest forms of dogmatism begin with an intuition of the original unity of subject and object. It follows from these respective presuppositions that, for critical idealism, it is the reality of Nature that proves to be problematic, while for dogmatism, the reality of freedom is what eludes clear conception. Either way, philosophy falls short of its goal of scientific knowledge of reality as a whole. For this reason, the young Schelling in his *System of Transcendental Idealism* (1800) provided the blueprint for Hegel's *Phenomenology of Spirit* (1807) by arguing that some higher perspective is necessary for such knowledge, an *absolute* idealism (which would be indistinguishable from absolute *realism*) that shows how freedom and Nature, subject and object, meet in a null-point of indifference.[70] In the course of articulating his own absolute

68. Kant, *Critique of Pure Reason*, 309, 328.
69. Whitehead, *Science and the Modern World*, 66.
70. Pinkard, *German Philosophy*, 179.

version of Kant's critical idealism, Schelling credits the "sagacious Berkeley" for his vision of light "as a converse of the soul with God" and regrets that his generation is no longer able to understand what the wise Bishop meant.[71] Despite Kant's hasty dismissal of Berkeley's "mystical" idealism, we will see below that the latter's concrete analysis of experience inspired Whitehead's critique of "simple location."[72]

Having made short work of Berkeley, Kant moves on to a more sympathetic treatment of Descartes' problematic idealism, which he respects as at least "rational" and so appropriate for philosophical reflection.[73] Indeed, Kant refers to Descartes as "a benefactor to human reason" because his thoroughgoing doubt of naive assumptions about the deliverances of the senses gave philosophy clearer sight of its own limitations.[74] Descartes' skepticism concerning the existence of external Nature is tempered only by his certainty concerning the inner existence of his own mind. By the sheer fact, or rather, *act* of his own thinking, Descartes is led immediately to a consciousness of his own existence as a thinking subject: "I think, I am."[75] From Kant's perspective, however, Descartes' consciousness of himself as a mere "I" or thinker is not yet a cognitive experience of himself as an actually existing being. In order to cognize himself as actually existing or even just as empirically real, his concept of himself as an "I" must be synthetically related to an inner intuition of himself as temporally determined. Thinking anything determinately, even oneself, requires an imaginative synthesis of the thinking "I" with its own intuition of itself in time.

The next step in Kant's refutation of idealism is to insist that the inner or temporal intuition of ourselves granting

---

71. Schelling, *Transcendental Idealism*, 153.
72. Whitehead, *Science and the Modern World*, 69.
73. Kant, *Critique of Pure Reason*, 326.
74. Kant, *Critique of Pure Reason*, 430.
75. Descartes, *Meditations*, 227.

Chapter 2: Inverting Kant: From a Mechanistic to an Organic Cosmology

us knowledge of our own existence presupposes something *persistent* relative to which the passage of time could be measured. This persistent thing cannot be in *me*, since for the recognition of myself I depend on first recognizing *it*. Thus my recognition of the thing must be related to more than a mere representation but a real thing outside me. It follows for Kant that my conscious experience of myself as temporally determined "is at the same time an immediate consciousness of the existence of other things outside me."[76] In other words, the synthesis of the ego in time is necessarily correlated with the solidity of the world in space.[77]

What does Kant mean when he refers to the "persistence" of actual things in our outer intuitions of space? Earlier in the *Critique*, in the section titled "First Analogy of Experience" focused on the synthetic *a priori* role of the concept of substance in the construction of our experience, Kant reiterates that "time cannot be perceived in itself," since "without that which persists [there can be] no temporal relation."[78] He then clarifies that that which is persistent in external things is the *substance* underlying their changing appearances. "That which persists," Kant writes,

> in relation to which alone all temporal relations of appearances can be determined, is substance in the appearance, i.e., the real in the appearance, which as the substratum of all change always remains the same.[79]

Kant adds that, since the underlying substratum of spatio-temporal appearances is unchanging, "its quantum is neither increased nor diminished in nature."[80] The flow of time is itself just the accidental alteration of the one underlying

---

76. Kant, *Critique of Pure Reason*, 327.
77. Schlutz, *Mind's World*, 87.
78. Kant, *Critique of Pure Reason*, 301.
79. Kant, *Critique of Pure Reason*, 301.
80. Kant, *Critique of Pure Reason*, 300.

substance. Nothing new ever truly arises in time, nor does anything perish, since all changes are only modes of the same underlying substance, the persistence of which, according to Kant, is what provides us with our only measure of change.[81] The substantial unity of the manifold of sensory appearances co-determines the unity of our own subjectivity, thus providing the conditions of the possibility of experience.

It should be noted that, despite his claims to be going beyond Descartes, Kant's approach closely resembles the former's famous argument about the concept of substance underlying the various appearances of candle wax in the second of his *Meditations on First Philosophy*.[82] But a closer look at Kant's explicit statements reveals a contradiction between what he says in the context of his "Refutation" and what he says elsewhere in the *Critique*. While in the Refutation he argues that "the perception of this persistent thing is possible only through a *thing* outside me and not through the mere *representation* of a thing outside me,"[83] in the context of the paralogisms of pure reason (unedited in the second edition), he writes that:

> external objects are merely appearances, hence also nothing other than a species of my representations, whose objects are something only through these representations, but are not something separated from them.[84]

Kant first claims that his view differs from both dogmatic and problematic idealism because an inner sense of ourselves presupposes not only the representation of things outside ourselves, but the *mind-independent existence* of these things. But he claims elsewhere that such a "thing-in-itself" or "nou-

---

81. Kant, *Critique of Pure Reason*, 303.
82. Descartes, *Meditations*, 20.
83. Kant, *Critique of Pure Reason*, 327.
84. Kant, *Critique of Pure Reason*, 427.

menon" can never be known with any certainty. The noumenon therefore remains merely a problematic idea whose reality is not determinable through any form of cognition available to us.[85] What is worse, Kant refers to the noumenon as "the *cause* of appearance" (my italics) while in the very same paragraph forbidding the application of phenomenal categories like substance and causality to things-in-themselves.[86] Causation cannot be employed to understand the noumenal source of our sensory experience without making improper use of the category, since such categories remain contentless logical forms when not brought into relationship with said sensory experience.[87] In short, there can be no such determinate concept as a "non-sensible cause." As Kant himself says, "we cannot . . . extend the field of the objects of our thinking beyond the conditions of our sensibility."[88] To be fair to Kant, he admits that "the mystery of the origin of our sensibility" is so deeply hidden that we, beings who know even themselves only as appearances, will never be able to bring clarity to its transcendental ground.[89] In all our attempts to do so all we can ever turn up are more appearances. No doubt, the profound obscurity of the aesthetic threshold mediating our encounter with a Nature outside us is what led Kant into contradiction when he attempted to think it through to the end.

The essence of Kant's "Refutation of Idealism" lies in his Subject-Substance correlation. He describes this correlation as the necessary bond between inner and outer intuitions that must be accepted *a priori* as the condition for the possibility of any experience at all.

85. Kant, *Critique of Pure Reason*, 380.
86. Kant, *Critique of Pure Reason*, 381.
87. The early critic of Kant, Salomon Maimon, was the first to notice this contradiction (Pinkard, *German Philosophy*, 173).
88. Kant, *Critique of Pure Reason*, 380.
89. Kant, *Critique of Pure Reason*, 376.

Whether or not his "Refutation" ultimately leads him into self-contradiction, Kant's transcendental deduction of the concept of Substance as the necessary correlate of subjective experience stands in unambiguous contradiction with Whitehead's experiential distillation of the idea of Creativity as the groundless ground or abyssal origin of experience. While Kant denies that time consists in the arising or passing away of actualities, Whitehead repeatedly affirms the doctrine that actual occasions are both self-creating and perpetually perishing. As we have seen, "the notion of an actual entity as the unchanging subject of change is completely abandoned" in Whitehead's philosophy of organism.[90] "No thinker thinks twice," Whitehead continues, "and, to put the matter more generally, no subject experiences twice." Whitehead goes on to state explicitly that his repudiation of the concept of Substance "directly contradicts Kant's 'First Analogy of Experience' in either of its ways of phrasing (1st or 2nd edition [of the *Critique of Pure Reason*])."[91]

Creativity is characterized by the concrescence of actual occasions, whereby the plurality of the universe disjunctively is unified in one occasion of experience, which is the universe conjunctively. Creativity is: "the advance from disjunction to conjunction, creating a novel entity other than the entities given in disjunction . . . . The many become one, and are increased by one."[92] By replacing the ancient Aristotelean category of "primary substance" with that of Creativity, Whitehead undercuts the premise of Kant's Refutation of Idealism. In the philosophy of organism it is not substance but *form* that is (at least relatively) permanent.[93] The underlying form of reality is given by the primordial na-

---

90. Whitehead, *Process and Reality*, 29.
91. Whitehead, *Process and Reality*, 27.
92. Whitehead, *Process and Reality*, 21.
93. Whitehead, *Process and Reality*, 29.

ture of God, which is not put forward as a mere speculative idea or object of religious belief in Whitehead's scheme, but is rather rooted in our experience of "real feelings derived from the timeless source of all order," feelings consisting in "an urge towards the future based upon an appetite in the present."[94]

Kant's argument that time-determination depends upon spatial intuition of something substantial and persistent (either figuratively through the tracing of an imaginary line in two dimensions or actually through the perception of the periodic movements of heavenly bodies) is, in essence, a spatialization of time: "we must order the determinations of inner sense as appearances in time in just the same way as we order those of outer sense in space."[95] Kant does admit that time itself is not a possible object of outer intuition (i.e., it cannot itself be reduced to motion); what he in fact argues is that we can only *represent* time to ourselves spatially. It follows that scientific knowledge of moving objects is only possible through the spatialization of time. Without granting the Subject-Substance correlation at the core of his Refutation of Idealism, Kant's cherished synthetic *a priori* knowledge would prove impossible. We can have determinate knowledge of the mechanisms of external Nature only because time can be spatially represented. Whitehead's process-relational ontology stands opposed to Kant's representational and seemingly remainderless translation of the intensity of time into the extensity of space. "Apart from time," writes Whitehead,

> there is no meaning for purpose, hope, fear, energy. If there be no historic process, then everything is what it is, namely, a mere fact. Life and motion are lost.[96]

---

94. Whitehead, *Process and Reality*, 32.
95. Kant, *Critique of Pure Reason*, 259.
96. Whitehead, *Modes of Thought*, 103.

As Schelling puts it, Kant's attempt to make a line drawn in space represent time only leads to "time *extinct* in space."[97] Whitehead joins Bergson's protest against the idea that the "fundamental [facts] of concrete nature" can be finally understood in terms of the "simple location of instantaneous material configurations."[98] But unlike Bergson, who assumes with Kant that the categories of the mechanical understanding are the only valid sources of scientific knowledge of Nature, Whitehead believes a more concrete account is possible. He endeavors upon his philosophic quest in an effort to construct novel categories making possible an alternative *organic* form of natural science. Instead of foregrounding perception in the spatialized mode of presentational immediacy, wherein time is projected onto the mechanical motion of substantial objects by an intentional-perspectival subject, Whitehead *temporalizes space* by grounding our subjective experience of Nature in the causally efficacious energy vectors streaming in from the encompassing cosmic community of other subject-superjects. Even our special form of human subjectivity is thus understood to grow out of the same subterranean prehensional currents as the rest of living Nature. It is important to note before moving on that Whitehead is not simply reversing Kant's preference for space with an absolution of time. He acknowledges that "apart from space, there is no consummation. Space expresses the halt for attainment. It symbolizes the complexity of immediate realization. It is the fact of accomplishment."[99] On Whitehead's reading, time and space refer to different phases of the experiential formation of an actual occasion. Time expresses the *transitional* essence of the universe from one occasion to the next, while space expresses each occasion's momentary achievement of concrescence. "The transition is real, and the achievement is real,"

---

97. Schelling, *Philosophy and Religion*, 33. Italics added.
98. Whitehead, *Science and the Modern World*, 50.
99. Whitehead, *Modes of Thought*, 102.

writes Whitehead. "The difficulty is for language to express one of them without explaining away the other."[100] As we will see in the next section (2.2), Whitehead's novel rendering of space and its relation to time are part of an organic alternative to the mechanistic view of Nature, an alternative which requires not only replacing Kant's foundational concept of Substance with that of Creativity, but also reimagining space according to a processual scheme more general than Euclid's (or Einstein's) geometry.

Returning to Berkeley, recall that it was his more concrete analysis of our intuitive experience of Nature that Whitehead found so helpful for his own critique of "the fallacy of simple location" resulting from the spatialization of time. This fallacy is a subset of Whitehead's famous "fallacy of misplaced concreteness," whereby the abstract is mistaken for the concrete.[101] The theory of space tacitly assumed by Newton and Kant alike (even if the latter transcendentalized Newton's real space into an ideal space) assigned to space the role of providing "the locus of simple locations" for bits of substantial material.[102] Whitehead writes:

> The enormous success of the scientific abstractions, yielding on the one hand *matter* with its *simple location* in space and time, on the other hand *mind*, perceiving, suffering, reasoning, but not interfering, has foisted onto philosophy the task of accepting them as the most concrete rendering of fact.[103]

The misplaced concreteness it has placed in the abstract concepts of "mind" and "matter" has led modern philosophy into ruin, according to Whitehead. Out of the confusion, three main metaphysical positions emerged, each with its own way

---

100. Whitehead, *Modes of Thought*, 102.
101. Whitehead, *Science and the Modern World*, 50.
102. Whitehead, *Science and the Modern World*, 52.
103. Whitehead, *Science and the Modern World*, 55.

of juggling the abstractions of the seventeenth century scientific scheme: dualism (which "[accepts] matter and mind as on an equal basis"), materialistic monism (which "[puts] mind inside matter"), and idealistic monadism (which "puts matter inside mind").[104] Descartes the skeptical dualist, Spinoza the pantheist, and Leibniz the panentheist provide examples of each of these three modern modes of thought.

Whitehead inherits the insights of each of these thinkers, but in his own cosmological scheme aims to avoid merely rearranging the abstractions of the modern tradition. When he inquires into Bishop Berkeley's conception of the realization of things in Nature, he isn't so much interested in Berkeley's conclusion that their "objectivity is grounded in the mind of God" as he is in Berkeley's definitive diagnosis of the fallacy of simple location.[105] Berkeley's theological solution to the problems raised by simple location creates as many new difficulties as already existed in the old materialistic scheme.[106] Further, like Descartes, Spinoza, Leibniz, and Kant, his reliance on Aristotelean subject-predicate logic and substance-property ontology hampered his metaphysical scheme's ability to give full concrete expression to the facts of Nature. But in questioning the comprehensibility of the notion of "the *absolute existence of sensible objects in themselves . . . without the mind,*"[107] Berkeley inspires Whitehead to articulate the novel concept of "prehension" as a replacement for Berkeley's importation of the unity of a divine mind as what constitutes the realization of things in Nature. "For Berkeley's mind [of God], I substitute a process of prehensive unification."[108] Whitehead's new

---

104. Whitehead, *Science and the Modern World*, 55.
105. Whitehead, *Science and the Modern World*, 67.
106. Whitehead, *Science and the Modern World*, 68.
107. Berkeley, *Human Knowledge*, section 24; as quoted in Whitehead, *Science and the Modern World*, 67.
108. Whitehead, *Science and the Modern World*, 69.

Chapter 2: Inverting Kant: From a Mechanistic to an Organic Cosmology

conception of prehension allows him to avoid the fallacy of simple location, as each prehensive unity or actual occasion of experience, while it "defines itself as a *here* and a *now*," also grasps its environing community into unity in such a way that this unity still carries "essential reference to other places and other times."[109] The concrete fact of Nature is thus the process of creative advance from one prehensive unification to the next along multiple routes of spatiotemporal inheritance. It follows that "the actual world is a manifold of prehensions," and that "space and time are simply abstractions from the totality of prehensive unifications as mutually patterned in each other."[110] No actual occasion can be understood in isolation from any other occasion, since the realization of each includes prehensive relations to all. A prehensive unity, or actual occasion, is not an independent substance with essential qualities and accidental changes. Whitehead replaces Aristotle's substance-property ontology with a process-relational one.[111] The present experience of each prehensive act of unification includes essential relations to actual occasions of its past and accidental relations to eternal possibilities relevant in the future. This implies that every actual occasion of experience—whether the mostly physical feelings in the nucleus of an atom, or a cell, or the mostly mental forms of experience arising in self-conscious human beings—includes some modicum of "memory of the past, immediacy of realization, and indication of things to come."[112] All the actualities of Nature—whether the actual occasions composing our own mind or the actual occasions composing the minds of other organisms—are thus bound up with one another in a real causal nexus. Unlike Kant, who responded to Hume's denial of necessary connection

109. Whitehead, *Science and the Modern World*, 69.
110. Whitehead, *Science and the Modern World*, 71.
111. Whitehead, *Interpretation of Science*, 138–39.
112. Whitehead, *Science and the Modern World*, 73.

between events in Nature by imposing causality *a priori* as an ideal condition of any possible experience, Whitehead generalizes from the psychological field of our own bodily event to derive the concept of prehension as a genetic condition of actual experience. "If you start from the immediate facts of our psychological experience, as surely an empiricist should begin," writes Whitehead, "you are at once led to the organic conception of nature."[113] In this sense, Whitehead is in full concordance with Hume when the latter argues that it is not reasoning which engages us to suppose that the past will resemble the future or which leads us to expect similar effects from causes that appear similar.[114] Not autonomous reason, but *communal feeling* is that through which we are granted comprehension of causation.

Our concrete experience is neither primarily inner intentional self-affection nor outer extensional affection by objects. It is these secondarily, perhaps, but primordially the nature of experiential realization is *affective tension* as such: the complex concrescent feeling of arising out of a given past of stubborn facts and perishing into an open future of creative possibilities. The affective tension generated by past actuality growing together with future possibility provides the genetic condition of actual experience. The tension manifest in our "advance from the past to the future through the medium of the present" is, according to Whitehead, "the ultimate baffling mystery of nature."[115] While the Substance-Subject correlation leads only to self-contradiction and confusion, Whitehead hopes the category of Creativity at least sheds some light on the mystery.

---

113. Whitehead, *Science and the Modern World*, 73.
114. Hume, *Human Understanding*, 55.
115. Whitehead, *Interpretation of Science*, 133.

2.2 From Geometric Conditions of Possibility to Genetic Conditions of Actuality

Although the skeptical Hume found nothing *a priori* in experience to justify the idea of necessary connection, even he could not deny the *a priori* status of mathematical knowledge. He went so far as to say that any works of philosophy lacking grounding in mathematical or experimental science should be "[committed] to the flames," for such works "can contain nothing but sophistry and illusion."[116] Kant also makes much of the *a priori* status of mathematics, but whereas Hume understood mathematics to be built up of analytic truths deduced from the principle of non-contradiction, Kant recognized mathematical propositions as constructive *synthetic* truths dependent upon our intuitions of the pure forms of space and time. Whitehead points to a startling passage in Hume's *Enquiry Concerning Human Understanding* wherein the latter argues that so-called primary qualities associated with physical extension and solidity, despite their mathematical basis, are no less subjective than the secondary qualities associated with sensory experience: "The idea of extension," Hume writes, "is entirely acquired from the senses of sight and feeling," meaning that it is produced "in the mind not in the object."[117] Whitehead "wonders whether this was one of the passages that awoke Kant from his dogmatic slumber."[118] Probably it was this passage along with the many others wherein Hume dismisses the *a priori* use of the concept of causality that compelled Kant to find a new foundation for scientific knowledge of Nature. As we have seen, Kant accepts Hume's argument that the spatial extension of objects (or any other quantitative measure of Nature's primary characteristics) is not a reflection of something existing outside

---

116. Hume, *Human Understanding*, 144.
117. Hume, *Human Understanding*, 135.
118. Whitehead, *Interpretation of Science*, 109.

Crossing the Threshold

and independent of experience. But Kant makes explicit what even Hume's philosophy of feeling (despite his denial that space, time, and causality refer to a mind-independent realities) nonetheless takes for granted: space and time are the *necessary and universal forms of our intuition* and as such provide the *conditions of the possibility of our experience*. Whitehead is in agreement with Kant's general response to Hume that space-time (as he renders it in post-Einsteinian terms) has an intrinsic character granting uniformity to the texture of our experience.[119] If it did not posses such a character, our experience of Nature would be ruptured by extrinsic contingencies, making scientific knowledge of the systematic course of Nature's passage impossible.[120]

Thus far, Whitehead and Kant are in agreement that Hume neglected to acknowledge his own presuppositions. For even if the constant conjunction between events is derived *a posteriori* from the inheritance of concrete feelings rather than grounded *a priori* by abstract thought, a "dominant space-time continuum" with a definite character must still be presupposed, at least if we hope to distinguish between a dreamworld and experience of Nature.[121] Aside from Whitehead's reformulated acceptance of Hume's rendering of causality in terms of feelings of inheritance, there is another important distinction to be made between Kant's and Whitehead's respective understandings of the relationship of mathematics to spatiotemporal intuition. Kant grounds the creative formation of arithmetical and geometrical knowledge in the

---

119. Whitehead, *Interpretation of Science*, 110.

120. It is for precisely this reason that Whitehead was a persistent critic of Einstein's identification of four-dimensional geometry with the supposedly real curvature of a physical space-time continuum. Since this curvature was thought by Einstein to depend upon the contingent distribution of centers of mass at various points in the continuum, the necessary uniformity of space-time, and thus the basis for accurate measurement, is thrown into question (see Whitehead, *The Concept of Nature*, 165).

121. Whitehead, *Interpretation of Science*, 111–13.

intuitive content provided by the formal structure of time and space, respectively:

> The essential feature of pure *mathematical* cognition, differentiating it from all other *a priori* cognition, is that it must throughout proceed *not from concepts*, but always and only through the construction of concepts. Because pure mathematical cognition, in its propositions, must therefore go beyond the concept to that which is contained in the intuition corresponding to it, its propositions can . . . never arise through the analysis of concepts, i.e., analytically, and so are one and all synthetic.[122]

Kant goes on to argue that spatial intuition is necessarily determinable *a priori* in Euclidian three-dimensional form. He thought Euclidean geometry provided the mind with synthetic *a priori* knowledge of physical space, meaning that the structure of space is not learned from actual experience but constructed in the mind prior to experience. Euclidean space, Kant argued, was the condition of all possible experience, not a contingent feature derived or abstracted from particular experiences. Once nineteenth-century mathematicians started to discover the implications of other parallel postulates and thus articulated non-Euclidean and even non-metrical projective geometries, something of a crisis ensued, as physicists could no longer be certain which geometry applied to real space. Euclid's "glorious mistake" had at least provided "our modern physical science" with the "simplification of presuppositions by means of which it could express itself," as Whitehead notes.[123] If there is no uniquely true geometry for measuring physical spatiality, scientific knowledge of Nature seemed to some to be impossible. The mathematical physicist Henri Poincaré was led to argue that we could never, in

---

122. Kant, *Prolegomena*, 20.
123. Whitehead, *Interpretation of Science*, 190–91.

principle, determine which geometry was "real." Our human minds have been shaped by social habit and natural instinct to interpret our experience in Euclidean terms, while intelligent species on other planets may have evolved to interpret their experience in entirely different, non-Euclidean terms. Poincaré showed that "the Euclidean and certain other geometries are interchangeable,"[124] so it makes no sense to claim one is truer than the other. Geometries are merely more or less useful conventions. Poincaré thus severed the necessary connection between Euclidean geometry and physical space presupposed by Kant. Any form of geometry could be applied with more or less success in the description of the physical world, but in an ontological sense we can never determine which of them is "true." Poincaré does agree with Kant that arithmetic is grounded synthetic *a priori* in our intuition of time, but argues in contrast to him that geometry (Euclidean or otherwise) develops analytically and so bears no essential relationship to any form of spatial intuition.

Other physicists thought there could be some empirical (*a posteriori*) test to determine which geometry described space accurately. Einstein was a product of this school. Russell and Whitehead were inheritors of and innovators upon another nineteenth-century development called (perhaps inaccurately) "projective geometry."[125] While Russell and Poincaré disagreed fiercely with one another about the relative status of deductive logic and inductive intuition in mathematics, Whitehead's views on the matter would diverge from those of his mathematical collaborator Russell after he moved on from their work together on the first three volumes of *Principia Mathematica*. As Whitehead describes his realization:

---

124. Whitehead, "On Mathematical Concepts of the Material World," in *An Anthology*, 11.
125. Calling non-metrical projective schemes a form of geo-"metry" is something of a contradiction in terms, so although awkward it might be better termed "geometry."

Chapter 2: Inverting Kant: From a Mechanistic to an Organic Cosmology

> There is a tradition of opposition between adherents of induction [or intuition] and of deduction [or logic]. In my view, it would be just as sensible for the two ends of a worm to quarrel. Both . . . are necessary [to] move one step in the formation of science.[126]

While Russell argued that there could be only one true geometry of space, Whitehead came to agree with Poincaré that the choice of geometries for the elucidation of Nature is purely conventional. Further, as Milič Čapek argues, Poincaré like Whitehead leaves open the possibility that "the plasticity of the human imaginative capacities" can grant us actual experience of non-Euclidean spaces (even if Euclid's geometry remains the most convenient for earthly purposes).[127] Whitehead eventually went beyond Poincaré by arguing for the synthetic *a priori* validity of a non-metrical or projective spatial scheme more general than all the special metrical systems derivable from it. Whitehead claimed that his non-metrical/projective approach was guided by an intuition of that "factor in nature which issues the pre-eminence of one congruence relation over the indefinite herd of other such relations."[128] Here Whitehead reasserts his process-relational ontology of space-time, deeming synthetic *a priori* not the specific metrical relations of Euclid's or any other geometry, but the more general non-metrical projective principle of "uniformed relatedness."[129]

As far as Kant had been concerned when he died in 1804, Euclid's geometry provides physical science with synthetic *a priori* knowledge of the structure of space (the sort of certainty he believed was required for natural scientific knowledge). After the discovery and articulation of other geometries,

---

126. Whitehead, "The Organization of Thought," in *The Aims of Education*, 116.
127. Čapek, *Bergson and Modern Physics*, 24.
128. Whitehead, *The Concept of Nature*, 124.
129. Whitehead, *The Principle of Relativity*, vi.

natural science seemed to be "haunted by the specter that the search for truth may be a search for phantoms," as the mathematician Morris Kline put it.[130] The epistemic situation may not be quite as stark as Kline's common sentiment suggests, however. Had Kant lived to see the developments in mathematics in the century after his death, he would have pointed physicists concerned about knowledge of "real" space to the arguments of his Transcendental Aesthetic regarding space's transcendental ideality. Kant never claims that Euclid's geometry is somehow *logically* true *a priori*, as though no other geometries are *possible*. He only denies that our type of spatial imagination can grant us any *actual experience* of such non-Euclidian spaces. His argument is that mathematical knowledge is based not on analytic, but on *synthetic a priori* judgments. The axioms of geometry involve and require the powers of the spatiotemporalizing imagination, meaning there is an ineradicably intuitive dimension to all mathematical knowledge.[131]

For his part, Whitehead not only struggled to interpret the new mathematical developments of the nineteenth and early twentieth centuries, he helped to initiate and bring several of them to fruition.[132] His later contributions to philosophy came "only after he was convinced that problems in the foundations of mathematics could not be solved mathematically"[133] but rather required the construction of an alternative categoreal scheme to replace that provided by Kant. Contrary to Kant's claim that Euclidean geometrical knowledge is grounded synthetically in our formal intuitions of space and time, Whitehead grounds our knowledge of a uniform spatiotemporal nexus on an entirely different conception of the mathematical imagination:

---

130. Kline, *Mathematics for the Nonmathematician*, 476.
131. Kant, *Critique of Pure Reason*, 286–89.
132. Henry, "Whitehead's Philosophical Response," 15.
133. Henry, "Whitehead's Philosophical Response," 14.

Chapter 2: Inverting Kant: From a Mechanistic to an Organic Cosmology

> In the absence of space-time there may still be consciousness aware of the truths of pure mathematics. It so happens that in fact we contemplate these mathematical truths in a temporal succession. But this order of precedence in our consideration of mathematics seems casual and irrelevant, so that we can easily imagine a timeless mathematical knowledge. In the same way the idea of a spaceless mathematical knowledge presents no difficulty.... Accordingly, we cannot maintain that knowledge in itself requires space-time, either as conditioning the mode of consciousness, or as an essential system of relations interconnecting things known.[134]

In his *Treatise on Universal Algebra with Applications* (1898) and his work with Russell on *Principia Mathematica* (1910–1913), Whitehead attempted to detach pure arithmetical and geometrical reasoning from all reference to intuitions of physical space-time. It is important to note that even in this earlier phase of his work, Whitehead balanced the formal or analytic aspects of pure mathematics with the intuitive component of applied mathematics. His claim to have freed mathematical reasoning of any necessary reference to our everyday spatial and temporal forms of intuition of the physical world still left open the possibility that another more general sub- or super-sensory form of intuition provides mathematical propositions with their synthetic *a priori* content. In *Universal Algebra*, Whitehead employed the new tools of his non-metrical projective scheme in an attempt to imaginatively construct a "common medium" providing a "content-ground" for all types of mathematical statements.[135] Under the influence of Russell and the formalist school in Europe, Whitehead began shifting his approach to search for such an intuitive content in the axioms of logic, rather than those of mathematics.

---

134. Whitehead, *Interpretation of Science*, 110.
135. Henry, "Whitehead's Philosophical Response," 15–18.

But the *Principia* project eventually ran aground, leading him into metaphysics in pursuit of an adequate intuitive content for mathematics.[136] He came to see that "even in arithmetic you cannot get rid of a subconscious reference to the unbounded universe,"[137] with the important difference from Kant that the unbounded universe subconsciously referenced need not necessarily be reducible to the metrical space of Euclid. In Whitehead's mature philosophy, he arrived at a definition of the "common medium" providing intuitive content to mathematics in terms of the realm of eternal objects as envisaged by the primordial nature of God.[138] God's primordial valuation of the infinite hierarchy of eternal objects grants the finite propositions of mathematics their synthetic *a priori* content. As summarized by Desmet, Whitehead came to see that "all mathematical understanding is intuition of pattern [or] formal similarity," such that both arithmetical and geometrical judgments are "intuitive judgments of pattern."[139] Recall that eternal objects describe the potential patterned relationships that actual occasions can enter into with one another. When specific eternal patterns are "ingressed" or become "ingredient" in the passage of actual Nature, we intuit their novelty then and there directly. God's primordial intuition or initial evaluation of the infinite realm of eternal objects influences but does not determine the final patterned character of the prehensive unifications of finite actual occasions. Aside from our intuitions of other finite actual occasions in physical space-time, we can also intuit relational patterns independently of their spatiotemporal actualization using the symbolic abstractions of mathematics, potentially putting us in touch with the infinite Creativity conditioning even God's primordial evaluation. The common medium of mathematical

---

136. Henry, "Whitehead's Philosophical Response," 20–21.
137. Whitehead, *Interpretation of Science*, 193.
138. Henry, "Whitehead's Philosophical Response," 16, 25.
139. Desmet, "Poincaré and Whitehead," 39.

relations is accessible through an intuition of the generative tension between infinity and finitude, between unlimited Creativity and its self-limiting concretion as God. I quote Whitehead at length:

> Apart from the finite, the infinite is devoid of meaning and cannot be distinguished from nonentity. The notion of the essential relatedness of all things is the primary step in understanding how finite entities require the unbounded universe, and how the universe acquires meaning and value by reason of its embodiment of the activity of finitude.... Creativity involves the production of value-experience, by the inflow from the infinite into the finite, deriving special character from the details and the totality of the finite pattern. This is the abstraction involved in the creation of any actuality, with its union of finitude with infinity. But consciousness proceeds to a second order of abstraction whereby finite constituents of the actual thing are abstracted from that thing. This procedure is necessary for finite thought, though it weakens the sense of reality. It is the basis of science. The task of philosophy is to reverse this process and thus to exhibit the fusion of analysis with actuality.[140]

Whitehead constructed both a more general and a more generative mathematical foundation for physics, a non-metrical but uniform projective space of topological possibility of which the geometries applicable to the physical space-time of this cosmic epoch are a particular expression. As we will see in the chiasmus and subsequent chapters, Whitehead's mathematical imagination put him in touch with the immeasurable Creativity underlying the physical cosmos.

---

140. Whitehead, *Interpretation of Science*, 196, 203.

Chiasmus

Descendental Aesthetic in Schelling and Whitehead: Crossing the Kantian Threshold

> "Space and time can never be mere side shows in philosophy. Their treatment must color the whole subsequent development of the subject."
> —Whitehead[1]

> That everything would, as much as is possible, become figural and be brought into visible, corporeal form, is the final intention. As the ancients expressed it, corporeality is the goal of the ways of God (*finis viarum Dei*), who wants to reveal Himself spatially, or in a place, as well as temporally.
> —Schelling[2]

> During such moments, [as when we unexpectedly stumble upon] a great tree ... in some ancient forest, we are suddenly caught up in something that has nothing to do with the human world. We feel something coming into us from *out there* .... We feel the touch of life, of a nonhuman awareness, upon us .... We experience in that moment what the ancient Greeks ... called aisthesis [sic], the touch of a nonhuman soul upon the deeps of us—and know that ours touches them in turn.
> —Stephen Harrod Buhner[3]

SCHELLING AND WHITEHEAD APPROACH THE AESTHESIS of Nature with systematic rigor but without deadening rigor mortis. They construct their systems not with fixed transcendental concepts imposed from beyond experience, but with imaginal schemas fluidly precipitated out of the tidal rhythms of aesthesis itself. Instead of beginning *from above* by founding knowledge of Nature's possibility upon the ahistorical

---

1. Whitehead, *Interpretation of Science*, 143.
2. Schelling, *The Ages of the World*, 93.
3. Buhner, *Plant Intelligence and the Imaginal Realm*, 356.

concepts of a transcendental mind, Schelling and Whitehead begin *from below*, experimenting with new metaphysical categories (always remaining in close conversation with the history of philosophy and attuned to advances in the natural sciences) in order to elucidate experience of actual Nature.[4] In their hands, philosophy becomes "nothing other than a *natural history of our mind*," as Schelling put it.[5] Experience and speculation are thus brought together in a "great synthesis," whereby we know the life of the Nature outside us through the life we experience in ourselves. Human consciousness is not the unique subjective center of agency around which all the determined objects of visible Nature revolve. Reflective or egoic consciousness of the sort critically dissected by Kant is rather itself one of productive Nature's products. As Iain Hamilton Grant puts it, "Nature is too large for finite reflective consciousness, precisely because it is nature that generates it anew with each electromagnetic pulse."[6]

It is not the human mind that is *a priori*; instead, according to Schelling, "Nature [as *Naturans*] is *a priori*."[7] The creativity of Nature thus "originally and necessarily underlies everything our species has ever thought about Nature."[8] Rather than making the freedom of the human ego of highest metaphysical import, both Schelling and Whitehead grant ultimate metaphysical generality to the creative generativity active in all creatures (human imaginative freedom being one of its most potent expressions). Their philosophy begins with an intuition of Nature from the inside out as an infinitely creative organic process, whereas the understanding at the helm of Kant's philosophy ultimately only reflects upon the external surfaces in its determination of Nature's apparently

4. Schelling, *Ideas*, 43.
5. Schelling, *Ideas*, 30.
6. Grant, *After Schelling*, 162.
7. Schelling, *Ideas*, 198.
8. Schelling, *Ideas*, 41.

mechanical products. In Whitehead's scheme, Creativity is the "ultimate notion of the highest generality at the base of all actuality" that is nevertheless "always found under conditions."[9] The infinite process of Creativity is conditioned by its own activity, thereby becoming its own creature. Its initial macrocosmic self-conditioning or primordial act of self-creation is referred to by Whitehead as "God's primordial nature." God is the primordial creature of Creativity, the original experiential entity that informs infinite potentiality with a definite character so as to inspire the emergence of an actual spatiotemporal cosmos composed of a democracy of fellow creatures.[10] God is not the material creator of actualities but the principle of concretion or limitation that grants the infinite passage into finite fact. God is the original macrocosmic act providing base notes for microcosmic actualities to riff on: their vibratory improvisations include the divine notes, and transcends them.[11] Creativity's divine act of macrocosmic self-conditioning thus simultaneously takes the microcosmic form of infinitely many particular creatures called "actants"[12] or "actual occasions"[13] of experience, each one resonating with the eternal "initial aim" of God's primordial act. God "at once limits and provides opportunity for" actual occasions.[14] While these actual occasions may appear finite as individuals, each one of them mirrors within itself the infinite activity of the whole.[15] The finite life of each actual occasion is made in the image of the infinite Life of God. Though God has the unique significance of being the eternal initiator of

9. Whitehead, *Process and Reality*, 31.
10. Whitehead, *Process and Reality*, 31.
11. Whitehead, *Process and Reality*, 128–29.
12. Schelling, *Philosophy of Nature*, 5.
13. Whitehead, *Process and Reality*, 18.
14. Whitehead, *Process and Reality*, 129.
15. Schelling, *Philosophy of Nature*, 18; Whitehead, *Science and the Modern World*, 91.

each temporal actuality, God is still a creature of Creativity, and as such is not unmoved by the creative agency of the finite occasions of experience composing the spatiotemporal pluriverse. God and the cosmic socius share in a single creative Life: they are dipolar co-creators of one another, with God achieving macroscopic universality while remaining in unison of becoming with the finite occasions striving for microcosmic individuality.[16] God's concrescence is eternal and ever-lasting, like a cresting wave that never crashes, while finite occasions arise and perish on the shores of time; but Whitehead intends the same categories to apply to both: "The presumption that there is only one genus of actual entities constitutes an ideal of cosmological theory to which the philosophy of organism endeavors to conform."[17] Whitehead here annunciates the main commitment of his adventure in cosmology: *there shall be only one genus of actual entity*. There shall be no special entities whose activity fails to exemplify Creativity or any of the other categories of his categoreal scheme. All of the categories composing his scheme must find exemplification at every level of actuality, whether the experiential occasion in question belongs to the life of a human person, to God, or to "the most trivial puff of existence in far-off empty space."[18] Schelling similarly grounds his *Naturphilosophie* on the idea that such "simple actants" or atoms of experience provide the generative "seed around which Nature can begin to form itself."[19] Schelling's "actants" or "dynamic atoms," like Whitehead's actual occasions, are "original and pure activities," not inert material particles. They are self-creating and other-prehending drops of experience. They are the final real things out of which Nature composes itself. Through erotically lured "reciprocal receptivity" (Schelling) or "mutual prehension" (Whitehead), these

16. Whitehead, *Process and Reality*, 167.
17. Whitehead, *Process and Reality*, 110.
18. Whitehead, *Process and Reality*, 18.
19. Schelling, *Philosophy of Nature*, 21.

actual entities grow together into ever-more complex collective products or "societies," enduring organisms capable of canalizing Nature's primordial creative urge with increasingly individuated experiential intensity.[20] "With all the various forms through which it metamorphoses," writes Schelling,

> creative Nature has in mind a common ideal operative in it to which the product gradually approximates itself; the various forms to which it commits itself will themselves appear only as the various stages of development of one and the same absolute organism.[21]

The ideal principle by which every experiential creature is genetically related to every other as an instance of the same divinely envisaged infinite Creativity is the hinge upon which Schelling and Whitehead attempt to re-open the doorway to philosophical cosmology in the wake of Kant's critiques. This genetic relation allows philosophy to break out of its transcendental cage and descend into the abyssal sources of human subjectivity in the enveloping cosmic process. Whitehead's reconstruction begins with an application of the method of "imaginative generalization": "the utilization of specific notions, applying to a restricted group of facts, for the divination of the generic notions which apply to all facts."[22] It goes without saying that the self-conscious experience of human organisms is highly specialized in Nature: "Clear, conscious discrimination is . . . of the essence of our humanity. But it is an accident of our existence."[23] Because the human being, body and soul, is itself composed of societies of actual occasions, human experience can still be taken "as an example upon which to found the generalized description required

---

20. Schelling, *Philosophy of Nature*, 24; Whitehead, *Process and Reality*, 89.
21. Schelling, *Philosophy of Nature*, 28.
22. Whitehead, *Process and Reality*, 5.
23. Whitehead, *Modes of Thought*, 116.

for metaphysics."[24] In order to avoid anthropomorphically projecting the more superficial dimensions of our uniquely human kind of conscious experience onto the cosmic substructures giving rise to us, we must subject consciousness to a process of alchemical distillation so as to reveal the deeper, universal dynamics of experience descriptive of actual occasions of every grade, whether they be associated with finite organic products or the cosmic organism: the World-Soul.

As we have seen, Whitehead laments the Kantian tradition's tendency to construe experience in general as

> the product of operations which lie among the higher of the human modes of functioning, [such that] the process by which experiential unity is attained is conceived in the guise of modes of thought.[25]

Whitehead notes that the one exception is to be found in the section of Kant's *Critique of Pure Reason*, discussed earlier, called the "Transcendental Aesthetic." Here Kant attempts to isolate the pure essences of space and time from our perceptual experience of spatiotemporal objects as they are determined by the conceptual categories of the understanding. Kant boils down what is given to us in sensory experience to reveal what he calls the "forms of intuition" of space and time.[26] To say he "boils down" sensory experience to these fundamental forms implies that he abstracts from the contingent existence of particular physical objects like planets and stars, plants and animals, and so on, in order to leave behind only what universally and necessarily conditions and makes possible the appearance of such objects. He searched not only for what holds true *in general* of all our particular sensory experiences of appearing bodies, but for what holds true *a priori*, in advance

---

24. Whitehead, *Process and Reality*, 112.
25. Whitehead, *Process and Reality*, 113.
26. Kant, *Critique of Pure Reason*, 157.

of any particular sensory appearance. He boiled down sensory experience until all that remained were its most formal and contentless arithmetical and geometrical possibilities, which he denoted as time and space, respectively. Kant argued that we do not have immediate sensory experience of either space or time. Look around you now, Kant would say: you can immediately sense only the disconnected movement of colored surfaces of various sizes and shapes. The forms of intuition of space and time underly and make possible all appearing things without themselves appearing. They are not empirically observed phenomena, but the transcendental conditions of phenomena. Space and time are the ideal conditions that first make possible the appearance of causally determined objects. We do not learn about space and time from our experience, argues Kant, since experience itself as we understand it already presupposes them. Kant further classifies space as the form of our "outer sense," and time as that of our "inner sense." Outer sense grants us experience of objects as they appear outside ourselves, while inner sense grants us experience of our own subjective stream of consciousness, the feeling of living duration, of flowing into the future without forgetting the past.

As should already be clear from the explication of Kant's critical philosophy in Chapter 1, space and time are not to be thought of as mind-independent realities. They apply only to reality as it is made to appear for us by what Kant calls the "transcendental imagination." Transcendental imagination is said to synthesize our experience of space and time with the categories of our understanding. Our experience of a geometrically ordered spatiotemporal world is then a synthetic product—a subjective construct—brought forth by the power of imagination. Space and time provide the *limits* of our human experience, which is to say that, for Kant, we can have no experiential knowledge of anything independent of our formal intuitions of space and time: we cannot even *conceive* of experience in any other form.[27] But it is precisely by limiting the formal structure of what it is possible for us to sense "out there" and "in here" that Kant's forms of intuition also provide the philosopher's stone from out of which he polishes his most prized transcendental jewel: synthetic *a priori* knowledge. Knowledge of this sort, which is achieved most readily by geometry and arithmetic, presupposes the formal structure of space and time. According to Kant, Euclidean geometry can be said to provide us with knowledge of external Nature only because the spatial world as it appears to us has always already been transmuted by the mind's innate faculty of outer sense. Similarly, arithmetic can be said to provide us with knowledge of numbers only because the time in which we solve arithmetic functions has already been provided by the mind's innate faculty of inner sense. The *synthetic a priori* knowledge of mathematics is possible, says Kant, only because space and time are themselves *a priori* forms providing the conditions for the possibility of any experience of objects. The example of mathematical knowledge is important for Kant, since his attempt to reground metaphysics on a scientific basis depends entirely on the existence of such synthetic *a priori* mathematical constructions.[28] And the reality of synthetic *a priori* constructions in mathematics depends entirely on Kant's argument for the transcendental ideality of space and time. The question of "real" space cannot be asked from within the Kantian framework. Reality as it exists in itself, independent of the mind, remains a mere "X" so far as Kant is concerned, inconceivable and unintuitable. Whitehead inverts Kant's answer to the question "How are synthetic *a priori* judgments possible?" For Whitehead, the spatiotemporal structure of experience "has not built itself up by the inclusion of [formal or conceptual] elements that are foreign to the [felt] reality from

27. Kant, *Critique of Pure Reason*, 331.
28. Kant, *Critique of Pure Reason*, 144–46.

which it springs."[29] He argues instead that the mathematical order exemplified in the interrelated activities of the cosmos emerges for the most part as a contingent achievement of those activities themselves.[30]

Despite its critical role in Kant's project, the Transcendental Aesthetic is the shortest section of the *Critique of Pure Reason*. From Whitehead's perspective, Kant's Transcendental Aesthetic (a mere sixteen pages in the first edition of the *Critique of Pure Reason*) provides only "a distorted fragment of what should have been his main topic."[31] By contrast, Whitehead's philosophy of organism "aspires to construct a critique of pure feeling, in the philosophical position in which Kant put his *Critique of Pure Reason*."[32] Whitehead concludes that such a critique of feeling—what I am calling a *descendental aesthetic*—would make the rest of the Kantian critiques redundant. While Kant began the task of critically examining aesthesis on its own terms in the *Critique of Judgment*, he pulled back from the more radical implications of what he discovered.[33] Even fifty years later, Schelling could claim that "the so-called *inner* sense"—that is, *feeling*—"still very much needs a critique."[34] Rather than search for formal *a priori* conditions of possible experience above aesthesis, a descendental approach dives into the actual conditions of aesthesis, namely the subconscious prehensive feelings out of which our reflective consciousness emerges as a finite selection. As Schelling argues, "A philosophy which starts from conscious-

---

29. Whitehead, *Adventures of Ideas*, 293.

30. Whitehead, *Process and Reality*, 91–92. "For the most part" because Whitehead still asserts as necessary a uniformly textured extensive continuum so as to secure fundamental congruence among relations, even if the specific shape this uniformity takes remains a contingent matter.

31. Whitehead, *Process and Reality*, 113.

32. Whitehead, *Process and Reality*, 13

33. Especially regarding the possibilities of human genius in art and organic purposiveness in Nature, discussed in Chapter 1.

34. Schelling, *Positive Philosophy*, 168.

ness," as Kant's does, will never be able to coherently explain the conformity of thought and object "without an original identity" between mind and Nature "whose principle necessarily lies beyond consciousness."[35] Schelling and Whitehead sought to return philosophy to the topic of aesthetic experience. There we must dwell on the concrete here-now of our perceptual encounter with the Universe instead of rushing ahead to construct a Transcendental Logic (which makes up the bulk of Kant's *Critique of Pure Reason*). Schelling and Whitehead articulate an *aesthetic ontology* rooted in the primal reality of feeling rather than the derivative abstractions of thought. They initiate a *descendental turn* in philosophy away from its transcendental obsession with reflection and toward the long-neglected feelings of organic embodiment.

Whitehead laments Kant's partial adoption of Hume's over-intellectualized account of perception, an account Whitehead refers to as the "sensationalist doctrine." According to this doctrine, the human sensory organs initially encounter reality as a patchwork of disconnected and unruly sensory impressions. "My senses convey to me only the impressions of colored points," says Hume; "If the eye is sensible of anything further, I desire it may be pointed out to me."[36] For Kant, the raw immediacy of these sensa must be mediated by the formal structure of reflective consciousness in order to mean anything. Sensations must be synthesized by imagination and systematized by the understanding to become law-abiding objects appearing in space and time. Prior to the mind's imposition of its transcendental order onto our otherwise chaotic sensorial encounter with reality, there simply is no perceivable "Nature," no conceivable "Cosmos" or world-system, there is only a disjoint manifold of unprocessed sense atoms (disconnected colors, sounds, etc.). For Hume, the mind contributes

---

35. Schelling, *Transcendental Idealism*, 135.
36. Hume, *Treatise*, Bk. 1, Part 3, Sec. 9. As quoted in Whitehead, *Process and Reality*, 117.

order and causality to its understanding of empirical Nature out of habitual associations, rather than transcendental determinations. But his difference on this point from Kant is incidental to Whitehead's critique of the sensationalist doctrine that Hume and Kant share. Contrary to this doctrine assumed by empiricists, rationalists, and transcendentalists alike, Whitehead argues that our sensorial encounter with reality "includes its own interconnections,"[37] which is to say that space, time, and causality are not projected upon sensory data by the mind (whether though the *a posteriori* perceptual habit of constant conjunction or the *a priori* concept of necessary connection in the formal construction of space and time). Causation is the transmission of feeling from one actual occasion of experience to another. The causal and the perceptual are thus combined into Whitehead's new category of prehension. Even Hume, who explicitly denies the reality of causality because, he claims, the eye sees nothing but randomly arrayed patches of color, implicitly presupposes that the *eye* sees, that the organ itself physiologically participates in the causal transmission of feelings as light pours through the cornea, drains into the retina, and flows down the optic nerve toward the back of the brain.[38] For Whitehead's philosophy of organism, it follows that "in human experience, the fundamental fact of perception is the inclusion, in the datum, of the objectification of an antecedent part of the human body with such-and-such experience."[39]

Whitehead accused modern philosophers, including Descartes, Hume, and Kant of committing a set of related mistakes: (1) they assume that the five senses are the only definite "avenues of communication" between human experience and the external world, and (2) they assume that conscious intro-

---

37. Whitehead, *Process and Reality*, 113.
38. Whitehead, *Process and Reality*, 117.
39. Whitehead, *Process and Reality*, 118.

spection is our sole means of analyzing experience.[40] The first mistake ignores the fact that "the living organ of experience is the living body as a whole."[41] The second mistake ignores the way that conscious introspection, though it "lifts the clear-cut data of sensation into primacy," for that very reason "cloaks the vague compulsions and derivations which form the main stuff of experience."[42]

The "living organ" Whitehead speaks of normally remains in unconscious causal contact with sub- and super-sensory modes of energetic transaction, with reflective consciousness distracted by its conceptual expectations. Later chapters speculate on the role of etheric imagination in bringing a descendental mode of consciousness to these transactions. Rather than imposing causality upon sense perception via the machinations of a transcendental ego, Whitehead re-interprets bodily sense-reception as already causally ordered. Causality is not an abstract category but an aesthetic power, the vague feeling of inheritance making up "the main stuff of experience."[43] Similarly, space and time cannot be mere forms of intuition projected upon an otherwise incomprehensible sensory chaos. Instead, our intuitions of space and time are the most aboriginal and generic feelings inherited in our bodily-aesthetic encounter with the contemporary universe. Whitehead terms the general character of space-time "the uniformity of the texture of experience,"[44] though unlike for Kant this experiential texture is not simply the construct of human minds or sense organs. From Whitehead's descendental perspective, "we know ourselves as a function of unification of a plurality of things which are other than ourselves."[45]

---

40. Whitehead, *Adventures of Ideas*, 225.
41. Whitehead, *Adventures of Ideas*, 225.
42. Whitehead, *Adventures of Ideas*, 226.
43. Whitehead, *Adventures of Ideas*, 226.
44. Whitehead, *Interpretation of Science*, 163.
45. Whitehead, *Science and the Modern World*, 151.

Space-time is the most generic pattern of possible experience realized thus far by the community of actual occasions constitutive not only of our bodily organism, but of the wider social order sheltering this cosmic epoch. We experience a more-or-less stable, causally-continuous spatiotemporal manifold because an enveloping cosmic community of physical actualities (e.g., the occasions associated with gravitational, electromagnetic, atomic, stellar, and galactic societies) is constructing, with mutual modifications accruing along the way, a suitable habitat within which a "concentrated efficiency and intensity of [experiential] satisfaction" can be realized in higher grade occasions (e.g., those associated with the complex physiology of conscious primates).[46] Our conscious awareness and scientific "cognition [of Nature] is the emergence, into some measure of individualized reality, of the general substratum of [spatiotemporalizing] activity, poising before itself possibility, actuality, and purpose."[47] There is no sharp boundary to be drawn between our consciousness, the human body, and the rest of Nature. "The truth," says Whitehead, "is that the brain is continuous with the body, and the body is continuous with the rest of the natural world," such that each moment of our human experience is "an act of self-origination including the whole of nature."[48] Space-time is not produced by the electrochemical patterns of activation within our skull or the transcendental forms of our mind. Rather, the entire organism-environment field—the whole cosmic socius—is involved in generating our spatiotemporal experience. The topology of space-time is an emergent product of the collective character of the individual drops of experience making up our cosmic neighborhood. The mathematical structure of the space-time continuum known to physics is not an *a priori* imposition of the mind nor a necessary law imposed upon Nature from

---

46. Whitehead, *Process and Reality*, 119.
47. Whitehead, *Science and the Modern World*, 153.
48. Whitehead, *Adventures of Ideas*, 225.

beyond, but an emergent pattern of mutual relations achieved by the most widespread society of occasions pervading this cosmic epoch. In other words, space and time as we experience them arise from reciprocal communication between electronic, protonic, and other widespread microcosmic actual occasions of experience "forming a background in layers of social order" for our more complex organic physiology.[49] The formal or mathematical structure of the spatiotemporal arena that these actualities bring forth is not eternally fixed, nor necessarily universal.[50] This structure is the result of emergent evolution, of the prehensive bonds and organizational habits achieved by the societies of actual occasions communicating with our experience.[51] Whitehead emphasizes the contingency of the evolved habits currently holding sway over the ecology of organisms shaping our cosmic epoch, no matter how general or universal they may appear at this time.[52] The so-called "laws" of Nature, including the specific causal structure of the space-time of our experience, are really *habits* that have developed within the societies of actual occasions "of increasing width of prevalence" constituting our cosmic epoch.[53]

The universe is thus "a complex of prehensive unifications," with space and time "[exhibiting] the general scheme of interlocked relations of these prehensions."[54] Each actual occasion "arises as an effect facing its past and ends as a cause facing its future."[55] Each occasion's prehension of stubborn

---

49. Whitehead, *Process and Reality*, 90–91.
50. Stengers, *Thinking With Whitehead*, 168.
51. Whitehead, *Process and Reality*, 98.
52. Stengers, *Thinking With Whitehead*, 169.
53. Whitehead, *Process and Reality*, 92, 106. While the continuous causal structure underlying the space-time of our experience is contingently emergent from the habits achieved during our cosmic epoch, Whitehead does recognize a metaphysically necessary form of relatedness that is discussed in chapter 2.2.
54. Whitehead, *Science and the Modern World*, 72.
55. Whitehead, *Adventures of Ideas*, 194.

facts together with open possibilities breathes new life into the present moment again and again, providing the eternal pulse driving nature's becoming. Whitehead writes:

> The oneness of the universe, and the oneness of each element in the universe, repeat themselves to the crack of doom in the creative advance from creature to creature, each creature including in itself the whole of history and exemplifying the self-identity of things and their mutual diversities.[56]

The most concrete reality of the cosmos is thus not a static structure or unbroken geometric continuum but a creative and relational process. The world is an open-ended creality, not a finished reality. Living nature is described most concretely by Whitehead as "the throbbing emotion of the past hurling itself into a new transcendent fact."[57]

As a result of this descendental inversion of Kant's transcendental aesthetic, "what forms the limit of our intuitive faculty no longer falls within the sphere of our intuition itself,"[58] as Schelling says. Instead, these limits are constellated by the wider community of actual occasions whose social order shelters our experience. The conditions of actual experience are not *a priori* cognitive principles but co-created relational patterns of cosmic composition. Such an account may seem to be a recursion to pre-Kantian realism, whereby space, time, and causality are ideas derived from generalizations of particular experiences. On the contrary, Whitehead and Schelling do not accept the modern bifurcation of Nature and related sensationalist doctrine shared by Descartes, Hume, Locke, and Kant alike. Space, time, and causality are not ideas derived from experience, they are conditions of experience.

---

56. Whitehead, *Process and Reality*, 228.
57. Whitehead, *Adventures of Ideas*, 177.
58. Schelling, *Philosophy of Nature*, 195.

In this sense neither Schelling nor Whitehead is a pre-critical thinker. But unlike Kant, whose forms of space and time and category of causality are constituted *a priori* by a transcendental mind, a descendental approach grounds these in our direct bodily perception of a cosmic community of other actual occasions of experience. Causal connection in Nature, whether within our bodies or across galaxies, is a function of sympathetic feelings between occasions disposed in interlocked community. "So far as concerns the causal efficacy of the world external to the human body," writes Whitehead, "there is the most insistent perception of a circumambient efficacious world of beings."[59] I perceive the universe spatiotemporally because my bodily perception directly inherits and recapitulates the universe's aesthetic achievement of such an order. While Kant tried to "balance the world upon thought,"[60] as though the process of perception were primarily a process of understanding, Whitehead rooted perception in pre-reflective, non-cognitive feeling. In his philosophy of organism, higher mental functions like reflective understanding or conscious knowing themselves become special forms of feeling.[61]

Whitehead distinguishes between "sense-perception" (a high grade form of mentality best characterized as "appearance" somewhat disconnected from "reality") and "sense-reception" (the primary form of causal transmission operative throughout the universe, best characterized as the "transference of throbs of emotional energy" from the settled past into the active present.[62] He describes the human body as a "complex amplifier"[63] of these throbs of emotional energy, its network of nerves canalizing the inflowing data into a coordinated hierarchy of feelings so as to produce an integrated and

59. Whitehead, *Symbolism*, 55.
60. Whitehead, *Process and Reality*, 151.
61. Whitehead, *Process and Reality*, 153.
62. Whitehead, *Process and Reality*, 116.
63. Whitehead, *Process and Reality*, 119.

predictive perspective on the world from moment to moment. "Our bodily experience is the basis of existence .... [It] is that portion of nature with which each moment of human experience intimately cooperates."[64] Whitehead's aesthetic ontology is thus grounded in our embodied experience of the encompassing cosmos.

Aesthesis, for the ancient Greeks, was related to the circular passive activity of breathing: we breathe in sensory impressions of the cosmic surround, and, thus inspired, we breathe out creative expressions. The universe is then not merely our "environment"; rather, it enters into and rhythmically transacts with the very heart of our being, beckoning us to partake in the call and response of the cosmogenetic ensemble. "There is an inflow and outflow of factors between the bodily actuality and the human experience, so that each shares in the existence of the other."[65] For this reason, Whitehead continues, "the human body provides our closest experience of the interplay of actualities in nature."[66]

Steiner describes the yogic breathing practices of ancient India as an attempt to become more conscious of the way these aesthetic bodily rhythms bind us to the wider cosmos. Human beings, according to Steiner, "find themselves oriented in a curious way between image and reality." By deepening into the boundary dissolving process of breathing, the ancients sought to develop "that part of the human being which is neither closed upon itself ... for the fashioning of images, nor closed off on the other side in order to experience reality." Unlike "our prevailing scientific paradigm," which "[contemplates] a world apart from us," Steiner continues, "they beheld a world for which our human rhythms became themselves an organ of perception."[67]

---

64. Whitehead, *Modes of Thought*, 114–15.
65. Whitehead, *Modes of Thought*, 115.
66. Whitehead, *Modes of Thought*, 115.
67. Steiner, *The Relation of the Diverse Branches of Natural Science to Astronomy*

Attending to the imaginal tides of aesthesis as they flow to-and-fro across the sublime edges of embodied experience helps bridge the otherwise gaping chasm between mind and matter. Attending only to conceptual thought, or to transcendental structures, artificially widens the gap. Dwelling instead upon the way aesthetic and emotional vectors vibrate sympathetically through and between bodies, we begin to realize that modern philosophy's abstract categories of mind and matter no longer hold any water. *They leak*.

It is all too easy to define aesthesis according to the misplaced concreteness, so prevalent among modern philosophers of both the empiricist and rationalist schools, which has it that our primary form of sensory experience is of bare patches of qualia free of all relations. As we have seen, Whitehead called this more superficial mode of perception "presentational immediacy" or "sense-perception," contrasting it with the primal mode of "causal efficacy" or "sense-reception." The latter mode of perception, as its name suggests, directly links us to the energetic expression of other actualities. Such direct links are denied by the modern thinkers Whitehead treats in *Process and Reality*, for whom perception is "mere appearance" and so causally epiphenomenal. From Whitehead's perspective, "experience has been explained [by modern philosophers] in a thoroughly topsy-turvy fashion, the wrong end first": because presentational immediacy (i.e., derivative appearances within subjects) provides us with clear and distinct ideas that are accessible to conceptualization by the understanding, it has been given genetic priority, when in fact, causal efficacy (i.e., primordial feelings of objects, which in Whitehead's scheme are other perished subjects or "superjects") deserves this honor.[68] "The philosophy of organism is the inversion of Kant's philosophy," according to Whitehead. While Kant endeavors to construe experience as a process

(CW 323), Lecture 5, 109–10. Translated as *Interdisciplinary Astronomy* (2020).
68. Whitehead, *Process and Reality*, 162.

whereby "subjective data pass into the *appearance* of an objective world," Whitehead's philosophy of organism describes experience as a process whereby the order of the objectively felt data pass into and provide intensity for the realization of a subject.[69] In short, in Kant's philosophy "[a merely apparent] world emerges from the subject," while "for the philosophy of organism, the subject emerges from [a real] world."[70]

Rather than treating the objective world as an appearance constructed by subjective activity, as Kant and most other modern thinkers do, Whitehead reverses the direction of the process of perception such that each subject is described as arising from its feelings of other objectified subjects.[71] "In the place of the Hegelian [or Kantian] hierarchy of categories of thought," writes Whitehead, "the philosophy of organism finds a hierarchy of feeling."[72]

On Whitehead's reading, Kant privileges perception in the mode of "presentational immediacy" and ignores or at least marginalizes the deeper and more ontologically relevant perceptual mode of "causal efficacy." "Presentational immediacy" displays reality in a way amenable to representational analysis, showing only the more or less clear and distinct surfaces of the extensive world as they are presented to a reflective subject here and now. It is the end product of a complex process of unconscious prehensive unification in our organism and nervous system. "Causal efficacy" unfolds behind the scenes of this Cartesian theater in the unrepresentable depths of reality, carrying vague but potent emotional vectors from the past into the present. Perception in the mode of presentational immediacy provides us with a freeze-frame of the surrounding world (hence its relative clarity and distinctness), while perception in the mode of causal efficacy is transitional, always

69. Whitehead, *Process and Reality*, 88.
70. Whitehead, *Process and Reality*, 88.
71. Whitehead, *Process and Reality*, 156.
72. Whitehead, *Process and Reality*, 166.

on the move (hence its vagueness). Presentational immediacy allows for *intentional* consciousness, the subjective capacity for attentional directedness toward the eidos of objects.[73] Causal efficacy is *prehensional*, the proto-subjective capacity to inherit the affective influences of objects, which themselves grow together into a novel subject. The former mode requires that a mind remain at a distance from things, relating to their essence rather than feeling their causal insistence. The latter mode reveals the interpenetration of things, the intimate assimilation of their past being into our present becoming. Schelling and Whitehead's alchemical distillation of consciousness uncovers an experiential dynamic deeper than reflective cognition, an ontologically basic and cosmically pervasive network of vector-feelings shared in by actualities of every grade. If anything is *a priori*, it is not the transcendental structures of human conceptuality as Kant argued, but the descendental processes of cosmic prehensionality.

The next chapter brings Schelling and Whitehead's process philosophy into conversation with several streams of post-modern thought that both exemplify the ontology of aesthesis articulated above at the same time that they challenge my cosmotheanthropic interpretation. My aim in the third chapter and first part of chapter four (4.1) is to lure Kant's transcendental approach to aesthetics a bit further than he was willing into a full-blown process ontology of organism. If, in Steiner's terms (see chapter 1), Kant's transcendentalism—that is, his coming-to-consciousness of the formerly unconscious way that the mind's own thinking, feeling, and willing contributes to the construction of our

---

73. Strictly speaking, intentionality or the object-directedness of consciousness as described by phenomenologists is accounted for by Whitehead in terms of a third, mixed mode of perception: "symbolic reference," whereby the spatial array of immediately presented objects is brought into relation with the temporal vectors of causal efficacy that underly them, thus granting us a conceptual grasp of enduring entities.

123

experience of the world—represents for philosophy the "lesser" guardian of the threshold, then the post-modern modes of thought expressed by Nietzsche, Sallis, and Deleuze confront philosophy as the "greater" guardian.[74] These figures thus test the metallurgic strength of Schelling and Whitehead's cosmotheanthropic process philosophy in the deconstructive fires of post-modernism.

That Kant was unwilling (per his devotion to the Good) to allow aesthetic feeling (Beauty) or scientific knowledge (Truth) an equal share in critical philosophy's transcendental foundation follows from his desire to subjugate the faculties of thinking (theoretical reason) and feeling (taste or aesthetic judgment) to that of willing (practical reason). The moral law derived from his critique of practical reason was Kant's keystone. He denied knowledge of Nature in order to make room for freedom. He thus gains experience of the formerly supersensible nature of freedom, but remains insensitive (or at least unwilling) to acknowledge the ontological significance of our imaginal experience of natural Beauty. Fearful of the sublime power of imagination, Kant restricts the mind to representations of a dead Nature manufactured by fixed categories of the understanding. Schelling and Whitehead were initiated into the lower transcendental mysteries of philosophy by Kant, but they did not stop there. They pressed on to imagine a living way of relating to reality. Unlike Kant, who indeed discovered but dared not disturb the Creativity at the abyssal root of mind and Nature, Schelling and Whitehead made it the lamp guiding their plunge into descendental philosophy.

---

74. Steiner, *Higher Worlds*, Ch. 11.

3

Descendental Philosophy and Aesthetic Ontology: Reimagining the Kantian Mode of Thought

> All Neoplatonists, Hermetic philosophers, alchemists and Kabbalists have asserted that the cosmos is animated by a collective soul which manifests now spiritually, now physically, now—daimonically—both at once; but which above all connects and holds all phenomena together. This is the true orthodoxy, they say, from which the erroneous orthodoxy of what the philosopher A. N. Whitehead has called "the last three provincial centuries" has deplorably lapsed.
> —Patrick Harper[1]

> "Philosophers have disdained the information about the universe obtained through their visceral feelings, and have concentrated on visual feelings."
> —Whitehead[2]

IN THIS CHAPTER, the most significant philosophical innovations of Kant's transcendental method are brought into conversation with the alternative process-relational mode of thought arising from Schelling and Whitehead, as well as several related thinkers, including Friedrich Nietzsche, Gilles Deleuze, John Sallis, and William Connolly. In the case of the latter three thinkers, the inheritance is direct and intentional. As for Nietzsche, there is little chance he had heard of Whitehead before dying in 1900 and he read little if any of Schelling's

---

1. Harper, *The Philosopher's Secret Fire*, 37; summarizing Whitehead, *Science and the Modern World*, vii.
2. Whitehead, *Process and Reality*, 121.

work directly (according to Walter Kaufmann the young Nietzsche was a follower of Schopenhauer, rather than Schelling).[3] It is probably true that some of Schelling's and Whitehead's theological language would ring hollow in Nietzsche's ears. But as Kaufmann notes, Nietzsche's aesthetic preference for Dionysus over Apollo (for creative ecstasy over measured self-possession) was prefigured in Schelling's *Philosophy of Mythology and Revelation*.[4] Despite their divergences over the cultural and philosophical importance of Christianity (more on this in the epilogue), I argue that many of the imaginative innovations of Schelling and Whitehead's process philosophy converge with Nietzsche's affirmation of an aesthetic ontology of power. Further, I make the case that their reconstruction of a process theology after the death of God is not vulnerable to many of the iconoclastic attacks leveled by the atheistic Nietzsche. As we will see in this chapter and again in the epilogue, Whitehead and Schelling's mobilization of Christian imagery is not the same old "monotono-theism" rightly rejected by Nietzsche.[5] "Religion will not regain its old power," writes Whitehead, "until it can face change in the same spirit as does science."[6] In Catherine Keller's terms, Schelling and Whitehead's is as much an "iconoplastic" as it is an iconoclastic theology.[7]

Simply put, the alternative mode of thought articulated by Schelling and Whitehead (and shared by Nietzsche, Deleuze, and Sallis) is aesthetically, rather than conceptually or morally grounded. They both challenge the orthodox plot of the philosophical soul's journey—that is, transcendental rationality's yearning for disembodied perfection—by reversing the vector of the soul's desire: their theology is not about a

3. Kaufmann, *Nietzsche*, 125.
4. Kaufmann, *Nietzsche*, 128n8.
5. Nietzsche, *The Anti-Christ*, 68.
6. Whitehead, *Science and the Modern World*, 189.
7. Keller, *Cloud of the Impossible*, 34.

fallen world longing for God, but the story of a lonely God longing for the world. For as Blake said, "Eternity is in love with the productions of time."[8] Their philosophy thus inhabits *descendental* conditions of *actual* experience, rather than dwelling on *transcendental* conditions of *possible* experience.

Bringing this descendental mode of thought into conversation with transcendentalism does not imply that Kant's critical method can simply be rejected as false. Obviously this would not make for productive conversation. Despite his profound dissatisfaction with Kantian philosophy, even Nietzsche admitted that the errors of great men like Kant "are worth honoring because they are more fruitful than the truths of small men."[9] Any attempt to reconstruct the bridge between physics and metaphysics in the wake of Kant's transcendental turn toward the subject must inoculate itself against the metaphysical illusions he warned about. Returning to the ideas of pre-Kantian philosophers like Spinoza and Leibniz (as both Schelling and Whitehead do) without first having been initiated into Kant's understanding of the *a priori* conditions of all experience (be it in the mode of thinking, willing, or feeling) puts us at risk of believing we have unproblematic access to the noumenal ground of Nature when, really, we are sleepwalking through a metaphysical dreamscape. On the other hand, while Kant's transcendental approaches to conceptual determination of Nature and to moral self-determination of the will may protect us from being carried away by speculative inflation, they also leave us with little means of affirming the value of actual embodied experience. The Kantian inheritance is thus decidedly double-edged.

From Schelling's perspective, the critical philosopher's epistemic alienation from actual Nature can be understood as a "necessary evil," a means to an end, since only through the strife of this separation can the philosophical soul initiate

---

8. Blake, "The Proverbs of Hell," in *The Portable William Blake*, 253.
9. Nietzsche, *The Nietzsche Reader*, 25.

the transformation from unconscious patient into conscious agent of the power of imagination.[10] Only when the sense-bound understanding or "*mere* reflection" of the critical method is treated as an end in itself does it become an "intellectual sickness."[11] Modern philosophy's bifurcated image of Nature becomes a moment in imagination's self-education, a goad to Spirit's overcoming of its split from matter. Without Kant's critical move calling all prior philosophizing into question, the creative synthesizing power of imagination would have remained unconscious, its secret art buried beneath the transcendental subject's reflection upon objects thought to be external to it.

Kant and especially his disciple Fichte argued that philosophy has no object other than itself, other than *the subject, the "I," doing the philosophizing*. The subject, "I," or Self, is of course no ordinary thing or object—if it can be so labeled at all. The Self—the protagonist of the Kantian approach to philosophy—is described by Fichte as an unconditioned (*unbedingt*) act rather than an objective fact.[12] It is literally unthingable (un-*ding*-able), the transcendental ground of all conditioned things.[13]

On Kant's reading, Nature is diametrically opposed to mind because it is ruled by necessity and causal determinism, while mind is free and self-determining, ruled only by itself. Schelling was unsatisfied by Kant and Fichte's attempt to account for the seeming externality and determinism of Nature by reference only to the *a priori* conditions of self-conscious experience. He refused to allow Nature's dynamically evolving creativity to be reduced to the transcendental activity of the reflective mind. On the other hand, Schelling also preserved many of Kant and Fichte's insights into the freedom of the

10. Schelling, *Ideas*, 11.
11. Schelling, *Ideas*, 11.
12. Förster, *Twenty-Five Years*, 181.
13. Bowie, "Translator's Introduction" to *Schelling's Modern Philosophy*, 7.

Self. For Schelling, human freedom and natural creativity must both be granted equal ontological weight.[14] But how can the two, Nature and freedom, be held together without contradiction?

Schelling begins trying to articulate the indifference of mind and Nature by critiquing Kantian accounts of selfhood. It became clear to Schelling that the already conscious ego, the Self after it has risen to an awareness of itself through the act of thinking "I am," could not possibly be responsible for "manufacturing" the external world, as Kant would have it.[15] The external world only appears as separate from the mind when the activity of the "I"s own coming-to-itself has ceased. The Self's alienation from a Nature outside it seems to be a necessary result of its initial coming-to-consciousness. In his own words, Schelling sought to

> explain the indestructible connection of the "I" with a world which is necessarily thought as external to it via a preceding transcendental past of real or empirical consciousness, an explanation which consequently led to a transcendental history of the "I."[16]

In other words, once the mind has said "I am" to itself, it forgets the path it traversed to get to that point, since only at the end of this path does consciousness emerge. The conscious ego finds only the "monuments" or "memorials" of the stages it passed through along the path, not the path itself. For Schelling, then, philosophy is principally an endeavor to remember *in full consciousness* what at first unfolded unconsciously. Similarly, for Whitehead,

---

14. Schelling, *Modern Philosophy*, 94–113.
15. Handwritten in the margin of a late fascicle of the *Opus Postumum*, Kant writes: "He who would know the world must first manufacture it—in his own self, indeed" (240).
16. Schelling, *Modern Philosophy*, 109.

> the creation of the world is the first unconscious act of speculative thought; and the first task of a self-conscious philosophy is to explain how it has been done.[17]

Schelling and Whitehead's approach to healing the bifurcation of mind from Nature thus hearkens back to Plato's original conception of philosophy as a work of *anamnesis*, only rather than remembering transcendent ideas, it descends into the depths of the past in search of mind's ancient archetypal roots in living Nature.

Schelling analogizes the ego's recollective attempt to overcome its own self- and world-alienation to Nature's divinely inspired dynamic evolution toward conscious freedom: "the monuments of [the ego's] successive overcoming [are] identical with the moments of nature."[18] Schelling's attempt to articulate an analogy between the processes of self-becoming and cosmic-becoming follow from his critiques of Cartesian-Newtonian conceptions of Nature, the very conceptions that Kant had taken for granted as the last word on the physical world. The fundamental natural phenomena of gravity and light are reinterpreted by Schelling in an organic, rather than mechanistic way as the first stirrings of mind as it emerges from Nature. The whole of Nature being organic, its apparently mechanical dimension is reinterpreted as giving only a partial glimpse of the universal polarity between gravity and light, where light as the formal/ideal force exists in dynamic tension with gravity as the material/real force. As Schelling puts it:

> The particular successions of causes and effects (that delude us with the appearance of mechanism) disappear as infinitely small straight lines in the universal curvature of the organism in which the world itself persists.[19]

---

17. Whitehead, *Aims of Education*, 164.
18. Schelling, *Modern Philosophy*, 112.
19. Schelling, "World-Soul," 70.

What appears at first to be inorganic matter, when considered in its full concreteness as always already conditioned by the universal communicability of light, is really just the germ of organic life.[20] As an illustration of the life-producing relationship between gravity and light, Schelling offers the example of the electromagnetic connection between Earth and Sun responsible for calling forth plant-life out of the planet.[21] In Schelling's scheme, gravity corresponds to the Self as first limited by itself, as caught up with itself, while light corresponds to the Self as it breaks free from its self-imposed restrictions. In this sense, light is "an analogy in the extended world for spirit or thought"; it is "thought on a lower step or at a lower potential" that later flowers as the human spirit.[22]

Schelling does not reject the transcendental approach to philosophy. He only relativizes its claims to Absolute knowledge by articulating a complementary approach that I am calling *descendental* philosophy. Schelling himself referred to his late "positive philosophy" as a *philosophia descendens*, opposing it to the merely logical or "negative philosophy" initiated by Kant, which he called *philosophia ascendens*.[23] Descendental philosophy "[descends] into the depths of Nature in order to raise itself from there to the heights of spirit."[24] Jason Wirth deploys Deleuze and Guattari's terminology to argue that, for Schelling, "Nature [is] the image of thought as such."[25] For Deleuze and Guattari, the confrontation with Chaos is the precondition of philosophy.[26] Chaos provides the

---

20. Schelling, *First Outline*, 186.
21. Schelling, *First Outline*, 185–86.
22. Schelling, *Modern Philosophy*, 119.
23. *Positive Philosophy*, 196n18. While negative philosophy "will predominately remain the philosophy of the academy," descendentalism "will be the philosophy for *life*" (ibid., 198).
24. Schelling, *Modern Philosophy*, 120.
25. Wirth, "Nature of Imagination," 457.
26. Deleuze and Guattari, *What Is Philosophy?*, 42, 207–8.

transcendental *Abgrund* or imaginal abyss from out of which emerge all a philosopher's concepts.[27] In Schelling, Chaos becomes the "abyss of freedom," the "dark precursor" of thought, "that which is absolutely mobile . . . which is continually an Other, which cannot be held on to for a moment."[28] For Schelling, then, the prime subject–object of philosophical thought is not the autonomous Self, as it was for Kant and Fichte. Nor is it simply an objectified deterministic Nature. Rather, in Schelling's *Naturphilosophie*, we are beckoned by the incomprehensible groundlessness preceding volitional selfhood and objectified physicality alike. This groundless abyss is the invisible and "unprethinkable" productivity of Nature.[29] Schelling also refers to it as the divine imagination.[30] Schelling was profoundly influenced both by Spinoza's identification of an infinite God with an infinite Nature ("*Deus siva Natura*") as well as his distinction between *Natura naturata* and *Natura naturans*.[31] Whitehead refers to this groundless unprethinkable infinity as Creativity. The creative abyss is the descendental condition of reflection and appearance alike, providing the groundless ground of Reason itself. The philosopher comes into contact with it directly at the sublime edges of sensibility, hence the early Schelling's claim that an "aesthetic act" provides the

---

27. "In philosophy, as in Dante's poem, the path toward heaven leads through the abyss [Abgrund]" (Schelling, *Philosophy and Religion*, 31).

28. Schelling, *Modern Philosophy*, 152.

29. "Das Unvordenklichkeit" is, according to Dale Snow, "one of the most difficult German expressions to translate." He suggests it might be "somewhat clumsily . . . rendered as 'the unpreconceivability of Being,' implying that there is always that in reality which will remain beyond thought" (Snow, *Schelling*, 235n8). My translation of "das Unvordenkliche" derives from Jason Wirth's translation of Schelling's *The Ages of the World*. Bruce Matthews renders it as "that before which nothing can be thought" (*Schelling's Organic Form*, 28). Terry Pinkard offers "the being that is un-thinkable-in-advance" (*German Idealism*, 328).

30. Schelling, *Human Freedom*, 18.

31. Literally, "Nature natured" and "Nature naturing," respectively. Or as Whitehead put it in Chapters 7 and 8 of *Modes of Thought*, "Nature Lifeless" and "Nature Alive."

keystone of philosophy and the late Schelling's defense of what he termed "metaphysical" or "higher empiricism."[32] This higher form of empiricism returns philosophy to experience, "not . . . in the formal . . . but in the material sense": it is only here, in actual experience of Nature, "rather than in an [*a priori*] metaphysics that floats in the air, lacking any foundation," that philosophy can achieve its highest goals (i.e., participatory knowledge of God, the Soul, and the Cosmos).[33]

According to Schelling, the fact that "everything in the sensuous world is grasped in number and measure does not therefore mean that geometry or arithmetic explain the sensuous world."[34] Whitehead similarly argues that "the general principle of empiricism depends upon the doctrine that there is a principle of concretion which is not discoverable by abstract reason."[35] The "higher empiricism" Schelling alludes to is not at all the positivistic empiricism of much modern science, wherein through "servile imitation," a reflective mind attempts to geometrically represent the objects of Nature as though their forms were "still born," as Wirth puts it.[36] Schelling and Whitehead have little patience for modern science's high altitude view of Nature as a collection of objects mechanically governed by externally imposed laws. Instead, both sought to return the philosopher to his or her concrete aesthetic encounter with Nature (to our "prehension" of Nature, in Whitehead's terms). It is here that Nature's creative natality shines through the superficial appearance of objective finitude. Our sensory experience, attended to in earnest, reveals its source to be infinite, sublime.[37] It is only

---

32. Schelling, *Positive Philosophy*, 169.
33. Schelling, *Modern Philosophy*, 190–91.
34. Schelling, *Modern Philosophy*, 147.
35. Whitehead, *Science and the Modern World*, 179.
36. Wirth, *Schelling's Practice of the Wild*, 134.
37. As I unpack in the pages to follow, the sublimity of sensory experience is rooted in a *descendental*, rather than transcendental reading of the sublime.

after reflective consciousness has manufactured for us a finite, ordered world that this infinity is obscured and covered over by abstract conceptual determinations.

In attempting to descend below the veil of intellectual reflection into the imaginal depths of the sensible, the philosopher puts their sanity at risk. According to Wirth, for Schelling "philosophy is the negotiation of madness, reason's ongoing encounter with what resists reason."[38] In this way, Schelling challenges the orthodox orientation of philosophy toward the intelligible by affirming that a certain kind of madness lurks within or behind intellect itself, giving it life. Intellect absent all madness would be mere mechanical understanding. Like Whitehead, Schelling is more concerned with keeping thought alive than with repeating stale truths of the merely logical sort. As Whitehead puts it, "in the real world, it is more important that a proposition be interesting than that it be true."[39] Of course, true propositions are liable to be more interesting than false ones. But it is precisely by *erring* that creativity disrupts repetitive habits so as to bring forth novelty.

Kant remains ever vigilant of the threat to transcendental philosophy posed by the madness lurking in the imaginal depths of the sensible. He juridically denounces the potential "offenses" (*Vergehungen*) of the aesthetic imagination: its unruly playfulness constitutes a revolt from the laws imposed by the understanding.[40] According to Kant, once imagination breaks free of the fixed world-determining laws of the understanding, the mind becomes imagination's "unfortunate victim," lost in irrational fantasies and thus on its way to insanity.[41] Although Kant came closer to unleashing the creative power of imagination than any philosopher prior,

---

38. Wirth, "Nature of Imagination," 466.
39. Whitehead, *Process and Reality*, 259.
40. Kant, *Anthropology*, 74.
41. Kant, *Anthropology*, 74–75.

when he reached the edge of the abyss, he became fearful of losing his balance and so retreated. In the A edition of the *Critique of Pure Reason*, Kant gave a central role to imagination's synthetic power, while in the B edition published several years later, he backtracked by erasing key passages on imagination's all-important mediating and grounding role.[42] Heidegger argues that Kant's recoil from the creative abyss of imagination is a result of his desire to "[preserve] the mastery of reason" over the senses.[43] As a result of his retreat from the power of imagination, the core distinction of his transcendental philosophy between sensation and cognition widens into an unbridgeable chasm.

In the conclusion to his *Critique of Practical Reason*, Kant writes:

> Two things fill the mind with ever-renewing wonder and awe, the more often and the more intensely the mind is drawn to think of them: the starry heavens above me and the moral law within me.[44]

He goes on to explain that neither the sky above him nor the freedom within him should be considered mere conjectures. Neither is beyond the horizon of conscious experience. We sense the celestial lights above through our eyes, and we feel the moral freedom within through our heart, the innermost source of our selfhood. Kant continues:

> The former view of a countless multitude of worlds annihilates my importance as an animal creature, which after it has been for a short time provided with vital power, one knows not how, must again give back the matter of which it was formed to the planet it inhabits (a mere speck in the

---

42. Kant, *Critique of Pure Reason*, 225–244; Heidegger, *Kant and the Problem of Metaphysics*, 113.
43. Heidegger, *Kant and the Problem of Metaphysics*, 119.
44. Kant, *Critique of Practical Reason*, 133.

> universe). The second, on the contrary, infinitely elevates my worth as an intelligence by my personality, in which the moral law reveals to me a life independent of animality and even of the whole sensible world, at least so far as may be inferred from the destination assigned to my existence by this law, a destination not restricted to the conditions and limits of this life, but reaching into the infinite.[45]

The intuitions he is attempting to express remain valid even if we are forced to reject the epistemological and metaphysical conclusions he draws from them. If human beings have any moral freedom and worth, it must be related to the creativity and value we share with animals. *For we are animals.* Accepting our creatureliness and our dependence on earthbound ecological relations does not require that we deny our participation in the infinite. It is our intuition of the infinite, both outside and within ourselves, that generates Beauty. Here, I follow Schelling in softening the distinction Kant sought to establish in his *Critique of Judgment* between the beautiful and the sublime.[46] Heidegger's argument above regarding the revised edition of the *Critique of Pure Reason* applies just as well to the *Critique of Judgment*: Kant sharply divides the finite form of the beautiful from the infinite depths of the sublime precisely in order to assure reason retains mastery over aesthetic imagination. A descendental aesthetic ontology requires that the sublime be released from its Kantian shackles. Kant took the aesthetic overflow resulting from encounters with the sublime (like the starry night) and tried to twist them into evidence of humanity's moral superiority over Nature. He comes so close to glimpsing the face of God in the imaginal depths of the cosmos only to turn away into abstract *a prioris* and artificial moralizing. As Deleuze suggests,

---

45. Kant, *Critique of Practical Reason*, 133.
46. Schelling, *System of Transcendental Idealism*, 225. For Schelling, beauty is the infinite finitely displayed.

> The analysis of the sublime has set us on the right track, since it showed us a common sense which was not merely assumed [like that generating formal beauty], but engendered.[47]

Instead of, like Kant, sharply dividing animal *aesthesis* from moral or spiritual *noesis*, we can recognize the sublime heights of the heavens and the sublime depths of the heart as equally aesthetic in nature. We can, as, Schelling put it, "grasp the god outside through the god within."[48] As the source of the Beautiful is infinite, no conceptual definition can capture or explain it. We cannot reach beyond or behind Beauty's inner and outer appearances to grasp the rules governing its aesthetic genesis. When we try to peer beyond the cosmos outside us, or plumb the depths of the psyche within us, we find only more appearances, an *infinite ingression* of appearances. When the understanding tries to reflectively grasp the infinity of aesthesis, it slips into an infinite regression. It fails to find an original ground or fundamental reason for the ongoing aesthetic genesis of the chaosmos. Only the creative imagination can intuit the meaning of the infinite aesthetic ingression of beautiful appearances.[49]

Schelling and Whitehead refuse to accept modern rationality's inability (or unwillingness) to know the divine life of Nature. For Schelling, after the Kantian revolution, philosophy began to deal "with the world of lived experience just as a surgeon who promises to cure your ailing leg by amputating it."[50] Instead of amputating the life of Nature, Schelling and Whitehead attempt to reform philosophy's bias toward abstraction by returning it to its senses. They strive to root philosophy in "that which precedes the logos of thinking,"

---

47. Deleuze, *Kant's Critical Philosophy*, 52.
48. Schelling, *Human Freedom*, 10.
49. Schelling, *First Outline*, 15.
50. Schelling, *System der Weltalter*, 92.

namely, "an aesthetic act of *poesis*" paralleling the creative *naturans* that underlies the putatively dead *naturata* of the physical world.[51] Schellingian philosopher Bruce Matthews likens the imaginative act at the generative root of Schelling's philosophy to "the explosive power of the sublime." "This initial moment of aesthetic production," continues Matthews,

> provides us with the very real, but very volatile stuff of our intellectual world, since as aesthetic, this subsoil of discursivity remains beyond the oppositional predicates of all thought that otherwise calms and comforts the knowing mind.[52]

Like Empedocles, Schelling and Whitehead launch themselves into the volcano and plunge into the creative power of living Nature, that is, into the divine imagination. The success of their descendental method depends upon philosophy's willingness to undergo a Dionysian journey through the underworld.

---

51. Matthews, *Schelling's Organic Form*, 5.
52. Matthews, *Schelling's Organic Form*, 5. I would qualify Matthew's claim that this aesthetic subsoil is "beyond" the oppositional predicates of thought (he himself here predicates it as "beyond" as opposed to, say, "before"). Aesthesis is not "beyond" or "before," not simply immanent or transcendent, but is better characterized simply as the soil from out of which thought flowers.

3.1 Aesthetic Ontology and Nietzsche's Encounter with Nihilism

> Pain is something universal and necessary in all life, the unavoidable transition point to freedom. We remember growing pains in the physical as well as in the moral sense. We will not shun presenting even that primordial being (the first possibility of God externally manifesting) in the state of suffering that comes from growth. Suffering is universal, not only with respect to humanity, but also with respect to the creator. It is the path to glory. God leads human nature down no other path than that down which God Himself must pass . . . . [In] its revelation, the divine being must first assume nature and, as such, suffer it, before it can celebrate the triumph of its liberation.
>
> —Schelling[53]

In this section, I argue that Nietzsche's valorization of becoming and musings on an ontology of power resonate with Schelling and Whitehead's process-relational, aesthetic ontology. But first, a few road blocks must be cleared. It is easy to read Whitehead's allegiance to Plato as something that, in Nietzsche's eyes, would have disqualified his scheme (which includes reformed conceptions of teleology, divinity, and eternal objects) from serious consideration. Schelling's theological orientation may also make his thought seem incompatible with Nietzsche's more theocidal project. Nietzsche saw himself as among the first Europeans to fully grasp and suffer through the death of the traditional image of God. His philosophy is a confrontation with the crisis of meaning that results when the transcendent illusions of dogmatic theism are no longer convincing enough to direct human thinking, feeling, and willing. Kant denies theoretical knowledge of God's existence, but his critical idealistic construal of God as the transcendental condition of human conscience and moral reasoning is still too priestly and disembodied for Nietzsche. Nietzsche is after more than a *critique* of dogma. His aim is to *destroy* dogma to make way for a new kind of human being

53. Schelling, *The Ages of the World*, 101.

capable of expressing ethical and aesthetic values that are not anchored on the transcendental sky hooks of a Highest Being. Whether or not the three thinkers finally diverge on the involvement of divinity in the becoming of reality, I believe that the convergence of their processual orientations makes for a fruitful comparison.

As Judith Norman argues, although Nietzsche largely dismisses the young Schelling's romantic idealism, had he read anything written by Schelling after the death of his wife Caroline of dysentery in late 1809, he may have reassessed him as a poetic and philosophical ally.[54] Norman summarizes Nietzsche's list of traditional philosophical errors in *Twilight of the Idols*: (1) the preference for being and hatred of becoming, (2) the distrust of the senses and devaluation of the body, (3) the privileging of a self-causing Creator above derivative creatures, and (4) the bifurcation of reality into a true world and an apparent world.[55] I agree with Nietzsche's diagnosis of the fundamental errors of traditional philosophy and argue in this section that Schelling and Whitehead's process-relational approach not only avoids these errors, but also at least indicates one way forward toward a post-Kantian and post-nihilistic philosophical outlook. Although Kant was already well aware that "the classical concept of God was on shaky ground,"[56] his attempt to justify religion on transcendental foundations comes at the cost of further alienating humanity

---

54. Caroline died just as Schelling was finishing the work that would signal his definitive break with idealism, titled *Philosophical Investigations into the Essence of Human Freedom*. A few weeks after her death, Schelling wrote,

> I now need friends who are not strangers to the real seriousness of pain and who feel that the single right and happy state of the soul is the divine mourning in which all earthly pain is immersed (Döderlein, *Brief über den Tod Carolines*; translated by Wirth, "Introduction," *The Ages of the World*, x).

Schelling would publish only a single pamphlet after *Human Freedom*, but intense writing and frequent lecturing continued unabated for 45 years.

55. Norman, "Schelling and Nietzsche," 90.
56. Howe, *Faithful to the Earth*, 19.

from the divinity animating Nature. In place of God, Kant substitutes an anesthetic "moral world-order," a substitution that in Nietzsche's eyes is the "very recipe for decadence" and signals "the final exhaustion of all life" in nihilism.[57]

Nihilism, according to Nietzsche, is a "psychological state" characterized by the feeling of "being ashamed in front of oneself, as if one had deceived oneself all too long" with the belief that the event we call "the universe" is *about* something—that "something is to be achieved through the process—and now one realizes that becoming aims at nothing and achieves nothing."[58] Nietzsche's first target in dismissing the supposed aim or telos of cosmic evolution is the notion, long cherished by philosophers and theologians alike, that humanity is at the center of things or is the end toward which all things move. His second target is the human desire to achieve a "unity" of knowledge based in some supposed ontological monism: "underneath all becoming there is no grand unity."[59] His third target is the metaphysical belief in a "true world." Instead of the classical philosophical dichotomy between the one true reality of Being and the many false appearances of becoming, Nietzsche affirms "becoming as the only reality." But in affirming the process of reality as aimless, Nietzsche finds himself stuck in a sort of nihilistic stasis unable to deny meaning altogether: "one . . . cannot endure this world though one does not want to deny it."[60] Nietzsche thus comes to see nihilism as "a pathological transitional stage." "What is pathological," Nietzsche continues, "is the tremendous generalization, the inference that there is no meaning at all."[61] In other words, once the three traditional categories of Reason—Aim, Unity, Being—have proven themselves incapable of capturing the

---

57. Nietzsche, *The Portable Nietzsche*, 11.
58. Nietzsche, *The Will to Power*, 12.
59. Nietzsche, *The Will to Power*, 13.
60. Nietzsche, *The Will to Power*, 13.
61. Nietzsche, *The Will to Power*, 14.

dynamism of the actual universe without remainder (applying instead to a mostly fictitious ideal universe projected by our psychological need for existential security), there remains the constructive task of *re-evaluating* the cosmos in accordance with more adequate categories. "Adequate" not according to the standards of transcendental reflection, which construes reality as though only human consciousness provides "the meaning and measure of the value of things"; rather, categories adequate to the standard of *life itself*, namely, the *will to power*. In Nietzsche's words:

> In order for a particular species to maintain itself and increase its power, its conception of reality must comprehend enough of the calculable and constant for it to base a scheme of behavior on it. The utility of preservation—not some abstract-theoretical need not to be deceived—stands as the motive behind the development of the organs of knowledge—they develop in such a way that their observations suffice for our preservation. In other words: the measure of the desire for knowledge depends upon the measure to which the will to power grows in a species: a species grasps a certain amount of reality in order to become master of it, in order to press it into service.[62]

Nietzsche's interpretation of the human intellect is similar to the evolutionary epistemology articulated by Henri Bergson and William James, perhaps Whitehead's two most important philosophical influences. This view of the intellect as a pragmatic survival mechanism rather than a judge of unchanging objective truth requires a total re-imagination of philosophy's methods and goals. For Bergson, it meant putting aside intellect (if not in science, then at least for the purposes of philosophy) and developing a new organ of perception: philosophical intuition.[63] For James, it meant construing philosophy "as

---

62. Nietzsche, *The Will to Power*, 266.
63. Bergson, *The Creative Mind*, 87–106.

Chapter 3: Descendental Philosophy and Aesthetic Ontology

more a matter of passionate vision than of logic . . . logic only finding reasons for the vision afterwards."[64] For Whitehead, despite his own logical acumen, it meant analogizing philosophy to "imaginative art."[65] With language as its medium, and logic as a check but not a master, philosophy strives to elucidate the texture of experience with novel turns of phrase. Whitehead continues, in a rather Nietzschean vein: "The degeneracy of mankind is distinguished from its uprise by the dominance of chill abstractions, divorced from aesthetic content."[66] Philosophy's role is then as a critic of abstractions working to prevent "the abstractive experience" achieved by rational consciousness from "destroying its own massive basis for survival," as Whitehead put it.[67] In Nietzsche's terms, a post-nihilist philosophy would remember that the concept "leaf" is but a passing puff of air compared with "the unique and wholly individualized original experience to which it owes its birth," that is, the encounter with the life of actual leaves, no two of which are ever the same.[68]

Nietzsche is extremely suspicious of the classical conception of teleology. But Whitehead's reformed concept of final causation is comparable to Nietzsche's own favorite concept: power. For Whitehead, the concept of power entails both efficient and final causation, where its efficient aspect is provided by the objective "ground of obligation" inherited by new actual occasions, and its finalist aspect by the "internal principle of unrest" expressed in the concrescence of each occasion.[69] Actual occasions do not wield power like a subjective capacity, controlling their behavior as if from a transcendental point of leverage beyond it. Power is not the capacity *of* a subject,

---

64. James, *Pluralistic Universe*, 176.
65. Whitehead, *Modes of Thought*, 117
66. Whitehead, *Modes of Thought*, 123
67. Whitehead, *Modes of Thought*, 123.
68. Nietzsche, *The Portable Nietzsche*, 46.
69. Whitehead, *Process and Reality*, 29.

but the capacity *productive* of a subject. Whitehead completely abandons "the notion of an actual entity as the unchanging subject of change"; instead, "an actual entity is at once the subject experiencing and the superject of its experiences."[70] Whitehead's is not the old concept of a design imposed by a transcendent, unmoved Creator standing distinctly above and apart from its creation. His reformed teleology is self-organizing, as each concrescence achieves its own joyful satisfaction while at the same time aiming beyond itself to influence the becoming of future occasions. This novel conception of teleology stems from his dipolar conception of divinity: God is described in its primordial pole as envisaging eternal objects as lures for the concrescence of finite occasions, but this envisagement is not a disinterested contemplation of ideas or a withdrawal into the "No" of unrealized possibility. Rather, God's primal act is erotic, the loving affirmation of actuality, a "Yay-saying" that embraces finite embodiment by aiding its initiation. Nietzsche is explicit that his philosophy involves both a "No-saying" and a "Yes-saying," both a rejection of anaesthetic modes of thought leading to life denying nihilism *and* the creation of new modes of thought sensitive to the meanings of *this* world.[71] As J. Thomas Howe points out, many critics attend only to the "No-saying" side of Nietzsche's thought, to the way he seeks out and destroys the metaphysical foundations of Western philosophy.[72] But there is also a metaphysically constructive side to his philosophizing, a desire to affirm and celebrate the value-creating power of the world's many creatures.[73]

For Nietzsche, as for Schelling and Whitehead, the processual concept of will or power replaces the classical concept of "Substance," that most abstract and stable of eternal ideas.

---

70. Whitehead, *Process and Reality*, 29.
71. Nietzsche, *Ecce Homo*, 1.
72. Howe, *Faithful to the Earth*, 71.
73. Howe, *Faithful to the Earth*, 72.

"This world is the will to power—and nothing besides!" proclaims Nietzsche.[74] While Schelling and Whitehead would certainly temper this claim by referencing divine lures toward goodness, truth, and beauty, they also do not shy away from acknowledging the ontological importance of power. "Will is primal being," writes Schelling.[75] In Whitehead's terms:

> The essence of power is the drive towards aesthetic worth for its own sake.... It constitutes the drive of the universe. It is efficient cause, maintaining its power of survival. It is final cause, maintaining in the creature its appetite for creation.[76]

Nietzsche, while he denies any overarching Meaning shaping all existence, does not deny meaning outright. Rather, *he pluralizes it*: the universe "has no meaning behind it, but countless meanings"[77] within it. Whitehead's rendering of the concept of power as not simply an efficient, but also a final cause, is not the imposition of a Single Destination toward which all creatures move. Rather, each individual creature creates its own meaning (even if the desire to create as such is initiated by God). Nietzsche argues that "every creature different from us senses different qualities and consequently lives in a different world from that in which we live."[78] Similarly, for Schelling, the primal will is not simply singular but composed of a community of many individual wills.[79] We should not misinterpret this pluralism of perspectives, this ontology of multiple meaning-makers, as the rather banal thesis that there are many perspectives on some underlying reality, be it material, ideal, or otherwise. This is not the shallow sort of pluralism where a

---

74. Nietzsche, *The Will to Power*, section 1067.
75. Schelling, *Human Freedom*, 21.
76. Whitehead, *Modes of Thought*, 119.
77. Nietzsche, *The Will to Power*, 305.
78. Nietzsche, *The Will to Power*, 305.
79. Schelling, *Human Freedom*, 23.

single stable reality is allowed to appear or be represented in many changing guises. "As if a world would still remain over after one deducted the perspectives!"[80] Instead, Schelling, Whitehead and Nietzsche affirm the most radical form of ontological pluralism, here given voice by the latter:

> Every center of force adopts a perspective on the entire remainder, i.e., its own particular valuation, mode of action, and mode of resistance.... There is no other mode of action whatever; and the "world" is only a word for the totality of these actions. Reality consists precisely in this particular action and reaction of every individual part toward the whole.... Appearance is an arranged and simplified world, at which our practical instincts have been at work; it is perfectly true of us; that is to say, we live, we are able to live in it: proof of its truth for us—the world, apart from our condition of living in it, the world that we have not reduced to our being, our logic and psychological prejudices, does not exist as a world "in itself"; it is essentially a world of relationships; under certain conditions it has a differing aspect from every point; its being is essentially different from every point; it presses upon every point, every point resists it.[81]

In this excerpt, Nietzsche could very easily have been describing Whitehead's process-relational ontology. There of course remains the issue of making Whitehead's conception of a creaturely God envisaging eternal objects compatible with Nietzsche's atheistic orientation. It is important to remember that Whitehead's God is constructed as a secular replacement for the supernaturalist images of the past. Whitehead's God cooperates and suffers with the world. It does not create *ex nihilo* an actual world from a transcendent heaven beyond the world. In Keller's terms, Whitehead's dipolar divinity effects a

---

80. Nietzsche, *The Will to Power*, 305.
81. Nietzsche, *The Will to Power*, 567.

"*creatio cooperationis*," rather than a *creatio ex nihilo*.[82] Similarly, Schelling's God is not one-sidedly spiritual, but includes and even longs for ever-increasing physical realization.[83]

William Connolly treats the conceptual correspondences and divergences between Nietzsche and Whitehead in *The Fragility of Things: Self-Organizing Processes, Neoliberal Fantasies, and Democratic Activism* (2013), from which the following summary excerpt is drawn:

> It must be emphasized that the positive spirituality Whitehead pours into his speculative philosophy is at least as affirmative as that of Nietzsche, and more consistently so. These two process philosophers are thus worthy protagonists from whom others can draw sustenance: they advance contending, overlapping cosmic creeds that speak to today; they address the spiritual quality through which a creed is lived in relation to others; and they throw up for grabs a set of established, complementary assumptions during a period when many constituencies both feel and suppress doubts about those assurances. Each, at his best, argues with the carriers of other creeds while inviting their proponents to fold positive spiritualities into their creedal relations. . . . Nietzsche and Whitehead articulate the planetary and cosmic dimensions in diverse concepts and affective tones that also touch. . . . Each expresses, in his inimical way, a spirit of deep attachment to a cosmos of dispersed, conditioned processes . . . [84]

Connolly counts Whitehead and Nietzsche as allies in his push for a pluralist cosmopolitics, that is, a politics open to the more-than-human realities within and around us.[85] He hears

---

82. Keller, *Face of the Deep*, 117.
83. Schelling, *Abyss*, 147.
84. Connolly, *The Fragility of Things*, 176–78
85. Cosmopolitics is not the cosmopolitanism championed by Kant (and the Stoics before him), but a more recent approach to the politics of Nature devel-

both Whitehead and Nietzsche calling us to "stretch human capacities by artistic and experimental means so as to respond more sensitively to other force fields."[86] But he also levels several potentially devastating critiques of Whitehead's thought. I must respond in particular to his attempts to "qualify" two of Whitehead's most enigmatic categories: God and eternal objects.[87] Some browsers of Whitehead's philosophical scheme (including Connolly) praise him for his categoreal innovations including "creativity," "prehension," "actual occasion," and "concrescence," but want nothing whatsoever to do with what they perceive to be his gratuitous theological constructions, most infamously his dipolar creaturely divinity and his existentially deficient but always ingressing eternal objects. Some materialists may argue that, if Whitehead's conceptual scheme cannot survive the removal of its theological elements, then it must be buried in the graveyard of history's bold but mistaken philosophical systems. If Whitehead's universe is really God-infused, the materialists say, then his speculative adventure in cosmology is for that reason also irrelevant for any modern scientific investigation of Nature.

The problem with this assessment of Whitehead's scheme is that, whatever may be the case with regard to religion, the story of modern scientific rationality and its alleged technological mastery over matter has itself already been made irrelevant by the planetary scale of the ecological crisis that it has

oped by Isabelle Stengers and Bruno Latour:

> The presence of *cosmos* in *cosmopolitics* resists the tendency of *politics* to mean the give-and-take in an exclusive human club. The presence of *politics* in *cosmopolitics* resists the tendency of *cosmos* to mean a finite list of entities that must be taken into account. *Cosmos* protects against the premature closure of *politics*, and *politics* against the premature closure of *cosmos*. (Latour, "Whose Cosmos, Which Cosmopolitics?", 454)

86. Connolly, *The Fragility of Things*, 161

87. See also Donald Crosby's critiques of these concepts in his own comparison of Nietzsche and Whitehead, "Two Perspectives on Metaphysical Perspectivism," in *The Pluralist*.

played an instrumental role in bringing about. Nature is not at all like what modern techno-scientists had thought she was. Her mechanical "laws" turn out to be more like organic tendencies—tendencies whose stability human beings are now altering at genetic and climatic scales. The mechanical conceptions of Nature imagined by thinkers like Galileo, Descartes, and Newton have proven to be incongruent with the thermodynamic, electromagnetic, evolutionary, quantum, relativistic, and complexity theories of nineteenth- and twentieth-century science.[88] Viewed in light of the process-relational philosophy articulated by Schelling and Whitehead, Nature can no longer be denuded of all subjective qualities, moral and aesthetic values, and creative potencies. Nature turns out to be more like a living organism than a programmed machine.

Whitehead asks us to take seriously his philosophical refusal to grant God any special powers not native to every other actual entity in the universe. God is not a separate category of entity to which we should offer "metaphysical compliments," but a creature of creativity like every other.[89] Schelling and Whitehead are often described as "panentheists" (for example, by Charles Hartshorne,[90] and more recently, Michael Murphy[91]) because of their insistence upon the immanent and processual character of the divine. Murphy likens the panentheism of thinkers like Schelling, Whitehead, James, Bergson, Charles Sanders Peirce, Pierre Teilhard de Chardin, and Sri Aurobindo to a temporalized evolutionary version of the ancient "Great Chain of Being."[92] Keller describes Whitehead's panentheism as a scheme in which God "trades omnipotence

---

88. See my *Physics of the World-Soul: Whitehead's Adventure in Cosmology* (2021) for more on how Whitehead's organic cosmology integrates these nineteenth- and twentieth-century paradigms.
89. Whitehead, *Science and the Modern World*, 179.
90. Hartshorne and Reese, *Philosophers Speak of God*.
91. Murphy, "The Emergence of Evolutionary Panentheism."
92. Murphy, "The Emergence of Evolutionary Panentheism," 555.

and impassivity for . . . sensitive interdependence," such that "God's own experience, God's open becoming, depends upon the becoming of [other] creatures."[93] Considering the processual basis of Schelling and Whitehead's theology, it may be better termed "pan*gen*theism," signaling the extent to which their cosmos is a *pantheogenesis* in which all things are not simply identical to God (as in Spinoza's view) but *becoming-with* God.

As we have seen, at the same time that he affirms the immanence of divinity, Whitehead also insists on the necessity of God's "unconditioned conceptual valuation of the entire multiplicity of eternal objects," an eternal act which assures the ingression of relevant novelty into the experience of finite actual occasions. "Apart from God," he writes,

> eternal objects unrealized in the actual world would be relatively non-existent for the concrescence in question. For effective relevance requires agency of comparison, and agency of comparison belongs exclusively to actual occasions.[94]

Whitehead often writes of God's primordial nature as "eternally fixed," as Donald Crosby complains.[95] But when read in imaginative conjunction with what Whitehead has to say about God's consequent nature—the way God is conditioned by and grows with the creative advance of the actual universe—this fixity quickly dissolves into something that looks a lot like Nietzsche's universe of "multiple interacting force fields ungoverned by an overriding center," as Connolly describes it.[96] Whitehead's own variety of perspectival panexperientialism is more Hesiodian than Connolly acknowledges when he contrasts Nietzsche's strong attraction to "the

---

93. Keller, *Cloud of the Impossible*, 33.

94. Whitehead, *Process and Reality*, 31

95. Crosby, "Two Perspectives on Metaphysical Perspectivism," in *The Pluralist*, 68.

96. Connolly, *The Fragility of Things*, 168.

contending gods of Hesiod" with the magisterial Whitehead's supposed preference for the settled order of eternal unity. "In Greek thought, either poetic or philosophic," Whitehead notes with regret, "the separation between physis and divinity had not that absolute character which it has for us who have inherited the Semitic Jehovah."[97] Whitehead and Schelling both celebrate Plato's proto-evolutionary cosmological insight into what the ancient Greeks referred to as "subordinate deities who are the animating principles for [certain] departments of nature."[98] Their schemes follow Plato's *Timaeus* in describing, in Schelling's terms, the way "anarchy still lies in the ground" and provides the birthplace of order and form.[99] On Whitehead's reading, Plato's cosmogonic dialogue describes:

> the creation of the world [as] the incoming of a type of order establishing a cosmic epoch. It is not the beginning of matter of fact, but the incoming of a certain type of social order.[100]

The order of the created universe is thus a historically emergent social achievement, not an *ex nihilo* emanation out of the Eternal One. It is "incoming," but not from somewhere else, some distant Eternal Realm separate from and prior to the creative advance of the actual universe. Eternal objects on their own (as pure potentials) are "deficient in actuality," such that it is only ever as a result of the decision of some actual occasion that they play a role in the creation of anything.

Despite Whitehead's tempering of eternity's role in the creative process, Connolly worries that Whitehead's concept of God as a "[conveyer] of new levels of complexity into the future" ignores the fragility of human civilization and indeed

---

97. Whitehead, *Process and Reality*, 94
98. Whitehead, *Process and Reality*, 94.
99. Schelling, *Human Freedom*, 29.
100. Whitehead, *Process and Reality*, 96

the inescapable eventual demise of life on Earth.[101] But Whitehead's categoreal scheme does not require the metaphysical preservation of the physical complexity aroused by any particular cosmic epoch's primordially evaluated potential. It is possible to creatively interpret his scheme such that each cosmic epoch has its own emergent divinity, or world-soul. It may be that some as yet undetected form of order is inherited from past epochs by newborn world-souls. It is also likely, however, that much order is lost in the cataclysmic transition from one epoch to the next. The apparently 13.8 billion year lifespan of our cosmic epoch can be imagined by analogy to the incarnate soul of an individual human being. Neither for our personal nor our cosmic soul can we be metaphysically certain what happens after death, that is, after the body has decayed and entropy has cooled all the energy in the visible universe. Intellect is here left in an antinomic aporia. Kant was correct in denying the mind theoretical knowledge of personal immortality and cosmic infinity. The important point for this experiment in descendental philosophy, however, is that the primordial character of God is a *contingent matter of fact*—that is, *a free deed*—and not a metaphysical necessity. This reframe of the Kantian problematic opens us again, after Kant, to the inevitability of coming to know the mind of God, but only if we are willing to *become God's body* by suffering with the entire cosmic community of experiential occasions. I do not know whether Whitehead himself would express discomfort with my proposed adjustment to his theology. But by the end of his life he admitted to being uneasy even about his own formulation of the divine function. My argument presently is that the coherence of Whitehead's scheme not only survives but may in fact be enhanced by this more Dionysian interpretation. Nietzsche challenges all one-sidedly Apollonian philosophies, and while Whitehead's dipolar divinity is clearly more in-

---

101. Connolly, *The Fragility of Things*, 175

volved in the chaotic tumult of cosmogenesis than traditional conceptions of the divine, committing to a processual and aesthetic orientation requires the explicit rejection of metaphysical fixity in the primordial nature of God. The Whiteheadian philosopher Michel Weber supports such a reading, pointing out that Whitehead nowhere attempts a demonstration of the necessary existence of God, as traditional theologians have for millennia:

> Since God belongs to Process and Reality's 'Derivative Notions,' not to its 'Categoreal Scheme,' it could...be argued that God is not a metaphysical necessity, only a contingent cosmological feature of our 'cosmic epoch.'[102]

This would mean that each divine envisagement of eternal creativity—that is, each incarnation of a world-soul—will eventually face death and dismemberment in the transition to a new cosmic epoch. Between the incarnations of each epochal soul, catastrophic fragmentation and loss is just as possible, metaphysically speaking, as enduring and harmonious organization. Even if the latter is what we happen to see in our cosmos today, it could all fall to pieces tomorrow. Nietzsche draws approvingly upon another process philosopher, Heraclitus, who compares "the world-forming force" of divine creativity to "a child at play, arranging and scattering stones here and there, building and then trampling sand hills."[103] While the metaphysical possibility of such tragic and chaotic forgetting always remains, the physical world we in fact inhabit displays tremendous intensities of aesthetic and mathematical order. The beauty of the world suggests that the achievements of prior cosmoi have been remembered and integrated within our own. The soul of our world may be more than a child, having matured over epochs by learning to preserve those patterns of

---

102. Weber, "On a Certain Blindness in Political Matters," 216.
103. Nietzsche, *The Nietzsche Reader*, 86 ("The Birth of Tragedy").

activity which increase the depth and intensity of its enjoyment of existence.[104] But again, this is an empirical proposal, and not a metaphysical principle. The risk of dismemberment remains indefinitely and is atoned for (if at all) only by the Love constituting God's consequent nature—that is, God's desire to save for eternity what otherwise would be lost in the creative flux of Nature. This Love is not a metaphysical decree, but a free deed affirmed here and now again and again in the passing of each and every occasion of our earthly experience. There is no eternal law compelling reality to love itself, or to become cosmically ordered. Reality does so, if it does so, because the creatures composing it desire it so.[105]

Connolly also complains that Whitehead's "doctrine of eternal objects reduces the scope of possible creativity in the

---

104. The philosopher Douglas Fawcett, shortly after discussing Whitehead's *Principles of Natural Knowledge* (1919), speculates on a similar scenario in his book *Divine Imagining* (1921):

> This present creative phase of our world-system may be its first; or it may be one of many like prior adventures which have alternated with rest-phases. This consideration, unfortunately for our convenience, cannot be ignored. For, if the system has gone through prior creative phases, it has had time in which to evolve superior orders of sentients and possibly that very exalted society of sentients which constitutes a limited or finite god. And these powers, entering into its present creative phase, must be making a vast difference to it. On the other hand, if it be a young system in its first creative phase, it may possess as yet no adequately evolved higher sentients of its own. We know that, in the case of our own and animal bodies, the organism begins and evolves for a long while before a conscious agent shows through it. Does Nature similarly precede god; the finite god of the system who arises and matures at a late stage in the process of the suns? There remains, withal, the suggestion that god and the superior sentients might come from beyond the system, the higher levels of which may not be so rigorously insulated or "encysted" as the lower. It seems that a human sentient may appear in a plurality of lives. Might not a god appear in a plurality of systems, continuing his evolution on the great scale? (166)

105. There is empirical evidence in the cosmic microwave background radiation studied by astronomers that is suggestive of the type of metaphysical scenario I am describing. Based on this evidence, mathematical physicist Roger Penrose has speculated on a cyclical model of the universe implying multiple big bangs in *Cycles of Time: An Extraordinary New View of the Universe* (2011).

world."[106] Terrence Deacon expresses identical concerns.[107] On my reading, Whitehead introduces the concept of God's primordial valuation of eternal objects specifically to make the experience of relevant novelty possible. Far from reducing the ingression of novelty into the universe, an actual occasion's initiatory experience of divine potentiality provides the descendental condition for such creative ingression. If prehensions were simply physical (that is, related only to past actual occasions), nothing new could ever happen in the world. Nature would remain utterly repetitive and habitual in its behavior. Further, without granting the distinct reality of potentialities alongside actualities, there would be no way to distinguish the future from the past. Time would be reversible and homogeneous, not a creative advance into novelty. The dynamic evolution of the universe is made possible by the creative decisions of actual occasions that conceptually prehend the givenness of the physical past in some more or less significant way as containing the potential to become *other* than it was. While physical prehensions relate to the settled facts of the past, conceptual prehensions relate to the formal possibilities of the future left open by those facts. As Heisenberg expressed it, the question is, How does "a unique actuality evolve from a matrix of coexistent potentia?"[108] Whitehead's answer is that each actual occasion, via the process of concrescence, makes definite (or concretely actual) what had been indeterminate (or abstractly possible), adding another fact of realized value to the ongoing evolution of this cosmic epoch.[109]

In the end, while it is possible to coherently read Whitehead's notion of God's primordial nature as contingently tied to the emergence of each cosmic epoch, I do not believe it is

---

106. Connolly, *The Fragility of Things*, 163.
107. Personal communication, April 25, 2012. See my essay *Physics of the World-Soul*, 49.
108. As quoted by Connolly, *The Fragility of Things*, 153.
109. See Segall, *Physics of the World-Soul*, 45.

possible to maintain coherence if the categories of eternal objects and God are left out altogether. In his book *Onflow: Dynamics of Consciousness and Experience* (2005), Ralph Pred attempts such a revision of Whitehead's cosmology by arguing that human valuation and aesthetic enjoyment can be accounted for without God's envisagement of eternal objects. Instead, value is explained solely through the "hybrid feeling of self [and] the memory and imagination, stirred by aim in the concrescence in question."[110] Whitehead's cosmotheanthropic philosophy includes these, but also affirms the highest aspiration and sublime intuition of the human spirit, that is, the feeling of God's Love luring us toward Beauty. In *Process and Reality* Whitehead explains that:

> [The primordial, non-temporal accident] is here termed "God" because the contemplation of our natures, as enjoying real feelings derived from the timeless source of all order, acquires that "subjective form" of refreshment and companionship at which religions aim.[111]

Pred attempts to naturalize Whitehead by explaining away the need for any divine function in cosmogenesis, but in critiquing Whitehead's speculative scheme, Pred focuses exclusively on the unconscious, primordial nature of God, leaving unmentioned the conscious pole of the Universe: God's consequent nature. The philosophical imagination can discover the divinity at the base of actuality only after having survived the crisis of nihilism and the deconstruction of all transcendently imposed values. When a philosopher is able to think, feel, and will in full consciousness of the grave implications of her own incarnation, then an actual, living God can be experienced. A philosopher whose will has been brought to its utmost extreme and who has thus "[stood] alone before the

110. Pred, *Onflow*, 178.
111. Whitehead, *Process and Reality*, 31–32.

infinite," as Schelling puts it, consciously participates in the becoming of God.[112] Paradoxically, to experience the divine life in all things, the philosopher must learn to die, as Plato suggests in the *Phaedo*. Encountering and embracing the sublime mystery of death *while still alive* awakens the embodied soul to the power of imaginative perception, granting it a metaxic bond with the soul of the world. The universe then openly displays itself as an ongoing expression of sublime aesthesis, an open-ended achievement of the immanent divine aim at play in the world. My body and its ego will die, but the soul of this world will inherit my actions and live on. Eventually, even this world-soul will die, and in so doing it will trace faint echoes of its adventures into the subtly ordered chaos preceding the next world-soul's awakening. "From the remnants of a dying, rigid world there sprouted the seeds of a new one," writes Steiner. He continues:

> That is why we have death and life in the world. The decaying portion of the old world adheres to the new life blossoming from it, and the process of evolution moves slowly. This comes to expression most clearly in man himself. The sheath he bears is gathered from the preserved remnants of the old world, and within this sheath the germ of that being is matured which will live in the future.[113]

The echoes of past cosmic and human incarnations flow into us as we become ever more enfolded into and ensheathed by God's consequent nature. As Keller describes the final phase of the dipolar process, "God in consequence feels, internalizes, *em-pathos*, each becoming as though in Her own body." The same God, she continues, who in the primal phase is "the one who entangles us in new possibilities" despite the stubbornness of the past, in the final phase becomes "entangled in

---

112. Schelling, *Werke*, 1/9, 227; excerpted and translated by Lawrence, "Philosophical Religion and the Quest for Authenicity," 22.
113. Steiner, *Higher Worlds*, Ch. 11, par. 1.

[the] spontaneous actualizations" of those possibilities as they open into the future.[114] There is no non-relational beginning to this process, no *creatio ex nihilo*: God is always already in creative relation with all creatures.

Just as God's dipolar nature must always be held in mind in order to grasp the meaning of Whitehead's categoreal scheme, the concepts of eternality and actuality must also be thought in polar tension. His cosmology becomes incoherent if divinely envisaged eternal objects are rejected and prehensions and finite actual occasions are made to do all the work of cosmogenesis, as Pred prefers. Contrary to Pred, I believe those who argue Whitehead's scheme cannot survive the removal of its theological components are correct: in regard to this issue, we must either swallow the scheme whole or spit it out whole and try something else. This is not to say Whitehead's scheme cannot or should not be tinkered with in order to improve or clarify it. Indeed, I have done just that in leaving open the possibility that each cosmic epoch is linked to a newborn God or world-soul. But for Whitehead, on a categoreal level, eternality (or potentiality) and actuality are the two poles of the magnet of explanation. If you try to break off either end of the explanatory scheme, you only end up with a smaller magnet. Which is to say that, at least if we are going to attempt to metaphysically explain our experiential situation, the polar tension between what is merely possible and what is in fact actual is an inescapable one. It is important to emphasize in this context that polarity is not the same as duality. Whitehead's ontology of process, like Schelling's, replaces the static dualism characteristic of Cartesian substance ontology with dynamic polarity. Experience is thus primordially rooted in *tension* as such, with intention and extension as its stems. Only when we have forgotten that the overripe fruits of intentional ego and extended matter have fallen off the same living

---

114. Keller, *Cloud of Possibility*, 188–89.

trunk do they appear to us like separate substances.

Returning to Schelling, his dipolar divinity is described by Norman as grounding Nature's temporality and as grounded by Nature's spatiality: "the grounding relation is chronological as well as ontological."[115] The divine is extended as space and intending in time, rather than remaining absent from the spatiotemporal universe. I would qualify Norman's choice of the word "chronological" to describe the temporal dimension of God, however. There is more than one modality of time, the "chronic" mode referring in particular to the spatialized time measured by mechanical clocks. The "temporal eternity"[116] of God's becoming is not adequately captured in the terms of the chronic mode. As Schelling describes it, God partakes of time through a "succession of eternities,"[117] rather than through a succession of measurable instants. Theogenesis is better described as an expression of the "aionic" or "kairotic" modes of time, modes that cannot be linearly or spatially measured in terms of "before" and "after."[118] Rather, for God, past, present, and future are mutually implicated in the creative renewal or concrescence of each moment of actuality. As Schelling writes:

> In the circle out of which everything becomes, it is no contradiction that that through which the One is generated may itself be in turn begotten by it. Here there is no first and last because all things mutually presuppose each other, no thing is another thing and yet no thing is not without

115. Norman, "Schelling and Nietzsche," 97.
116. Wolfson, *Alef, Mem, Tau*, 41.
117. Schelling, *The Ages of the World*, 76.
118. For a more detailed discussion of the various modalities of time, including chronic, kairotic, and aionic, see my essay "Minding Time in an Archetypal Cosmos," in *Archai*, Volume 5. See also Schelling's discussion of the "system of times" in *Philosophy of Mythology*, 162–64, and Panikkar's about the difference between "chronological" and "kairological" time in *The Cosmotheandric Experience*, 20–21.

another thing. God has in himself an inner ground of existence that in this respect precedes him in existence; but, precisely in this way, God is again the *prius* [what is before] of the ground in so far as the ground, even as such, could not exist if God did not exist *actu*.[119]

Norman compares Schelling's conception of the birth of God to Nietzsche's conception of self-creation in that both show "striking and unexpected fidelity to Kant" in construing the productive process (of God and of the Self) as one of temporal synthesis.[120] But unlike in Kant, where synthesis works "in service of stability and identity," in Nietzsche as in Schelling, synthesis roots divine power in Nature and the fate of the human soul in the fate of the whole. "The fatality of human existence," writes Nietzsche, "cannot be extricated from the fatality of everything that was and will be" because "[each] person belongs to the whole."[121]

Nietzsche elsewhere imagines a future God whose power comes from becoming-with and so suffering alongside finite creatures, a God whose growth "could make our old earth more agreeable to inhabit."[122] His vision of a "powerful future feeling" that human beings are just beginning to awaken to resonates deeply with Whitehead's sense of the consequent nature of God, God's "universal feeling" inclusive of the world's sufferings, sorrows, failures, triumphs, and joys alike, a "tender care that nothing be lost."[123] In Nietzsche's terms:

> he who is able to feel the history of man altogether as his own history feels in a monstrous generalization all the grief of the invalid thinking of health, of the old man thinking of

---

119. Schelling, *Human Freedom*, 28.
120. Norman, "Schelling and Nietzsche," 190.
121. "The Four Great Errors." Quoted and translated by Norman. "Schelling and Nietzsche," 100.
122. Nietzsche, *The Gay Science*, 337.
123. Whitehead, *Process and Reality*, 346.

the dreams of his youth, of the lover robbed of his beloved, of the martyr whose ideal is perishing, of the hero on the eve after a battle that decided nothing but brought him wounds and the loss of a friend. But to bear and to be able to bear this monstrous sum of all kinds of grief and still be the hero who, on the second day of battle, greets dawn and his fortune as a person whose horizon stretches millennia before and behind him ... to take this upon one's soul—the oldest, the newest, losses, hopes, conquests, victories of humanity. To finally take all this in one soul and compress it into one feeling—this would surely have to produce a happiness unknown to humanity so far: a divine happiness full of power and love, full of tears and laughter, a happiness which, like the sun in the evening, continually draws on its inexhaustible riches, giving them away and pouring them into the sea.... This divine feeling would then be called—humanity![124]

While in some of his moods Nietzsche may have dismissed Schelling and Whitehead's "deification of becoming" as an all too metaphysical consolation,[125] towards the end of his life, he remarked in a notebook that "everything seems far too valuable to be so fleeting: I seek an eternity for everything.... My consolation is that everything that has been is eternal."[126] In response to these remarks, David Krell writes: "How close the communication of Dionysian affirmation brings us to the Redeemer type."[127] In mythic terms, Christ seems to be the divinity situated at the chiasmus of Apollo and Dionysus. Christ is not pure light, like Apollo, but light mixed with darkness, spirit incarnate, a rainbow binding heaven and earth.

---

124. Nietzsche, *The Gay Science*, 337.
125. Nietzsche, *Human, All Too Human*, 114.
126. Nietzsche, *The Will to Power*, 1065.
127. This and the prior excerpt were quoted in Howe, *Faithful to the Earth*, 166–67.

3.2 Aesthetic Ontology in Sallis' Elemental Phenomenology

"I beseech you, my brothers," Nietzsche has Zarathustra say, "*remain true to the earth!*"[128] In his account of "How the 'True World' Finally Became a Fable," Nietzsche traces the historical development of the dualism between the True and the apparent world from Plato, through Christianity, to Kant. Finally, in Nietzsche's day, the subordination of appearance to Truth had come to be refuted:

> The true world—we have done away with it: what world was left? the apparent one perhaps? . . . . But no! *with the true world we have also done away with the apparent one!*[129]

In line with the efforts of Whitehead and Schelling to articulate an aesthetic ontology, the elemental phenomenologist John Sallis makes good on Nietzsche's call for a return to the sensible that is not a simple reversal, placing appearances above intelligibles. Such an inversion is nonsensical. Rather, the very dichotomy must itself be overcome to make way for a new interpretation of the sense of the sensible.[130] Sallis suggests that this new orientation to the sensory world requires also a new orientation to *logos*, to speech. His work toward a "logic of imagination" is largely an attempt to reconstruct the sense of speech so that it is no longer "subordinated . . . to an order of signification absolutely anterior to it."[131] Instead of the meaning of speech being thought of as a derivative of some preconstituted intelligible order, its meaning is to be brought forth out of the sense of the sensible itself. "What is now required," writes Sallis, "is a discourse that would double the sensible—interpret it, as it

---

128. Nietzsche, as quoted by Sallis, *Force of Imagination*, 22.
129. Nietzsche, *The Nietzsche Reader*, 465.
130. Sallis, *Force of Imagination*, 33.
131. Sallis, *Force of Imagination*, 23.

Chapter 3: Descendental Philosophy and Aesthetic Ontology

were—without recourse to the intelligible."[132]

Sallis admits that such a logic of imagination, in that it "[disturbs] the very order of fundamentality and [withdraws] from every would-be absolute its privileging absolution,"[133] places philosophy in a somewhat unsettled, even *ungrounded*, position. Indeed, Nietzsche's call to return to our senses by being true to the Earth should not be read as an attempt to erect a new foundation for philosophy on more solid ground. Nietzsche sought a new beginning for philosophy in groundless becoming—the world of "death, change, age, as well as procreation and growth."[134] Even Earth is made groundless by the tectonic forces that slowly turn it inside out. Nietzsche subjected all prior philosophers to the earthquakes of his hammer, showing mercy only to Heraclitus, perhaps the first process philosopher, for challenging Parmenides' emphasis on static Being with his declaration that *all things flow*.

Although Sallis articulates his logic of imagination largely in the context of Nietzsche's anti-foundationalism, Schelling and Whitehead's aesthetically-oriented process ontology may provide a more constructive example of how to philosophize after the "True world" has become a fable. In contrast to Nietzsche's more demolitional approach to "[philosophizing] with a hammer," you might say Whitehead and Schelling philosophize with a paint brush in an attempt to recolor a coherent vision of the human soul's relationship to a God-infused universe.

For Whitehead, the dichotomy between appearance and reality is not as metaphysically fundamental as has been assumed from ancient Greek philosophy onwards.[135] The over-emphasis on this dichotomy is based upon the misleading notion that perception in the mode of "presentational

---

132. Sallis, *Force of Imagination*, 33.
133. Sallis, *Force of Imagination*, 21.
134. Nietzsche, "Twilight of the Idols," *The Nietzsche Reader*, 462.
135. Whitehead, *Adventures of Ideas*, 209.

immediacy" is the source of the raw data of experience, when in fact, unconscious bodily reception in the mode of "causal efficacy" is more primordial. Instead of understanding consciousness to be the highly refined end product of a complex process of experiential formation rooted in vague feelings of bodily inheritance streaming in from an expressive environment, philosophers have made the clear and distinct concepts of conscious attention their starting point. "Consciousness," writes Whitehead,

> raises the importance of the final Appearance [presentational immediacy] relatively to that of the initial Reality [causal efficacy]. Thus it is Appearance which in consciousness is clear and distinct, and it is Reality which lies dimly in the background with its details hardly to be distinguished in consciousness. What leaps into conscious attention is a mass of presuppositions about Reality rather than the intuitions of Reality itself. It is here that the liability to error arises.[136]

The obsession with achieving certainty and avoiding error is characteristic of the representational paradigm to which modern philosophy in its rational, empirical, and transcendental modes adheres. Derivative appearances in the form of sensory universals displayed before a merely reflective ego are thus mistaken for the primary particular realities unfolding beneath the surface of conscious intentionality. Representational consciousness tends to abstract from these prereflectively intuited realities such that, by the time the ego reflects upon them, their once-occurrent and self-existent uniqueness has been scrubbed clean and forgotten, leaving only the concept of a universal for thought. For example, a hand-carved chair made from Brazilian mahogany by a master craftsman becomes simply another instance of the category

---

136. Whitehead, *Adventures of Ideas*, 270.

"chair," a thing whose meaning comes not from its own being and history, but from its value to me as a thing for sitting on; or perhaps an even more telling example, a living mahogany tree is perceived as merely another instance of the category "raw material" used for making furniture. Unfortunately for modern philosophy and its obsession with conceptual certainty, Nature, even as *Natura naturata*, "does not remember to remain itself, to repeat its identity again and again," as Wirth puts it. Nature's *natality*, *Natura naturans*, always undoes the temporarily fixed forms of Nature natured, "[contesting] the habits of representation that maintain identities in the present."[137] Modern philosophy's obsession with attaining certain knowledge of the truth and avoiding error at all costs must be replaced with the more pragmatic pursuit of *efficacious* ideas—that is, the pursuit of ideas that ameliorate alienation by allowing for more intimate aesthetic participation with living Nature. In short, philosophy must return to its ancient soteriological roots rather than remaining stuck in epistemological abstractions.

3.3 Aesthetic Ontology in Deleuze's Transcendental Empiricism

Whitehead and Schelling's aesthetically-oriented philosophies were an important influence on Gilles Deleuze's "transcendental empiricism." Deleuze's response to the Kantian mode of thought provides a model for the descendental philosophy I am attempting to articulate. Deleuze, like Whitehead and Schelling, follows Leibniz in beginning philosophy, not with the crystalline clarity of eternal essences, but with the confused sway of empathic perceptions (i.e., with causal efficacy rather than presentational immediacy). The perceived world, as Merleau-Ponty described it in a discussion of Schelling's debt to Leibniz, "teaches us an on-

---

137. Wirth, *Schelling's Practice of the Wild*, 71.

tology that it alone can reveal to us."[138] Perception is thereby treated as "an original world,"[139] rather than a derivative copy. "All the bodies of the universe are in sympathy with each other," writes Leibniz,

> and though our senses are in response to all of them, it is impossible for our soul to pay attention to every particular impression. This is why our confused sensations result from a really infinite variety of perceptions. This is somewhat like the confused murmur heard by those who approach the seashore, which comes from the accumulation of innumerable breaking waves.[140]

Given the aesthetic basis of knowing, Deleuze forgoes the pretense of a scientific transcendental method seeking certain knowledge and instead articulates a *pedagogical* method attentive to the fact that "learning is, after all, an infinite task." For Deleuze, "it is from 'learning,' not from knowledge, that the transcendental conditions of thought must be drawn."[141] His pedagogical method is not based on Kant's fixed table of logical categories, the *a priori* conditions for all possible knowledge of objects, but rather on an experimental set of aesthetic categories that provide *genetic* conditions for new becomings-with objects. Deleuze mentions Whitehead's categoreal scheme as an example of a new transcendental aesthetic (or a descendental aesthetic, in my terms) where, unlike representational categories, it is not only *possible* experience that is conditioned, but *actual* experience. He calls Whitehead's categories "phantastical," in that they represent novel creations of the imagination never before encountered by philosophers.[142] For Whitehead, because each experient

---

138. Merleau-Ponty, *Nature*, 40.
139. Merleau-Ponty, *Nature*, 40.
140. Leibniz, *Philosophical Papers*, 325.
141. Deleuze, *Difference and Repetition*, 166.
142. Deleuze, *Difference and Repetition*, 284–85

is a perspective on the world *and* an element in the world, the categories of an experientially adequate philosophical scheme must elucidate the "paradox of the connectedness of things:—the many things, the one world without and within."[143] In other words, while Whitehead accepts modern philosophy's focus on the self-created perspective of the subject—that, in some sense, *the world is within the subject* (as in Kant's transcendental idealism)—he holds this insight in imaginative polar tension with the common sense presupposition that the subject is *within* and *emerges from* the world. This refusal to remove subjective experience from the world of actual entities brings Whitehead's descendental panexperientialism very close to Deleuze's transcendental empiricism.

Contrary to Kant, the mind is not the only problem solver. It is not the sole intelligent observer and manipulator of a stupid and passive Nature. The formative forces driving Nature's evolutionary "education of the senses" are just as creative and problematically arrayed as are the imaginative forces shaping the historical education of the human mind. As Deleuze argues,

> problematic Ideas are precisely the ultimate elements of nature and the subliminal objects of little perceptions. As a result, "learning" always takes place in and through the unconscious, thereby establishing the bond of a profound complicity between nature and mind.[144]

Mind thus becomes a more complexly folded Nature. The proper maintenance of the conscious complicity of mind and Nature depends upon what Deleuze calls the "education of the senses," by which he means the raising of each of the soul's powers to its limit so that, through their mutual

---

143. Whitehead, *Adventures of Ideas*, 228.
144. Deleuze, *Difference and Repetition*, 165.

intra-action, the imagination is quickened and freed from the preformed conceptions of identity normally produced by the understanding into creative perceptions of difference in itself. The path of the learner is "amorous" (we learn by heart), but also potentially fatal,[145] since the creation of difference—though free from the anxieties of method, free of having to know with certainty—for precisely this reason always risks the creation of nonsense, or worse, the descent into madness. But in the end, the philosopher must take these risks, since "to what are we dedicated if not to those problems which demand the very transformation of our body and our language?"[146]

Deleuze's transcendental empiricism does not privilege the thinking or willing faculties, as does Kant's transcendental idealism. While thought concerns itself with the domains or levels of virtuality (what Whitehead refers to as the hierarchy of eternal objects), it is the faculty of imagination that "[grasps] the process of actualization," that "crosses domains, orders, and levels, knocking down the partitions coextensive with the world, guiding our bodies and inspiring our souls, grasping the unity of mind and nature."[147] Imagination, continues Deleuze, is "a larval consciousness which moves endlessly from science to dream and back again."[148] Deleuze's faculty of imagination is no mere conveyer belt, however, merely transporting fixed categories back and forth along the schematic supply line between reflection and sensation. By bringing the imagination face-to-face with the chaotic wilderness of existence, Deleuze forces it to rediscover the wildness within itself. Faced with what Schelling called "the unprethinkable" (*das Unvordenkliche*), the sublime elemental forces of the universe, the imagination becomes

---

145. Deleuze, *Difference and Repetition*, 23.
146. Deleuze, *Difference and Repetition*, 192.
147. Deleuze, *Difference and Repetition*, 220.
148. Deleuze, *Difference and Repetition*, 220.

unable to perform its domesticated role in service to the *a priori* concepts of the understanding. "That which just exists," writes Schelling, "is precisely that which crushes everything that may derive from thought, before which thought becomes silent . . . and reason itself bows down."[149] It is upon confronting the unprethinkability of these elemental forces that "imagination finds itself blocked before its own limit: the immense ocean, the infinite heavens, all that overturns it, it discovers its own impotence, it starts to stutter."[150] But, continues Deleuze, imagination's sublime wounding is not without consolation:

> At the moment that imagination finds that it is impotent, no longer able to serve the understanding, it makes us discover in ourselves a still more beautiful faculty which is like the faculty of the infinite. So much so that at the moment we feel our imagination and suffer with it, since it has become impotent, a new faculty is awakened in us, the faculty of the supersensible.[151]

Brought to the edge of sanity, the soul's cognitive powers are thus transfigured, potentially laying a bridge across the gulf between physics and metaphysics. The path remains perilous, however. "The recourse to metaphysics," writes Whitehead, "is like throwing a match into the powder magazine. It blows up the whole arena."[152] Deleuze's pedagogical metaphysics indeed quickens the philosophical imagination's powers into "a harmony such that each transmits its violence

---

149. Schelling, *Werke*, 1/3, 161; excerpted and translated by Matthews, *Positive Philosophy*, 48.
150. Deleuze, "Kant seminar."
151. Deleuze, "Kant Seminar," par. 14 (4/4/1978). Instead of an entirely new faculty awakening, I would say that imagination itself comes to operate at a higher potency.
152. Whitehead, *The Concept of Nature*, 29.

to the other by powder fuse."[153] Rather than converging on a common sense, as Kant demanded of imagination, Deleuze's education of the senses approaches the point of "para-sense," where "thinking, speaking, imagining, feeling, etc." overcome themselves in a continual process of learning generative of new modes of thought and perception, modes capable of incarnating paradoxical Ideas as transformative symbols.[154] Deleuze would here seem to approach Schelling's understanding of the Idea's gradual incarnation in the course of an evolutionary cosmogenesis: "the time has come for a new species, equipped with new organs of thought, to arise," as Schelling argued more than two centuries ago.[155]

For Whitehead and Schelling, as for Deleuze, "the ultimate realities are the events in their process of origination."[156] Whitehead calls this process of origination *concrescence*. Concrescence refers to the process of "growing together" whereby "the many become one and are increased by one."[157] Each individual concrescing event, according to Whitehead, "is a passage between two ... termini, namely, its components in their ideal disjunctive diversity passing into these same components in their [real] concrete togetherness."[158] Similarly, Deleuze describes the incarnation of a problematic Idea as an event that unfolds in two directions at once, along a *real* and an *ideal* axis: "At the intersection of these lines," writes Deleuze, "where a powder fuse forms the link between the Idea and the actual—the 'temporally

---

153. Deleuze, *Difference and Repetition*, 193.
154. Deleuze, *Difference and Repetition*, 194. As I unpack in the epilogue, Deleuze's hostility to common sense should be checked by Schelling and Whitehead's concern, not only to creatively disrupt old habits of thought, but to seek social recuperation so as to build new habitats for thinking.
155. Schelling, *Einleitung in die Philosophie*; translated by Grant, *After Schelling*, 55.
156. Whitehead, *Adventures of Ideas*, 236.
157. Whitehead, *Process and Reality*, 21.
158. Whitehead, *Adventures of Ideas*, 236.

eternal' is formed."[159] Whitehead's event ontology, wherein eternal objects intersect with or ingress into actual occasions in the process of concrescence, can be read in terms of Deleuze's account of the incarnation of Ideas, whereby concrescence becomes a temporary solution achieved through the condensation of the fragmentary multiplicity of past actualities and future possibilities into a precipitated drop of unified experience. The problematically condensed occasion of experience cannot long endure in its unity since, according to Whitehead's categoreal scheme, all entities necessarily find themselves perpetually perishing into objective immortality. This leads "the solution to explode like something abrupt, brutal and revolutionary," in Deleuze's terms.[160] Upon perishing, each entity becomes experiential debris to be gathered up again by the occasions to follow it.

Deleuze also describes incarnating Ideas as two-faced expressions of both the power of *love* (the ideal principle which seeks progressively to harmonize the fragmented times of past and future to form a unified "temporally eternal" solution) and the power of *wrath* (the real principle which angrily condenses these solutions until they explode, creatively issuing in revolutionary new problems). He argues that the most important aspect of Schelling's process theology is his consideration of these divine powers of love and wrath, where love relates to God's *existence* and wrath to God's *ground*.[161] Schelling conceives of both love and wrath as *positive* powers which therefore do not simply negate one another as opposed concepts in a Hegelian dialectic of contradiction, where wrath would struggle with love before both were sublated in some higher Identity. Rather, the eternal encounter between divine love and divine wrath leads to their mutual potentialization into a dynamic succession

---

159. Deleuze, *Difference and Repetition*, 189.
160. Deleuze, *Difference and Repetition*, 190.
161. Deleuze, *Difference and Repetition*, 190–91; Schelling, *Human Freedom*, 64.

of evolutionary stages in Nature (*Stufenfolge*). According to Schelling:

> These two forces [infinitely expanding love and infinitely retarding wrath], clashing or represented in conflict, leads to the Idea of an *organizing*, self-systematizing *principle*. Perhaps this is what the ancients wanted to hint at by the *soul of the world*.[162]

For Deleuze, "Ideas no more than Problems do not exist only in our heads but occur here and there in the production of an actual historical world."[163] Ideas are not simply located inside the head. Nor can Ideas be entirely captured inside the grammatical form of a logical syllogism, even if that syllogism is dialectically swallowed up and digested in the course of history by an Absolute Spirit. Even though the primary instrument of speculative philosophy is language, Ideas should never be reduced to verbal propositions, nor should philosophy be reduced to the labor of "mere dialectic."[164] Dialectical discussion "is a tool," writes Whitehead, "but should never be a master."[165] According to Schelling, the age old view that "philosophy can be finally transformed into actual knowledge through the dialectic . . . betrays more than a little narrowness."[166] That which gets called from the outside "dialectic" and becomes formalized as syllogistic logic is a mere copy, "an empty semblance and shadow" of the authentic mystery of the philosopher, which, for Schelling, is *freedom*. Freedom is the original principle underlying both mind and Nature, the archetypal scission generative of all Ideas through the "secret circulation" between the knowledge-seeking soul and

---

162. Schelling, "World Soul," translated by Grant, *After Schelling*, 145.
163. Deleuze, *Difference and Repetition*, 190.
164. Whitehead, *Adventures of Ideas*, 228.
165. Whitehead, *Adventures of Ideas*, 228.
166. Schelling, *The Ages of the World*, xxxvii.

its unconsciously knowing Other.[167] The authenticity of the philosopher's "inner art of conversation" depends upon this doubling of the soul into I and Other through a creative act of imagination. Without this imaginal doubling, the original scission of freedom is repressed and philosophy devolves into the formulaic dialectical refinement of the customary sayings and conceptual peculiarities of common opinion.[168]

As Whitehead describes it, "the very purpose of philosophy is to delve below the apparent clarity of common speech"[169] by creatively imagining "linguistic expressions for meanings as yet unexpressed."[170] Whitehead's adventure of Ideas, like Schelling's and Deleuze's, is not a search for some original opinion, or for the "complete speech" (*teleeis logos*) of encyclopedic knowledge.[171] Ideas are not merely represented inside an individual conscious mind, they are detonated in the imaginal depths of the world itself. Exploding Ideas seed symbolic vibrations that reverberate along the cosmic membrane (or "plane of immanence") and unfold at the level of representational consciousness as a profound complicity between mind and Nature.

It follows that Ideas, for Whitehead as for Deleuze, "are by no means essences," but rather "belong on the side of events, affections, or accidents."[172] As Steven Shaviro writes of Whitehead's "eternal objects," they ingress into events as "alternatives, contingencies, situations that could have been otherwise."[173] Ideas, that is, are tied "to the evaluation of what is

---

167. Schelling, *The Ages of the World*, xxxvi.
168. Schelling, *The Ages of the World*, xxxvii.
169. Whitehead, *Adventures of Ideas*, 222.
170. Whitehead, *Adventures of Ideas*, 227.
171. Magee, *Hegel and the Hermetic Tradition*, 12.
172. Deleuze, *Difference and Repetition*, 187.
173. Shaviro, *Without Criteria*, 40. "Ideas" in Deleuze's sense should be understood as *actualized* or *ingressed* eternal objects. While Whitehead's category "eternal object" (especially when considered in abstraction from the rest of his categoreal scheme) may bare some resemblance to the Aristotlean category of

important and what is not, to the distribution of singular and regular, distinctive and ordinary."[174] "The sense of importance," writes Whitehead, "is embedded in the very being of animal experience. As it sinks in dominance, experience trivializes and verges toward nothingness."[175] The Western philosophical tradition's obsession with pinning down general essences instead of open-endedly investigating particular experiences—its emphasis on asking "what is . . . ?" instead of "how much?," "how?," "in what cases?" in its pursuit of Ideas—has fostered some insight but also much confusion.[176] "Ideas emanate from imperatives of adventure," writes Deleuze, not from the banality of encyclopedic classification.[177] The mistaken identification of Ideas with dead essences has led to the inability of modern philosophy to grasp the utter dependence of rationality on "the goings-on of nature," and to the forgetfulness of "the thought of ourselves as process immersed in process beyond ourselves."[178] The dominant view since the Enlightenment has been to affirm the natural origins of the human mind. But the "Nature" to which this Enlightenment mentality seeks to reduce itself is only a mechanical abstraction constructed by the mind.[179] The mechanical model of Nature made in our mind is mistaken for the living process of Nature that, indeed, has given birth to mind.

"essence," equating the two would be a misreading. "Eternal objects" must be considered in the context of the whole cosmological scheme, most importantly Whitehead's "ontological principle" and category of the "actual occasion." "Eternal objects" are meaningless without "actual occasions." There are no eternal essences independent of actual experiences. The two depend upon one another for their conceptual meaning and their ontological importance.

174. Deleuze, *Difference and Repetition*, 189.

175. Whitehead, *Modes of Thought*, 9.

176. Deleuze, *Difference and Repetition*, 188–90.

177. Deleuze, *Difference and Repetition*, 197.

178. Whitehead, *Modes of Thought*, 8.

179. The Enlightenment's scientific and materialistic mentality thereby falls victim to Whitehead's "fallacy of misplaced concreteness."

Chapter 3: Descendental Philosophy and Aesthetic Ontology

Despite the shared conceptual emphasis of much of Deleuze, Schelling, and Whitehead's philosophical work, Deleuze's dismissive attitude toward methodological knowledge in favor of a culture of learning may at times fall prey to Whitehead's "fallacy of discarding method." Though Whitehead was also critical of tradition-bound and narrow-minded methodologies (as is evidenced by his corresponding "dogmatic fallacy"), he distances himself from philosophers like Nietzsche and Bergson (perhaps Deleuze's two most important influences) because they tend to assume that intellectual analysis is "intrinsically tied to erroneous fictions" in that it can only proceed according to some one discarded dogmatic method.[180] "Philosophers boast that they uphold no system," writes Whitehead. "They are then prey to the delusive clarities of detached expressions which it is the very purpose of their science to surmount."[181] "We must be systematic," Whitehead writes elsewhere, "but we should keep our systems open [and remain] sensitive to their limitations."[182]

---

180. Whitehead, *Adventures of Ideas*, 222.
181. Whitehead, *Adventures of Ideas*, 222.
182. Whitehead, *Modes of Thought*, 6.

4

Etheric Imagination in Naturphilosophie: Physics of the World-Soul

> All merely embryonic life is in itself full of yearning and desires to be elevated out of the mute and inactive unity and into the expressed and acting unity. In this way we see nature yearning. In this way the earth so ardently sucks the force of heaven to itself. In this way the seed strives toward light and air in order to gather a spirit for itself. In this way flowers sway in the rays of the sun in order to shine the rays back as fiery spirit and as color.
> —Schelling[1]

Earlier chapters outlined how Kant's transcendental method led him to determine the spatiotemporal conditions of possible experience according to the axioms of Euclid's geometry or "mathematics of extension."[2] Kant argues that the *a priori* geometrical construction of our pure intuition of the form of space grants us certain and precise knowledge of the extensive character all the objects that could be encountered in sensory experience. What geometry says about objects in space, he claims, is valid *prior to actual experience*, such that "evasions, as if objects of the senses did not have to be in agreement with the rules of construction in space . . . must cease."[3] While Kant accepted the *logical* possibility of non-Euclidean geometries, he denied that forms of spatial intuition other than that defined by Euclid could ever be imagined or

---

1. Schelling, *The Ages of the World*, 72.
2. Kant, *Critique of Pure Reason*, 288.
3. Kant, *Critique of Pure Reason*, 289.

perceived by the human mind. They can never make intuitive *sense* to us. The question of what the structure of space might be independent of what Whitehead would call our human "modes of emphasis"[4]—that is, what space is *in itself*—should not even be asked so far as Kant is concerned. Asking what is "outside" our form of outer intuition literally makes no sense given his transcendental premises. We also saw that when Kant is forced by his earliest critics to address the question of what transcends experience, he ends up overstepping his own transcendental method by attributing the cause of our sensory experience to things outside our formal intuition of outerness. He is "tempted" into the very same "childish endeavor of chasing after soap bubbles" that he accused his critics of for mistaking "appearances, which after all are mere representations," for "things in themselves."[5] As long as appearances are determinable by the rules of Kant's Euclidian-Aristotelean understanding, they can bring forth truth. But, Kant continues, as soon as our understanding of appearances "passes beyond the boundaries of experience and becomes transcendent, [it] brings forth nothing but sheer illusion."[6] Kant could not help himself: he, too, was tempted by the transcendent into speculating about what lies beyond experience, since otherwise he could not distinguish his critical idealism from the dogmatic idealism his critics accused him of.

In his introduction to the *Prolegomena*, Hatfield argues that Kant's intention is not to "turn bodies into illusion," as his critics had claimed, but to erect a transcendental system of philosophy upon the synthetic *a priori* knowledge granted by mathematical intuitions of space and time determining *for us* the properties of solid bodies in empty space.[7] Whitehead ultimately does not disagree with Kant that pure mathematics

---

4. Whitehead, *Interpretation of Science*, 195.
5. Kant, *Prolegomena*, 44.
6. Kant, *Prolegomena*, 44.
7. Hatfield, "Introduction," *Prolegomena*, xxix.

can provide us with some synthetic *a priori* knowledge of the spatiotemporal passage of physical Nature. But instead of conceiving of the logic of objects in Aristotelean terms, arithmetic and geometry in Euclidean terms, and space and time in idealized Newtonian (i.e., quasi-Spinozistic[8] and quasi-Leibnizian[9]) terms, Whitehead employed a process-relational logic, allowing him to conceive of counting in serial time and drawing lines in simultaneous space as special modes of a more general form of mathematical intuition. Further, he built upon the relativistic and quantum paradigm shifts in physics to reframe the monistic and monadic insights of Spinoza and Leibniz as part of a novel rendering of space-time as an abstraction from the "organic extensive community" constituting the "creative advance of Nature."[10]

Perhaps the most important catalyst generating the metaphysical thrust of his later years as a philosophical cosmologist was Whitehead's construction of a non-metrical, topological "extensive scheme,"[11] a scheme he argued rested upon synthetic *a priori* truths more general than the specific limitations Kant imposed upon imaginal experience of possible spaces. Whitehead's scheme of extensive connection granted him intuitive access not just to any finished form of space (Euclidean or otherwise), but also to the generative source of all possible spaces, a certain subset of which could be fruitfully applied to the physical world of our cosmic epoch as

---

8. See Omri Boehm's *Kant's Critique of Spinoza*, wherein he argues that "the metaphysical structure of the first *Critique's* Ideal of Pure Reason . . . as the regulative idea of that entity through which all possibility is grounded" commits Kant "to what can be called 'regulative Spinozism'" (17).

9. See Grant's essay "Philosophy Becomes Genetic" wherein he argues that, in the course of his attempt to provide the metaphysical foundations for natural science, Kant almost ceases to be Kantian and, in a certain manner, reverts to Leibniz, whose own "transition between metaphysics and physics" was similarly accomplished by way of the actions of a *potentia agendi*, an active force within the monads (130).

10. Whitehead, *Process and Reality*, 289.

11. Whitehead, *Process and Reality*, 288.

a matter of pragmatic convention, rather than *a priori* necessity or unique experimental verification. The metaphysically necessary aspect of extensiveness has to do with the general topological rules defining congruence and "the mutual implication of extensive whole and extensive part."[12] But these general rules say little about the particular three- or four-dimensional spatiotemporal form of our experience, which is an evolutionary specification creatively realized by the community of actual occasions composing our cosmic epoch and which can only be experienced and measured *a posteriori* through the use of clocks and rulers.[13] The contingencies of our cosmic epoch presuppose only the *a priori* rules of extensiveness. These rules provide the condition allowing the universe to be systematically conceived "as a medium for the transmission of influences."[14] The synthetic *a priori* rules of Whitehead's topological scheme thus establish the descendental conditions required for causal relationship among actual occasions. Whitehead elsewhere refers to the uniform medium required for extensive connection between actualities, and thus the generative source of our spatiotemporal experience, as the "ether of events."[15] Whitehead's metaphysical ether of events can give rise to any number of physical spatiotemporal orders: "So far as mere extensiveness is concerned," writes Whitehead, "space might as well have three hundred and thirty-three dimensions, instead of the modest three dimensions of our present epoch."[16] Unlike Kant's scheme, wherein the primary transcendental *attribute* of physical objects is their *extension* in three-dimensional space, in Whitehead's philosophy of organism "the primary *relationship* of physical occasions is

---

12. Whitehead, *Process and Reality*, 288.
13. "Measurement is a systematic procedure dependent upon the dominant societies of the cosmic epoch" (Whitehead, *Process and Reality*, 332).
14. Whitehead, *Process and Reality*, 286.
15. Whitehead, *The Principle of Relativity*, 38.
16. Whitehead, *Process and Reality*, 289.

extensive connection" in the ether of events.[17] Causal connection, rather than being imposed conceptually upon apparent objects by the transcendental structure of the human mind, arises affectively through the etheric medium providing a scheme of uniform relatedness for all actual occasions of experience. Contrary to the bifurcation between the phenomenal and noumenal realms that is central to Kant's critical philosophy, in Whitehead's philosophy of organism, *there is but one reality*, namely that provided by the creative ether of events constituting the essential uniform relatedness underlying the spatiotemporal experience of the actual occasions of our cosmic socius.[18]

4.1 Traces of the Ether in Kant's *Opus Postumum*

With his first *Critique* in 1781 (bolstered by the *Prolegomena* in 1783), Kant believed he had secured the possibility of a new form metaphysics. Following upon his discovery of our capacity for reflective judgment of Nature's transcendental purposiveness in the *Critique of Judgment* (1790), he began attempting to articulate a transition from the metaphysical foundations of natural science laid bare by his transcendental critique of theoretical reason to the possibility of physics as such. Several years earlier, Kant had already published his *Metaphysical Foundations of Natural Science* (1786), wherein he sought the metaphysical principles that would allow him to transcendentally construct the concept of matter. Whereas the Transcendental Aesthetic of Kant's *Critique of Pure Reason* had provided the *form* of all outer intuition as space, in the *Metaphysical Foundations* he sought to provide the *matter* of such intuition, i.e., "that in the outer intuition which is an object of sensation."[19] Kant deduced the *a priori* attributes of ma-

---

17. Whitehead, *Process and Reality*, 288.
18. Desmet and Eastman, "Relativity Physics," 250.
19. Kant, *Metaphysical Foundations*, 16.

terial bodies using nothing but the four categories of quantity, quality, relation, and modality employed by the understanding to determine all possible experience of objects. This provided physics with apodictic certainty regarding its knowledge of objects. What remained lacking until Kant's discovery of our capacity for reflective judgment of Nature's transcendental purposiveness in the *Critique of Judgment* was an *a priori* basis for the systematic unity of Nature as a whole.[20] Without both *a priori* certainty of the necessary determinations of physical objects (provided by the *Metaphysical Foundations*) and the unity of their lawful relationships within Nature (not yet provided), Kant did not believe physics could remain genuinely scientific. While the laws governing particular natural processes were only discoverable through experience and thus *a posteriori*, our capacity for such discovery presupposes that Nature can appear to us as always already determined by the categories of our organ of understanding and shaped by the spatiotemporal form of our intuition. As Kant put it in the preface to the *Critique of Pure Reason*, which I quote at length due to its seminal importance for his argument, Bacon, Galileo and other early modern initiators of the scientific revolution had comprehended that:

> Reason, in order to be taught by nature, must approach nature with its principles in one hand, according to which alone the agreement among appearances can count as laws, and, in the other hand, the experiments thought out in accordance with these principles—yet in order to be instructed by nature not like a pupil, who has recited to him whatever the teacher wants to say, but like an appointed judge who compels witnesses to answer the questions he puts to them. Thus even physics owes the advantageous revolution in its way of thinking to the inspiration that what reason would not be able to know of itself and has to learn

---

20. Förster, "Introduction," *Opus Postumum*, xxxiv.

from nature, it has to seek in the latter (though not merely ascribe to it) in accordance with what reason itself puts into nature. This is how natural science was first brought to the secure course of a science after groping about for so many centuries.[21]

The systematic unity of Nature must be presupposed by physical science ("put into nature" Reason), not discovered through experiment or observation. Kant thus realized that his construction of the matter of all objects of sensation in the *Metaphysical Foundations* was not enough to put physics on a sound metaphysical footing. An *a priori* principle specified by Nature itself had to be found to secure its unity.[22] In his *Critique of Judgment* Kant had unwittingly discovered such a unifying principle in our reflective judgments of the teleological wholeness implied by Nature's beautiful appearance. The concept of Nature's purposive organization is not known to the understanding independently, but instead first arises as an imaginatively produced schema elicited by our harmonious feelings upon encountering Nature's beauty. The conceptual schema of purposiveness attributes nothing at all to Nature in itself, it only represents the unique way our human organ of cognition must proceed in its reflection upon Nature if it hopes to secure a unified and coherent (i.e., systematic) account of its possibility. Nature conceived teleologically is then the result of what Kant calls a "subjectively universal" principle or maxim of our power of judgment. We must, in order to secure a ground for the transition between metaphysics and physics, judge Nature and its products as purposeful unities, as wholes reciprocally determining their parts, even though we can have no determinative knowledge of such a possibility. Kant remarks on the surprised delight a scientist experiences when he encounters a systematic unity in Nature's empirical

21. Kant, *Critique of Pure Reason*, 108–9.
22. Förster, "Introduction," *Opus Postumum*, xxxiv.

laws, such as Newton experienced when he first grasped the law of universal gravitation.[23] The scientist may think such discoveries are merely happy accidents, but, given Kant's transcendental critique of our organ of cognition, science *must* assume such a unity *a priori* as universal and necessary for any scientific inquiry into Nature to be possible at all. Empirical physics may discover the unity of particular laws, but it cannot discover the universal law of Nature's unity as such. For Kant, this *a priori* unity is a result of our mind determining the way we come to know Nature in advance of any experience. In doing so, the power of judgment prescribes an *a priori* law, not to Nature, but to itself. Thus, while the experience of Nature's beauty broadens our *concept* of Nature, it offers us no new *knowledge* of natural objects.[24]

Since the principle of Nature's and her objects' unity is derived from an aesthetic intuition of natural beauty in the subject, this principle does not itself bridge the chasm between the transcendental possibility of physics and actual physics that Kant realized he needed to provide. It remains merely a regulative principle of subjective judgment about Nature as a mere product, rather than a constitutive decision produced in and by Nature itself (as in Whitehead and Schelling's doctrine of a creative advance composed by actual occasions or dynamic atoms). The subjectively universal principle only prepares the ground for the transition Kant sought. He thus began work at some point in the 1790s on a new text seeking the transition between metaphysics and physics. Soon after beginning, however, Kant found himself struggling to articulate this transition, as he was drawn into reflections "far beyond the problem he initially set out to solve."[25]

The manuscript Kant labored on for more than a decade was eventually published in a jumbled order long after his

---

23. Kant, *Critique of Judgment*, 18.
24. Förster, *Kant's Final Synthesis*, 10.
25. Förster, "Introduction," *Opus Postumum*, xxxvii.

death under the title *Opus Postumum*. According to one of its most insightful interpreters, Eckart Förster, early reviewers of the unfinished manuscript compared their efforts to make sense of it to "inferring the pattern of an oriental rug from the confusing array of knots on its back."[26] The manuscript shows evidence of many false starts and revisions as Kant's struggle to find a transition between metaphysics and physics forced him to revisit and reconsider almost every aspect of his transcendental philosophy. Of particular interest for the purposes of this book are Kant's enigmatic "ether proofs."

Kant had already speculated on the status of the ether in both the *Critique of Pure Reason* and the *Critique of Judgment*. In the first *Critique*, Kant dismisses the idea of an etheric substance or "intermediate thing between matter and thinking beings" because, he then thought, its possibility is without any ground in experience.[27] In the third *Critique*, Kant discusses Euler's analogy between tones of music as vibrations in the air and colors of light as vibrations in an ether filling cosmic space.[28] Förster points out that, while in the first two editions Kant wrote that he doubted such an analogy "very much," in the third edition, he revised the text to say he "did not doubt at all" Euler's analogy.[29] This revision allowed Kant to claim that colors, like musical tones, should be judged beautiful rather than merely pleasurable, the difference being that judgments of beauty imply that reflection upon the sensation of color discovers therein a mathematical proportion in the vibrations of the ether, while the experience of mere pleasure implies no such proportion.[30]

Kant begins reconsidering the ether dynamically as a fluid system of moving forces, rather than mechanically as

26. Förster, *Kant's Final Synthesis*, x.
27. Kant, *Critique of Pure Reason*, 324.
28. Kant, *Critique of Judgment*, 44.
29. Förster, *Kant's Final Synthesis*, 29–30.
30. Förster, *Kant's Final Synthesis*, 31.

a collection of many minute and exceedingly fine impenetrable particles (like Euler's version).[31] This follows from Kant's attempt to replace Newton's mathematico-mechanical atomism with a metaphysico-dynamical account of matter as the construction of two opposing forces.[32] I should note here that Schelling's early works on *Naturphilosophie* build upon and correct Kant's still merely *formal* dynamical account by adding a third principle to the construction of *actual* matter.[33] They both agreed that conceiving of material atoms as distinct from forces presupposed more than Kant's new transcendental method could permit. Schelling and Whitehead go beyond Kant, however, in articulating a *dynamic atomism* as a novel synthesis inclusive both of Nature's infinite productivity and its finite products. Schelling offers the following analogy, which I quote at length because of its clear parallels with Whitehead's organic process philosophy:

> A stream flows in a straight line forward as long as it encounters no resistance. Where there is resistance—a whirlpool forms. Every original product of nature is such a whirlpool, every organism. The whirlpool is not something immobilized, it is rather something constantly transforming—but reproduced anew at each moment. Thus no product in nature is fixed, but it is reproduced at each instant through the force of nature entire. (We do not really see the subsistence of Nature's products, just their continual being-reproduced.) Nature as a whole co-operates in every product. Certain points of inhibition in Nature are originally set up—consequently, perhaps there is only *one* point of inhibition from which the whole of Nature develops itself—first of all, however, we can think infinitely many points of inhibition—at each such point, the stream of Nature's activity will be broken, as it were, its productivity

---

31. Förster, *Kant's Final Synthesis*, 32.
32. Kant, *Metaphysical Foundations*, 75.
33. Schelling, *Ideas*, 192.

annihilated. But at each moment comes a new impulse, as it were, a new wave, which fills this sphere afresh.[34]

Indeed, a better extended metaphor for Whitehead's organic cosmology could hardly be imagined. Schelling even hints at what in Whitehead's scheme is described as the influence of the primordial nature of God on actual occasions when he speculates that the whole of Nature developed from one original inhibition or limitation of the sphere of Creativity which is further actualized into infinitely many points of inhibition.[35]

In Whitehead's *Principles of Natural Knowledge*, he dismisses materialistic conceptions of the ether (like Euler's, and before him, Descartes') as "merely the outcome of a metaphysical craving" for continuity. In its place he offers an "ether of events," whereby the transmission of energy in Nature results, not from the mechanical vibration of material substance, but from the "reciprocal interaction" of coextensively creative occasions of experience.[36] In his ether proofs in the *Opus Postumum*, Kant also rejects mechanical forms of the ether in favor of a dynamical account, but what further support he hopes to derive from the concept for the sake of his transcendental project remains somewhat obscure. Kant was clear enough that "there must be something like an *a priori* 'elementary system' of the moving forces of matter if physics is to be possible as a systematic science," a point which eventually leads him to the idea that such an elementary system is already contained in the concept of the transcendental unity of experience.[37] After repeated false starts in an attempt to justify this claim, Kant finally concludes that the "elementary system of the moving forces of matter" that makes physics possible as a science is in fact the ether. The

---

34. Schelling, *Philosophy of Nature*, 18.
35. See Whitehead, *Science and the Modern World*, 177–79.
36. Whitehead, *Principles of Natural Knowledge*, 25.
37. Förster, *Kant's Final Synthesis*, 11.

ether is thus not a mere hypothesis devised to explain contingent features of Nature, but rather provides the necessary transcendental condition of our experience of Nature as such. In Kant's terms:

> [The ether] is given by reason, not as a hypothesis for perceived objects, for the purpose of *explaining* their phenomena, but rather, immediately, in order to found the possibility of experience itself.[38]

Kant further argues that because the moving forces of the world-ether are in fact dynamically *self*-moving, an analogy can be drawn between them and our experience of ourselves as self-moving organisms. The forces of the ether are thus *organic* forces.[39] Kant even speculates that the organic nature of the all-pervasive etheric fluid makes it equivalent to the world-soul, or *anima mundi* as it was known to the ancients.[40] Kant insists that the etheric soul of the universe must be a "dull" vegetal soul rather than an animal or thinking (spiritual) soul, a connection I explore in Section 4.4 in conversation with Michael Marder's vegetal metaphysics. Förster points out that Kant's use of the ancient doctrine of the world-soul was almost certainly a result of his having read Schelling's book *On the World-Soul: An Hypothesis of Higher Physics for Explaining Universal Organism* (1798), wherein Schelling notes that ancient physicists took this "common soul of nature ... to be one and the same as the underlying, form-giving ether."[41]

As Grant describes it, Kant attempts to transition between transcendental metaphysics and actual physics by pointing to "the interaction of subjective-bodily and ethereal forces."[42] In

---

38. Kant, *Opus Postumum*, 89.
39. Kant, *Opus Postumum*, 118.
40. Kant, *Opus Postumum*, 85, 147–48.
41. Translation by Förster, from "Factual Notes," in Kant's *Opus Postumum*, 274n89; Schelling, *Weltseele*, 168.
42. Grant, "Philosophy Become Genetic," 130.

the *Critique of Pure Reason*, Kant had limited our knowledge of the *real* unity of Nature to the regulative use of the *idea* of Nature's unity via Reason's projection of a *focus imaginarius* or imaginal point toward which the understanding could strive but which it could never in fact reach (since such a point was not a possible object of experience).[43] In the *Opus Postumum*, Kant (at least in some places in the text) breaks through this limitation and argues that Nature's systematic unity is known *a priori* and constitutively because our experience of this unity emerges from the imaginal depths of the ether. The ether, in other words, becomes "the principle from which the systematic unity of all the moving forces of matter is thought to emerge."[44] Kant here revisits the foundational assumptions of his Transcendental Aesthetic regarding the pure form of space. Contradicting his earlier view, Kant realizes that, if space itself is not somehow sensible, then experience of outer objects would be impossible, for through what sensible medium could we be affected by anything outside ourselves? By way of the ether, Kant now conceives of space, not as a pure and empty ideal form, but as actually filled with real moving forces, forces which provide the condition for outer (and thus also inner) intuition since they provide a medium through which we may be affected by things outside us.[45] He also re-imagines intuition in *active*, rather than merely passive terms, meaning that the organic forces within us must meet and reciprocally interact with the etheric forces outside us for spatiotemporal experience to be possible. Thus, according to Förster,

> we find Kant now characterizing space and time not simply as forms of our intuition . . . but as "forms of our effective forces"; space and time are also forms of the forces by which I move and react to affection of the senses. If the pure

---

43. Kant, *Critique of Pure Reason*, 591.
44. Förster, *Kant's Final Synthesis*, 84.
45. Förster, *Kant's Final Synthesis*, 87.

motion of the productive imagination underlies the space of geometry, organic self-motion must underlie all experience of the moving forces of matter.[46]

In the end, however, due to the unfinished state that the *Opus Postumum* was left at the time of his death, Kant wavers on the issue of whether or not the self-moving forces of the ether are a real feature of Nature or merely a transcendental ideal imposed by the mind. Förster argues convincingly for the latter option, showing how Kant came to connect (if not equate) the theoretical function of the ether with the transcendental ideal of God.[47] The latter serves an epistemic role as a merely regulative principle of reason allowing us to interpret the connection between each of our experiences of Nature as if they originated from some all-sufficient necessary cause.[48] Thus, despite his flirtation with the ether as an actually existing and indeed *living* soul of the world, Kant finally reverts to the strictures of the same critical idealism he had inaugurated two decades earlier. We must turn instead to Schelling and Whitehead to develop the philosophical and cosmological implications of the ether.

---

46. Förster, *Kant's Final Synthesis*, 109.
47. Förster, *Kant's Final Synthesis*, 95.
48. Förster, *Kant's Final Synthesis*, 82.

4.2 Etheric Imagination in Schelling and Whitehead

A tree that draws strength, life, and substance into itself from earth may hope to drive its topmost branches hanging with blossom right up to heaven. However, the thoughts of those who think from the beginning that they can separate themselves from nature . . . are only like those delicate threads that float in the air in late summer and that are as incapable of touching heaven as they are of being pulled to the ground by their own weight.

—Schelling[49]

Schelling shared the cosmological ether theory with most of his natural scientific contemporaries.[50] He identified the infinite elasticity of the ether with the original polarity of forces animating both the one soul of the universe and the many souls within it.[51] Schelling describes the relation between the universal world-soul and individual organisms by analogy to a ruling star and its subsidiary planets. Like all stars, our Sun obtained its "self-illuminating" quality by precipitating a universally distributed "common solvent medium."[52] The Sun serves as the local source of the positive force of light for our solar system, a force which bathes the entire system in a common atmosphere.[53] This positive light-force exists in etheric tension with the negative force of gravity associated with each planetary body. "In all nature," writes Schelling,

> neither of these forces exists without the other. In our experience, as many individual things (particular spheres,

---

49. Schelling, *Clara*, 5.
50. Grant, "Introduction to Schelling's *World Soul*," in *Collapse*, 65.
51. Vassányi, *Anima Mundi*, 143, 384; Beiser, *German Idealism*, 541–47.
52. Schelling, "World Soul," translated by Grant in *Collapse*, 87.
53. Schelling speculates that all stars, including the Sun, "yet belong to a higher system, governed from a common central body" with its own even more widely distributed etheric atmosphere ("World Soul," 90). Contemporary astrophysics now knows these higher systems to be galaxies with their central supermassive black holes and mysterious "dark matter" envelopes (dark matter=the negative pole of galactic ether?).

as it were, of the universal forces of nature) arise as there are different degrees in the reaction of the negative force. Everything terrestrial has this property in common: that it is opposed to the positive force that radiates to us from the sun. *In this original antithesis lies the seed of a universal world organization.*[54]

For Schelling, like Kant, the ether is not just a scientific hypothesis about a particular feature of the natural world; rather it is the speculative philosophical principle required to justify the pursuit of scientific knowledge of the physical world in the first place. If there were no organic unity to Nature as a self-organizing whole—if Nature was just an accidental assemblage of externally related parts—then we could never learn anything by way of natural scientific investigation. Schelling's ether theory secures the possibility of natural science through the organ of etheric imagination, whereby the spiritual ether "in me" finds its point of indifference with the natural ether "out there."[55] Or as Schelling himself put it, "What in us *knows* is the same as what *is* known."[56] Conscious human knowing is thus but a higher potency of the original antithesis animating unconscious Nature. Light, according to Schelling, though not yet conscious, "is itself already a seeing, and the original seeing at that."[57] In his lectures on Schelling's *Naturphilosophie*, Merleau-Ponty comments that light:

> penetrates everywhere, [exploring] the field promoted by our gaze and [preparing] it to be read. Light is a sort of

---

54. Schelling, "World Soul," translated by Grant in *Collapse*, 92. Italics added.
55. According to Beiser, Schelling thereby "[reintegrates] the transcendental 'I' into nature" by showing how human self-consciousness is a more intense expression of Nature's original etheric forces (*German Idealism*, 541–42, 559).
56. Schelling, *Modern Philosophy*, translated by Bowie, 130.
57. Schelling, *Transcendental Idealism*, 75. See also Merleau-Ponty's quotation of Schelling's understanding of light as "the symbol of primordial and eternal knowing which is imaginatively replicated [*einbildet*] in Nature" (Jaspers, *Schelling*, 291).

concept that walks among appearances; it does not have a
subjective [i.e., conscious] existence, save when it becomes
for us . . . . Nature is lent to our perception. We are the
parents of a Nature of which we are also the children. It is in
human being that things become conscious by themselves;
but the relation is reciprocal: [the evolution of the] human
being is also the becoming-conscious of things.[58]

Schelling's account of the dynamic series of stages (*Stufenfolge*) leading from the unconscious ground of Nature to the freedom of human consciousness requires for its coherence, according to J.-F. Marquet, that there exist a "'first force of nature,' a naturally expansive and centrifugal fluid, the ether, of which light will be the phenomenal manifestation."[59] Following Marquet, William Hamrick and Jan Van Der Veken contrast Schelling's attribution of primal knowing (*Urwissen*) to Nature's etheric fluid with Kant's account of the cognitive role of imagination: whereas for Kant, *transcendental* imagination is a subjective faculty responsible for synthesizing the soul's experience of a fundamentally withdrawn reality, for Schelling, *etheric* imagination is "a knowing that is not separate and distinct from its object because the former [etheric knowing] is simultaneously the production of the latter [etheric nature]."[60]

The luminiferous ether remained the foundation of science's understanding of electromagnetic phenomena until Einstein dismissed it as "an unnecessary burden on space" in 1905.[61] In 1916, Whitehead began articulating a new cosmological ether theory as a direct response to Einstein's replacement of the traditional "material ether" with a pre-given "space-time fabric." By 1918, Einstein also began

---

58. Merleau-Ponty, *Nature*, 42–43.
59. Marquet, "Schelling," *Encyclopedia Philosophique Universelle*, 2085–93.
60. Hamrick and Veken, *Nature and Logos*, 136–37.
61. Lederman, *The God Particle*, 101, 375.

to recognize that his general theory of relativity had in effect replaced the old mechanical ether with a new ether, which he explicitly identified with the gravitational field of space-time.[62] However, in place of Einstein's geometrical space-time fabric, Whitehead reconstructed "time-space"[63] as an "ether of events" on the basis of his own novel process ontology.[64] "On the old theory of relativity," Whitehead writes, "Time and Space are relations between materials; on our theory they are relations between events."[65] Whitehead's ether of events is not the undetectable "shy ether behind the veil" hypothesized to exist by nineteenth century physicists; rather, "the ether is exactly the apparent world, neither more nor less."[66] The ether, in other words, is that which grants rational coherence and causal connection to "the whole complex of events" constituting the experiential universe.[67] For Whitehead, as for Schelling, the ether is no mere scientific hypothesis about a supposedly mind-independent external world. Instead, it is a metaphysical principle constructed precisely to avoid the "unfortunate bifurcation" between subjective mind and objective nature by "[construing] our knowledge of the apparent world as being an individual experience of something which is more than personal."[68] "Nature," Whitehead continues,

> is thus a totality including individual experiences, so that we must reject the distinction between nature as it really is

---

62. Desmet, "The Rebirth of the Ether" in *Chromatikon 3*, 76.

63. A term I draw from David Abram, who borrows it from Merleau-Ponty, Heidegger, and an anthropological study of Navajo semantics (*Spell of the Sensuous*, 115, 125, 127, 187n31). Unlike the Einsteinian term "space-time," the inversion, "time-space" signals the irreducibility of concrete becoming to any spatialized representation.

64. Whitehead, *The Principle of Relativity*, 36–38; Whitehead, *The Principles of Natural Knowledge*, 25.

65. Whitehead, *The Principles of Natural Knowledge*, 26.

66. Whitehead, *The Principle of Relativity*, 37.

67. Whitehead, *The Principles of Natural Knowledge*, 66.

68. Whitehead, *The Principle of Relativity*, 62.

and experiences of it which are purely psychological. Our experiences of the apparent world are nature itself.[69]

As we have seen, Whitehead continued throughout his career to develop a precise mathematical description for the ether of events using the tools of projective geometry. Whitehead was among the first to wonder whether the constructions of projective geometry could be fruitfully applied to actual processes in the physical world.[70] He originally articulated the ether in terms of what he called "anti-space" in his 1898 book *A Treatise on Universal Algebra*.[71] In a review of this book in 1899, Hugh MacColl referred to Whitehead's concept of the "manifold" (derived originally from the non-Euclidean geometry of Riemann) as "the *ether* of mathematical conceptions."[72] The anthroposophist and mathematician George Adams, who studied with Whitehead at Cambridge,[73] argues that to understand the etheric dimension of Nature, science must first decathect itself from any static geometry, Euclidian or otherwise. Euclid's conceptual picture of space as an empty container of rigidly extended objects, while perhaps practically useful for engineers, must be replaced for the purposes of cosmology with a *new geometry*, variously termed *projective, synthetic,* or *dynamic*. This new process-oriented geometry would "[apprehend] 'space in becoming'" by penetrating to the intensive "space-creative process" underlying extensive metrical space-time.[74] "We must learn to see in Nature," Adams writes,

> not only what is ready-made (and therefore dying) but what is new-becoming in her life. We have to liberate

---

69. Whitehead, *The Principle of Relativity*, 62.
70. Zucker, "Three Counter Strategies," in *Mind in Nature*. See also Whitehead's 1905 essay *On Mathematical Concepts of the Material World*.
71. Whitehead, *Universal Algebra*, 354, 365.
72. As quoted in Desmet, "The Rebirth of the Ether" in *Chromatikon III*, 5n33.
73. Whicher, *George Adams*, 12–13.
74. Adams, *Physical and Ethereal Spaces*, 6.

> imagination from the bondage of the finished forms of space.[75]

Steiner argues in his 1920 lectures on the links between astronomy, mathematics, and other sciences (lectures attended by Adams) that the rigidified three-dimensional space first described by Euclid (and later presupposed by Kant) is at best "a kind of approximation to reality that we ourselves construct in our inner life."[76] Steiner goes on to suggest that natural science must find a more concrete way of imagining space that does not ignore the important *qualitative* differences between the various perspectives that space takes upon itself. For example, the vertical spatial orientation of human and plant organisms is different in kind from the horizontal orientation of animals and the spherical orientation of single cells. Space comes in a variety of species, each of which is genetically related through a non-local cosmic ecology of mutual prehensions. Real cosmic space cannot be adequately grasped only through the quantitative measurements of telescopes and the ideal mechanics of calculus, since through these methods only an abstract picture of dead parts is produced. "A clear indication of the real movements in celestial space," according to Steiner, requires an aesthetic attunement to the form-generating etheric forces streaming into the perceptual organs of the human organism, perhaps the "most sensitive of instruments" in Nature.[77] "Ordinary mathematics," Steiner continues,

> based as it is on rigid forms calculated within a rigid Euclidean space, would help us little if we tried applying it to organic forms. Only by seeking, as it were, to carry

---

75. Adams, *Physical and Ethereal Spaces*, 6.
76. Steiner, *The Relation of the Diverse Branches of Natural Science to Astronomy* (CW 323), Lecture 7, 137. Translated as *Interdisciplinary Astronomy* (2020).
77. Steiner, *The Relation of the Diverse Branches of Natural Science to Astronomy*, Lecture 7, 139–42.

life itself into the realms of mathematics and geometry as such . . . shall we make progress.[78]

Whitehead began to recognize the need to overcome the scientific bifurcation of Nature between living mind and dead matter while developing his own alternative version of Einstein's theory of relativity. As noted earlier, he overcame this bifurcation by replacing the Einsteinian notion of insensate and durationless material instants with the notion of etheric events of perspectival prehension as basic to Nature. In Adams' terms, the new dynamic topology underlying Whitehead's ether theory "[imagined] every point of space as a potential eye-point able to receive into itself all forms and pictures of surrounding space."[79] In Hamrick and Veken's terms, building on Merleau-Ponty's late Whiteheadian ontology, overcoming the bifurcation of Nature requires coming to *conceive* space as we *perceive* it—not as an objective thing "laid out simultaneously as *partes extra partes*," as though "our living spatiality [derived] from [the] more ontologically primary" metrical space of Euclid—but rather as a polymorphic non-metrical topological or projective space that, because of its "enveloping, overlapping, encroaching, coiling over, [folding], and intertwining" character is "organically bound up with us," continually metamorphosing with the changing perceptual contours brought forth by the intra-action of the community of living organisms composing the cosmos.[80] In Schelling's terms, the intuition of this living spatiality "cannot be compared to a universal geometrical figure" because it is "particular to each soul like the perception of light in each eye" and as such is "a merely individual revelation"; but, he continues, "in this individuality there is

---

78. Steiner, *The Relation of the Diverse Branches of Natural Science to Astronomy*, Lecture 11, 212.
79. Adams, *Physical and Ethereal Spaces*, 13.
80. Hamrick and Veken, *Nature and Logos*, 94–96.

also a *universal* revelation, just as light is for the empirical senses."[81]

This "intertwining" of lived space with living organisms follows from Whitehead's critique, rooted in his novel interpretation of relativity and quantum theories, of the related doctrines of "simple location" and "external relation." These doctrines are derived from the Euclidian mentality and provide the basis of Newton's cosmology, wherein individual bits of matter are "conceived as fully describable apart from any reference to any other portion of matter."[82] In contrast, the new, non-metrical imagination of time-space developed by Steiner, Adams, and Whitehead describes a universe in which, while a physical event can rightly be ascribed to a "focal region," it must be added that the influence of any physical event

> streams away from it with finite velocity throughout the utmost recesses of space and time . . . . [The event] is a state of agitation, only differing from the so-called external stream by its superior dominance within the focal region.[83]

The denial of the doctrine of simple location implies that every physical event is in some sense a superposition of the innumerable multitude of other events making up the universe: "Thus the physical fact at each region of [time-space] is a composition of what the physical entities throughout the Universe mean for that region."[84] Every organic process, according to Whitehead, "repeats in microcosm what the universe is in macrocosm."[85] In Steiner's terms, "Every cell . . . is nothing less than an image of the form of the whole

---

81. Schelling, *Philosophy and Religion*, 15.
82. Whitehead, *Adventures of Ideas*, 156.
83. Whitehead, *Adventures of Ideas*, 157.
84. Whitehead, *Adventures of Ideas*, 158.
85. Whitehead, *Process and Reality*, 215.

universe."[86] Whitehead adds that these interrelated organic processes are not compositions of "mere formulae"; rather, the concrete composition of things merely "illustrate formulae," such that "the fact is more than the formulae illustrated."[87] Turning to non-metrical, topological formulations of time-space as an "ether of events" allows philosophers of Nature to avoid committing the "fallacy of misplaced concreteness" that results from mistaking one's favored geometry (whether Euclidean, Reimannian, or otherwise) for the concrete composition of the physical world (as both Newton and Einstein did).[88] The difficultly of grasping the concept of the non-metrical ether put forward by Schelling and Whitehead will be lessened, according to Adams, only if we stretch the old geometrical imagination by "developing the pure mathematical thought-forms of ethereal space," thereby allowing us to "acquire a new spatial feeling" that will in turn "fertilize our knowledge of external Nature."[89] Contrary to Kant, then, Steiner, Adams, Whitehead, and Schelling all conceived of the human mind as caught up with Nature in an ongoing process of evolution. Unlike Kant, they argued that the human mind is capable of cultivating and transforming its intuitions of Nature. Etherically attuned human imagination is capable of perceiving time-space as a prehensive nexus of living processes, rather a set of fixed forms.

---

86. Steiner, *The Relation of the Diverse Branches of Natural Science to Astronomy*, Lecture 1, 31.

87. Whitehead, *Adventures of Ideas*, 158.

88. As Merleau-Ponty, building on Whitehead, points out: "different geometries are metrics, and metrics are neither true nor false and, therefore, the results of these different metrics are not alternatives" (*La Nature*, 103, 141; translated by Hamrick and Veken).

89. Adams, *Physical and Ethereal Spaces*, 26.

4.3 Nature Philosophy as "Spiritual Sensation"

By what right do you declare the world finished without thinking? Does not the world bring forth thinking in human heads with the same necessity as it brings forth blossoms on the plant? Plant a seed in the earth. It puts forth roots and stem. It unfolds into leaves and blossoms. Set the plant before you. It links itself to a specific concept in your soul. Why does this concept belong to the plant any less than the leaves and blossoms do? You might reply that the leaves and blossoms are present without a perceiving subject, while the concept appears only when a human being confronts the plant. Very well. But blossoms and leaves arise in the plant only when there is earth in which the seed can be laid and light and air in which leaves and blossoms can unfold. Just so, the concept of the plant arises when thinking consciousness approaches the plant.

—Steiner[90]

So long as I myself am *identical* with Nature, I understand what a living nature is as well as I understand my own life. As soon, however, as I separate myself, and with me everything ideal from nature, nothing remains to me but a dead object, and I cease to comprehend how a *life outside* me can be possible.

—Schelling[91]

Like Schelling, Whitehead argues that understanding the life of the actual occasions composing Nature requires first becoming conscious of the etheric dynamism underlying *our own* conscious experience and then imaginatively generalizing it to *all* the individualities of Nature. Such generalization allows for the creation of experiential categories applicable to the etheric life of *any* actual occasion.[92] Etheric imagination allows the process philosopher to intuit the formative forces flowing through the natural world subtly enfolded within its outward sensory surfaces. Such an imaginative thinking represents the individual's discovery within themselves of the etheric forces of *Natura naturans*, the *inner* potency of Nature that is always in dynamic tension, sloughing off external Nature (*Natura*

---

90. Rudolf Steiner, *Intuitive Thinking as a Spiritual Path*, 79–80.
91. Schelling, *Ideas*, 36.
92. Whitehead, *Adventures of Ideas*, 221.

naturata) like a snake shedding its skin. "Nature alive,"[93] as Whitehead called it, never sits still long enough to be caught in the conceptual net of merely reflective sense-bound understanding. "Nature speaks to us the more intelligibly the less we think of her in a merely reflective way," writes Schelling.[94] To think nature as living, our own thinking must come to life, must become *etheric*.

According to Owen Barfield, the forces of the etheric organ of perception can be understood as

> imagination operating in reverse . . . . Whereas imagination [typically] uses the spatial to get to the non-spatial, what the organic [etheric] force is doing is moving out of the non-spatial realm (the creative logos, if you like) to convert it into space–[it moves out] of the immaterial producing a material, spatial world . . . . What the etheric does is, to put it crudely, convert time into space.[95]

As the spiritual source of the force of imagination, the etheric organ and its formative-forces, when properly cultivated, can release the philosopher from the Kantian restrictions placed on knowing by opening the normally sense-bound understanding to the sub-sensory "intensive depth"[96] or super-sensory "inner infinitude"[97] of living Nature, there revealing the invisible creative forces animating her from the inside out. As we have seen, Kant did at least glimpse the creative depths of Nature in the Transcendental Aesthetic, but as Whitehead complains, he should have expanded this short section of the *Critique of Pure Reason* on the imaginal genesis of space and time into the centerpiece of his transcendental philosophy. Had he done so, Kant may have been remembered today as

---

93. Whitehead, *Modes of Thought*.
94. Schelling, *Ideas*, 35.
95. Barfield, "*Towards* Interviews," 9.
96. Bortoft, *The Wholeness of Nature*, 69.
97. Adams and Whicher, *The Plant Between Sun and Earth*.

the author of the *Critique of Feeling*, and the originator of a philosophy I am calling *descendentalism*.[98]

In the terms of Whitehead's three-fold theory of perception, sense awareness of the environment in terms of bare qualia or universals adhering to material surfaces is perception "spatialized" in the mode of "presentational immediacy," while etheric perception of sub-sensory emotional currents or what Whitehead calls "vector feelings"[99] is perception in the temporal mode of "causal efficacy." Whitehead's third mode of perception, "symbolic reference," imaginatively synthesizes our intuitions of these emotional currents into the meaningful and coherent world of everyday life.[100] The synthetic work (or play) of the force of imagination can be in service either to the maintenance of the habits of everyday conscious experience (common sense), or else to the creative disruption of those habits in favor of alternative imaginations of the flow of etheric time-space. The cultivation of an etheric organ of perception is aimed at raising the normally unconscious vector feelings of causal efficacy to consciousness, thus providing for more living symbolic formations.

The etheric forces animating Nature and her organisms are each and all alive, just as I am (though perhaps to differing degrees). The etheric imagination which participatively perceives organic Nature is then not simply the transcendental ground of our ego's sensory intuitions of the physical world—*it is the genetic principle of the universe itself*, the *poetic root of all life*, a creative fountain rather than a stable foundation. Unlike Kant's transcendental faculties of the understanding, Reason, and judgment, which provide only the necessary universal conditions of *possible* theoretical, ethical, or aesthetic experience, etheric imagination provides the genetic conditions of *actual* experience (whether

---

98. See Whitehead, *Process and Reality*, 113.
99. Whitehead, *Process and Reality*, 116, 163.
100. See Whitehead, *Symbolism*, 13–18.

of truth, goodness, or beauty). Etheric imagination not only schematizes the formal and abstract, it bodies forth the material and concrete—that is, it not only makes possible the universal and impersonal, it actualizes the unique and individual.

Schelling and Whitehead's approach to natural philosophy is rooted in aesthetic intuition and thus could be called an empiricism of imagination. What Wirth says of Schelling is equally true of Whitehead, that he is "through and through a thinker of the problem of imagination, of the emergence into image of that which itself has no image."[101] Their aesthetic (un)grounding of philosophy destabilizes the Hegelian notion that philosophy ought to overcome itself by arriving at a conceptually complete "system of science." Schelling and Whitehead's *Naturphilosophie* is an infinite creative task, not a finished system. *Naturphilosophie* is not a philosophy about Nature but "Nature itself philosophizing" (*autophusis philosophia*). "None of our spiritual thoughts transcend the earth," says Schelling.[102] Unlike so much modern philosophy, Schelling and Whitehead put Nature, rather than Mind, at the generative core of thought. Where modern philosophy put the human subject at the center, Schelling realized that the true subject of humanity is Nature herself: "Nature is *a priori*." Even if human thinking "stands at the limits of nature," the human mind remains "the ideal aspect *of the universe*."[103] The human being is unique among earthly creatures in that it knows reality's ground is incomprehensible. With this knowledge, we can either use our new-found freedom to flee upwards by way of anti-physical idealistic transcendentalism, or we can fall deeper in love with cosmogenesis via a descendental naturalism. The former option,

---

101. Wirth, "Nature of Imagination," 458.
102. Schelling, *Answer to Eschenmayer*, translated by Wirth and Christopher Lauer in *Schelling's Practice of the Wild*, 179.
103. Grant quoting Schelling, "Philosophy Become Genetic," 146n16.

freedom without love, quickly devolves into alienated nihilism. Idealists like Kant and Fichte tried to overcome this devolution by privileging practical over theoretical philosophy. To save the possibility of moral responsibility among humans they had to deny the possibility of a sympathetic knowledge of Nature. Schelling moved away from modern technoscience's conception of knowledge as power in favor of what Goethe termed a "gentle empiricism," or what might be called a loving knowledge. Rather than recoiling from the abyss of the sensible to a supposedly stable intelligible ground, as critical philosophy does, Whitehead and Schelling dive heart first into its radiant darkness. Theirs is a creative, rather than a critical philosophy. As I have argued, however, critical philosophy is not simply to be rejected. It is indispensable for clearing the way and preparing consciousness for its encounter with etheric reality. But critical reason alone cannot take us all the way. Schelling is clear on this point: "Without intellectual intuition, no philosophy!" The capacity for this sort of intuition, usually experienced only in artistic geniuses and mystical initiates, depends on a certain character trait, Schelling tells us. As such, it cannot be taught to just anyone, as geometry or arithmetic can. It can, however, be developed in those with a heartfelt sense for the "nullity" of all finite knowledge. Because of his tendency to rest philosophical insight on the capacity for genius or mystical sensitivity, Schelling may fall victim to Hegel's criticism that such a philosophy would prove useless and unteachable.[104] Mystical experience (Greek: *musterion*) is "secret" experience, known only in silence. As such it is difficult if not impossible to communicate about to those who have not encountered it for themselves.

Whitehead similarly likens philosophy to "imaginative art,"[105] implying that it is only a unique personality who can

104. Wirth, "Nature of Imagination," 462.
105. Whitehead, *Modes of Thought*, 117.

philosophize creatively (just as it takes a certain inborn ability to write inspired poetry or compose beautiful symphonies). Despite Hegel's critique and insistence that philosophy must rest on a universal and easily teachable method or set of principles (which itself may sway too far in the opposite direction), both Schelling and Whitehead were rigorous thinkers committed to developing their ideas in public. They simply rejected the idea that the creative abyss at the heart of Nature could be finally explained or captured in a geometric proof. "Philosophers can never hope to finally formulate [their] metaphysical first principles," admits Whitehead. No matter how technical and precise our language, the speculative propositions of philosophers "remain metaphors mutely appealing for an imaginative leap."[106] As Merleau-Ponty suggested in his late lecture course on Whitehead, "Nature is always new in each perception," even while it is "never without a past."[107] An ever-new Nature cannot be captured once and for all by any fixed verbal statement or logical formula, no matter how dialectically sophisticated. As is said of Isis, Goddess of Nature: "I am all that has been, and is, and shall be, and my veil no mortal has yet uncovered."[108] Isis/Nature is not a true Being hidden behind the illusory appearances of becoming. Her myth is not the story of bifurcation, but provides the imaginative background for an aesthetic ontology. Isis *is* the becoming or creative advance of living Nature. She is the ongoing underlying creative tension or polarity powering the eternal movement of contractive concealment and expansive revelation known as cosmogenesis.

Schelling and Whitehead share an intuition about eternity's participation in time, and about God's (or Goddess') participation in Nature. "No thing has an external time," writes Schelling.

---

106. Whitehead, *Process and Reality*, 4.
107. Merleau-Ponty, *Nature*, 118.
108. Plutarch, *Moralia*, 25.

> Rather, each thing only has an inner time of its own, inborn and indwelling within it. The mistake of Kantianism with respect to time consists in it not knowing this *universal* subjectivity of time and hence it delimits time in such a way that it becomes a mere form of our representations. No thing comes to being in time. Rather *in* each thing time comes to being anew and does so immediately from out of eternity.... The beginning of time is in each thing, and, indeed, each thing is the same as the eternal beginning. Every single individual comes to being through the same cision [*Scheidung*] through which the world comes to being, and therefore does so right from the beginning with its own epicenter of time.[109]

As with the initial aim granted to actual occasions by Whitehead's primordial nature of God, Schelling sees each actual entity as inwardly resonant with eternity. Whitehead's primordial nature is the original rhythm or rhyme scheme uttered by the divine poet that still resounds within each finite actual occasion. It is through an intellectual intuition that we hear this silent song—"silent" because it provides the ground-tone for our entire existence, its humble humming hardly noticeable but for special moments of mystical insight. God is "the poet of the world," as Whitehead puts it, the cosmic myth-maker or whisperer of secrets gently goading us toward Nature's ever-revelatory meaning. Whitehead's primordial nature of God is the eternal at play in Nature, revealing itself in the joy of the present as well as the promise of a future. According to Wirth, "Nature . . . **is the life of imagination**,"[110] a statement not unlike William Blake's: "to the eyes of the man of imagina-

---

109. Schelling, *Weltalter*, 78–79; excerpted and translated by Jason Wirth, *Schelling's Practice of the Wild*, 86. Though usually translated as "divorce," Wirth translates *Scheidung* with "cision," as in "de-cision." Elsewhere in this book, I have used the normal spelling "scission" to translate *Scheidung*.

110. Wirth, *Schelling's Practice of the Wild*, 29.

tion, Nature is imagination itself."[111] In the same letter, Blake defines imagination as "spiritual sensation," a more poetic translation of *intellektuelle Anschauung* into English than the usual "intellectual intuition."

4.4 Etheric Imagination and Vegetal Metaphysics

Process philosophers can become rooted in the etheric forces of imagination by learning to think like a plant. Michael Marder's "vegetal metaphysics" provides a contemporary example of the power of plant-thinking to (re)turn modern philosophy to its etheric senses. Marder's critical account of the history of Western metaphysics exhaustively details philosophy's theoretical incoherences and practical inadequacies as regards the vegetal dimension of reality. For example, he criticizes Aristotle for the "violence" his formal logic of identity and non-contradiction "unleashed against plants,"[112] diagnoses Hegel's negative dialectic as a symptom of his "[allergy] to vegetal existence,"[113] and regrets Husserl's essentializing "failure to think the tree" itself.[114]

To be fair to these philosophers, Aristotle's psychological anthropology as described in *De Anima* includes descriptions of how "physical ... vegetative, sensitive and intellectual souls" are each set to work within the whole human being,[115] and in the end Husserl's etheric imagination hearkened to a form of post-Copernican geocentrism: "the original ark, earth, does not move."[116] As for Hegel, Jonael Schickler points to Steiner's mediating conception of a living ether circulating

---

111. Blake, "To the Revd. Dr. Trusler, August 23, 1799," in *The Portable William Blake*.
112. Marder, *Plant-Thinking*, 21.
113. Marder, *Plant-Thinking*, 126.
114. Marder, *Plant-Thinking*, 75–78.
115. Schickler, *Metaphysics as Christology*, 162.
116. Husserl, "Foundational Investigations," in *Husserl, Shorter Works*, 222–33. See also, Abram, *Spell of the Sensuous*, 34–35.

between mind and Nature as a cure for Hegel's allergic reaction to the supposed linearity of plants (by which he understood them to be closer to crystals than to animals).[117] According to Marder, Hegel's dialectical logic forces him to leave the blind growth of plant-life outside the autopoietic circle of the Concept, thereby alienating the self-conscious mind from a natural world demoted to "petrified spirit."[118] Unlike Hegel and the idealist tradition, which "[retreated] from the world of the senses" and so failed "to consider an ontology intrinsic to life," an organic philosophy aesthetically inspired by etheric imagination reaches below the surface to the invisible but prehensible vital forces out of which the visible sensory arena is later abstracted.[119] In Marder's terms, philosophy must learn to think like a plant: "The plant sets free the entire realm of petrified nature, including mineral elements, if not the earth itself."[120]

David Hume, though not mentioned in Marder's historical account, had his own bout of vegetal thinking in the midst of composing his *Dialogues on Natural Religion*. In this dialogue, Cleanthes at one point is made to deploy an ontophytological critique of Philo's over-determined analogization of the universe to an animal. Unlike an animal, argues Cleanthes, the universe we experience has "no organs of sense; no seat of thought or reason; no one precise origin of motion and action." "In short," Cleanthes jests, "[the universe] seems to bear a stronger resemblance to a vegetable than to an animal."[121] Cleanthes' does not really believe the universe is a self-generating plant, he only suggests as much in order to undermine

---

117. Marder, *Plant-Thinking*, 124–26.
118. See *Petrified Intelligence* by Alison Stone. Marder is perhaps exaggerating Hegel's admittedly idealistic perspective. It should be noted that in his lectures on the philosophy of Nature in the *Encyclopedia of the Philosophical Sciences*, Hegel remarks that "the very stones cry out and raise themselves to Spirit" (15).
119. Schickler, *Metaphysics as Christology*, 143.
120. Marder, *Plant-Thinking*, 127.
121. Hume, *Natural Religion*, 417.

the credibility of Philo's animal analogy.[122] Philo responds by accepting the critique of the animal analogy, but then opportunistically turns the relative credibility of the vegetable analogy against Cleanthes' own argument for design: "The world plainly resembles more . . . a vegetable, than it does a watch or a knitting-loom," says Philo.

> Its cause, therefore, it is more probable, resembles . . . generation or vegetation . . . . In like manner as a tree sheds its seed into the neighboring fields, and produces other trees; so the great vegetable, the world, or this planetary system, produces within itself certain seeds, which, being scattered into the surrounding chaos, vegetate into new worlds.[123]

Philo, of course, is no more sincere in his vegetal speculations than Cleanthes was in his. He doubts whether philosophy will ever have enough data to determine the true nature and cause of the universe. In the intervening two centuries since Hume published his *Dialogues*, mathematical and technological advances have allowed scientific cosmology to drastically expand and complexify the range of data available to assist the natural philosopher's speculative imagination. Modern scientific cosmology, especially when interpreted in light of Marder's "plant-nature synecdoche," which posits that plants are "the miniature mirror of *physis*,"[124] has only made Hume's vegetal conjecture more scientifically plausible. Despite the breadth of his "ontophytological" deconstruction of Western metaphysics, Marder makes no mention of Hume's imaginatively generative double gesturing toward plants.

Hume was not the first to philosophize about the vegetal life of the universe. At least in the Western tradition,[125] such

---

122. Cleanthes really believes the universe to be a law-abiding machine designed, built, and maintained by a perfect God.
123. Hume, *Natural Religion*, 421.
124. Marder, *Plant-Thinking*, 120.
125. The Indian *Bhagavad Gita* used the image of an inverted Ashwattha tree to

Crossing the Threshold

speculations date at least to Plato, who wrote in *Timaeus* that the philosopher is a "heavenly plant" or "heavenly flower." "We declare," Plato has Timaeus say,

> that God has given to each of us, as his daemon, that kind of soul which is housed in the top of our body and which raises us—seeing that we are not an earthly but a heavenly plant—up from earth towards our kindred in the heaven. And herein we speak most truly; for it is by suspending our head and root from that region whence the substance of our soul first came that the divine power keeps upright our whole body.[126]

The next to carry forward Plato's plant-thinking was Plotinus, into whose philosophy Marder writes that

> there is no better point of entry . . . than the allegory of the world—permeated by what he calls "the Soul of All"—as a single plant, one gigantic tree, on which we alongside all other living beings (and even inorganic entities, such as stones) are offshoots, branches, twigs, and leaves.[127]

Plotinus' World-Tree grows from a single inverted root. The inverted root of the World-Tree is an image of the ever-living One that, though it "gives to the plant its whole life in its multiplicity,"[128] itself remains forever "unaffected by the dispersion of the living."[129] Neither Marder, Whitehead, nor Schelling accepts Plotinus' emanational monism. Marder calls

---

describe the cosmos earlier than Plato. While some Hindu historians suggest the *Gita* was conceived (if not written down) in the third or fourth millennium BCE, most scholars place its origins around the sixth century BCE (see Radhakrishnan and Moore, *Indian Philosophy*, 99). "The branches of this cosmic tree extend both below and above (below in the material, above in the supraphysical planes)" (Aurobindo, *Gita*, 15.2).

126. Plato, *Timaeus*, 90a–b.
127. Marder, "Plotinus' Anonymous 'Great Plant.'"
128. Plotinus, *Enneads* 3.8.10, 5–15.
129. Marder, "Plotinus' Anonymous 'Great Plant.'"

for an "anarchic radical pluralism,"[130] a title which could just as well describe Whitehead and Schelling's process ontology. Nonetheless, though they reject monism in favor of pluralism, all three carry forward Plotinus' root image of an archetypally informed vegetal universe.

Marder, like Schelling and Whitehead, conceives of Nature "as suffused with subjectivity."[131] He likens the life of the plant (*phytos*) to the whole of Nature (*physis*), arguing that plant-life "replicates the activity of *physis* itself."[132] "*Physis*," continues Marder, "with its pendular movement of dis-closure, revelation and concealment, is yet another ... name for being."[133] Hume had Philo argue against the plausibility of divining the Nature of the whole based on an acquaintance with its parts,[134] but in daring to ontologize the vegetal life of the whole of Nature (making its "life" more than a mere metaphor), Marder displays his allegiance to the ancient hermetic principle of correspondence (shifting its verticality into a mereotopological register, as Whitehead himself does[135]): as it is above, so it is below; as it is below, so it is above.[136]

The hermetic principle of polar correspondence between the one above and the many below is not simply an abstract mental concept. It is a magical symbol whose power is enacted not only in the ideal meanings of the mind, but in the living movements of Nature. These movements are made most obviously apparent by the mystery of the seasonal life cycle of the plant realm. Though Hume recognized that plant-life

---

130. Marder, *Plant-Thinking*, 58.
131. Marder, *Plant-Thinking*, 35.
132. Marder, *Plant-Thinking*, 28; both "plant" and "nature" derive from the same Greek prefix (*phuo-*) and verb (*phuein*), meaning "to generate," or "to bring forth."
133. Marder, *Plant-Thinking*, 28–29.
134. Hume, *Natural Religion*, 416.
135. Whitehead, *Process and Reality*, Part 4.
136. Hermes, *The Emerald Tablet*, line 2.

presented a definite limit to traditional metaphysical speculation, he remained uninitiated into the death/rebirth mystery esoterically encrypted in this vegetal threshold. Whitehead also invoked the hermetic principle of polarity by balancing Plato and Plotinus' preferential treatment of the One with his own more Heraclitan "Category of the Ultimate": *Creativity* is an ultimate category that dissolves the classical metaphysical dichotomy separating the single supreme Creator from Its many subsidiary creatures. "Creativity," writes Whitehead,

> is the universal of universals characterizing ultimate matter of fact. It is that ultimate principle by which the many, which are the universe disjunctively, become the one actual occasion, which is the universe conjunctively.[137]

Through this process of creative advance from disjunction to conjunction, a novel entity is created that was not present in the prior dispersion. "The novel entity," continues Whitehead,

> is at once the togetherness of the "many" which it finds, and also it is one among the disjunctive "many" which it leaves; it is a novel entity, disjunctively among the many entities which it synthesizes. The many become one, and are increased by one.[138]

The many down below thereby enter into and pass through the one up above, just as the one up above enters into and passes through the many down below. "The way up and the way down is one and the same," as Heraclitus put it.[139] Schelling also creatively inherits the hermetic principle of correspondence by analogizing the metaphysical polarity of the many below and the one above to the physical pulsation

---

137. Whitehead, *Process and Reality*, 21.
138. Whitehead, *Process and Reality*, 21.
139. Fragment 123; translated by Panikkar, *The Rhythm of Being*, 266.

—the "systole" and "diastole" rhythm—of living nature. "The antithesis eternally produces itself," writes Schelling,

> in order always again to be consumed by the unity, and the antithesis is eternally consumed by the unity in order always to revive itself anew. This is the sanctuary, the hearth of the life that continually incinerates itself and again rejuvenates itself from the ash. This is the tireless fire through whose quenching, as Heraclitus claimed, the cosmos was created.[140]

Schelling offers the telling example of a tree to show how this cosmogenetic rhythm resonates through the whole to the parts and back again:

> Visible nature, in particular and as a whole, is an allegory of this perpetually advancing and retreating movement. The tree, for example, constantly drives from the root to the fruit, and when it has arrived at the pinnacle, it again sheds everything and retreats to the state of fruitlessness, and makes itself back into a root, only in order again to ascend. The entire activity of plants concerns the production of seed, only in order again to start over from the beginning and through a new developmental process to produce again only seed and to begin again. Yet all of visible nature appears unable to attain settledness and seems to transmute tirelessly in a similar circle.[141]

Schelling is not only one of a handful of philosophers to escape deconstruction by Marder's vegetal anti-metaphysics, he even earns Marder's praise for defending the continuity between life and thought.[142] Schelling suggests that "every plant is a symbol of the intelligence,"[143] and that this symbolic

---

140. Schelling, *The Ages of the World*, 20–21.
141. Schelling, *Ages*, 21.
142. Marder, *Plant-Thinking*, 157.
143. Schelling, *Transcendental Idealism*, 122.

intelligence finds expression precisely in the plant's power of "sensibility," which—even when the pendulum of organic Nature has swung toward its opposite but complimentary pole of "irritability"—remains the "*universal* cause of life."[144] According to Elaine Miller, another plant-thinker, while Hegel approaches plant-life and Nature more generally as appearances to be taken up and sublated by human reason, Schelling's *Naturphilosophie* approaches Nature as possessed of its own kind of intelligence:

> Schelling does not claim that the human intellect works in the way that a plant grows, but rather that the growth of a plant exhibits the kind of intelligence that nature is. Nature itself is a visible manifestation of the ideal, a manifestation of a power of reason that is not limited to human consciousness.[145]

Miller argues that Schelling's main problem with Hegel's dialectical understanding of Nature stemmed from the latter's "[reduction of] nature to a passing moment of spirit." "Human subjectivity," she continues, "insofar as it believes it can overcome its plantlike fragility, loses sight of its connection to the life-and-death rhythms of nature."[146]

As we saw above, Schelling offers the etheric connection between Earth and Sun as an illustration of the life-producing relationship between gravity and light that is responsible for calling forth intelligent plant-life out of the planet.[147] Steiner similarly remarks that any attempt to understand the inorganic, mineral dimension of Earth independently of the plant-life it supports will remain hopelessly abstract: "Just as our skeleton first separates itself out of the organism," says Steiner, "so we have to look at the earth's rock formations as

---

144. Schelling, *Philosophy of Nature*, 146.
145. Miller, *The Vegetative Soul*, 124.
146. Miller, *The Vegetative Soul*, 147.
147. Schelling, *Philosophy of Nature*, 185–86.

the great skeleton of the earth organism."[148] Steiner further argues that the cultivation of etheric imagination will allow the philosopher to come to see "the plant covering of our earth [as] the sense organ through which earth spirit and sun spirit behold each other."[149] The mineral and plant realms are to Earth what the skeletal and sensorial organs are to the human body. As Plotinus wrote, "earth is ensouled, as our flesh is, and any generative power possessed by the plant world is of its bestowing."[150] Plant-life has all too often been relegated to the margins of natural philosophy, attended to only to insult it rather than to be inspired by it. And so the natural philosophical imagination has withered and disintegrated into a mind/matter dualism. Rejuvenating *Naturphilosophie* will require that plant-life become the matrix from which all philosophical thinking emerges. Plants are transitional organisms, not quite material and not quite spiritual. They force the mind to loosen the seals separating its categories, allowing it to perceive the etheric life actively mediating every fold of Nature's self-organization.

A process philosophy rooted in the power of etheric imagination requires an inversion of our ordinary experience of the universe. It is as if the world were turned inside out, or as if we were walking upside down upon the Earth, with our head rooted in the ethereal soil of formative forces streaming in from the cosmos beyond, our limbs yearning for the living ground below, and our heart circulating between the two in rhythmic harmony. Rather than stretching for the abstract heights of the intelligible as if to steal a glimpse of heaven, the force of etheric imagination returns philosophy's attention to the earth beneath its feet, and to the roots, branches, leaves, flowers, fruits, and seeds of *plants*, Earth's most generous life forms, and indeed the co-generative source (with the Sun, Moon, and

---

148. Steiner, *The Spirit in the Realm of Plants*.
149. Steiner, *The Spirit in the Realm of Plants*.
150. Plotinus, *Enneads* 4.2.27.

other stars) of Life itself. Thinking with etheric imagination is thinking with a plant-soul. Plant-souls, according to Marder, partake of a "kind of primordial generosity that gives itself to all other creatures, animates them with this gift, . . . allows them to surge into being, to be what they are."[151]

Heraclitus' oft cited fragment 123, "nature loves to hide" (*physis kryptesthai philei*), should not be understood as a negation of the generous growth of the plant realm described by Marder.[152] As with the natural world, there is more to Heraclitus' paradoxical statement than first meets the eye. The earliest recorded use of *physis* in ancient Greek literature is in Homer's *Odyssey*, where it refers specifically to the "magic" and "holy force" of the *molü* plant given by Hermes to Odysseus to keep his "mind and senses clear" of Circe's sorcery. The *molü* plant grows duplicitously into "black root and milky flower" and can be safely uprooted only by the gods.[153] As we have seen, then, *physis* suggests not only a tendency toward concealment in the darkness of the soil, but also a tendency toward revelation in the light of the Sun. As is typical both of the plant-life of Nature and of the semantic structure of his sentences, there is an underlying polarity to Heraclitus' fragment. Understanding the poetic meaning of his occult philosophy, or of a plant's process of growth, is impossible without cultivating a polar relational logic of etheric imagination. The logics of techno-scientific manipulation and abstract conceptual analysis, in attempting to uproot and expose the etheric dimension of mind and Nature to total illumination, succeed only in making it evaporate.[154] Instead of objectifying Nature, etheric imagination approaches her hermeneutically, not by "[shying] away from darkness and obscurity," but by letting plants "appear in their own light . . . emanating from

---

151. Marder, *Plant-Thinking*, 46.
152. Marder, *Plant-Thinking*, 28.
153. Homer, *Odyssey*, Book 10, lines 328–42.
154. Marder, *Plant-Thinking*, 30.

Chapter 4: Etheric Imagination in Naturphilosophie

their own kind of being."[155] Marder's plant-thinking approaches a logic of imagination, in that he aims to begin his vegetal philosophizing, not from the putatively purified perspective of disembodied rationality, but *in media res*, always in the middle of things:

> To live and to think in and from the middle, like a plant partaking of light and of darkness ... is to ... refashion oneself—one's thought and one's existence—into a bridge between divergent elements: to become a place where the sky communes with the earth and light encounters but does not dispel darkness.[156]

Only by finding its vegetal roots can philosophy become *planetary*, true to the Earth and to the plant-like, etheric forces of imagination. But because the etheric imagination is in fact abyssal/ungrounded, its plant-like growth must be inverted: it has "underground stems" and "aerial roots," as Deleuze and Guattari put it.[157] Or, as Gaston Bachelard suggests (echoing Plato in *Timaeus*), the properly rooted philosopher is like "a tree growing upside down, whose roots, like a delicate foliage, tremble in the subterranean winds while its branches take root firmly in the blue sky."[158] For Bachelard, the plant is the *root image* of all life: "The imagination [must take] possession of all the powers of plant life," he writes. "It lives between earth and sky ... [it] becomes imperceptibly the cosmological tree, the tree which epitomizes a universe, which makes a universe."[159]

Marder argues that "plants are resistant to idealization."[160] He dwells upon "the vegetable vein" of Plato's philosophy

---

155. Marder, *Plant-Thinking*, 30.
156. Marder, *Plant-Thinking*, 178.
157. Deleuze and Guattari, *A Thousand Plateaus*, 15.
158. Bachelard, *Poetic Imagination*, 85.
159. Bachelard, *Poetic Imagination*, 85. The inverted tree is a common motif in hermetic literature.
160. Marder, *Plant-Thinking*, 13.

in an attempt to re-envision the latter's oft-characterized two-world metaphysical theory as through it were a transformative "pedagogic endeavor."[161] The real import of Plato's dialogues, in other words, is not the theoretical content defended by Socrates' various conversation partners, but the soteriological metanoia the dramas aim to spark in the reader. The *Republic*'s Myth of the Cave, for example, is often read as Plato's most extravagant metaphor for the otherworldly role of the philosopher, who "descends to the gloomy underworld to initiate a prison break by delivering those living in the shackles of the senses to the heights of intellection."[162] But Marder challenges any straightforward metaphysical interpretation of Plato's metaphor as a call to detach our souls from the appearances of this world by reminding us that Socrates, our constant companion throughout all Plato's dialogues, hardly fits the model of the ivy tower intellectual. Socrates, an eager participant in the aristocratic *sympósia* and the democratic *agorá* alike, "came back to the cave of appearances to give those imprisoned there a chance to emerge into the broad and luminous expanses of Ideas."[163] Marder reads the Myth of the Cave as "a story of . . . seed germination" describing "how heavenly plants sprouted from the dark soil of appearances to the light of Ideas."[164] In Plato's *Theaetetus*, Socrates describes himself as a midwife of ideas who helps guide the growth of concepts out of the soil of his interlocutors' souls and into the light of the Good.[165] In the *Timaeus*, Plato describes perhaps the most mysterious of his dialogue characters, the Receptacle, in a similar way as "the wet-nurse of becoming."[166] It is as though Socrates is Plato's human personification of the

---

161. Marder, *The Philosopher's Plant*, 16–17.
162. Marder, *The Philosopher's Plant*, 16.
163. Marder, *The Philosopher's Plant*, 18.
164. Marder, *The Philosopher's Plant*, 17.
165. Plato, *Theaetetus*, 149a.
166. Plato, *Timaeus*, 52d.

cosmic matrix or etheric receptacle of divine Ideas. By providing resistance to and suffering with the elemental powers of ingressing Ideas, a process of growth is allowed to unfold as Ideas learn through the trials of experience what in eternity they did not know: the idea of Fire sees light, shadow, and color; the idea of Water flows and feels wet; Air blows and feels dry; and Earth rests heavy.[167] Plant-life is resistant to idealization because it displays the same ambiguous process-relational character as Socrates and the Receptacle. All are expressions of the resistance providing matrix that, in the course of evolutionary history, gradually raises unconscious Nature to consciousness of itself as Spirit. Etheric imagination is the esemplastic power[168] through which eternal Ideas become incarnate in the concrescing occasions of the world, like seeds taking root in the ground, growing skyward through branch, leaf, flower, and fruit, only to fall again into the soil to be born again, and again . . .

Marder's "post-metaphysical task of de-idealization" makes him especially attentive to the association between the aesthetic power of plant-life (particularly flowers) and the pathos of death: flowers—"the free beauties of nature,"[169] as Kant called them—have since the beginning of history been customarily "discarded along the path of Spirit's glorious march through the world," "abandoned" and thereby "freed from dialectical totality."[170] "In contrast to the death borne by *Geist*," continues Marder, plant-life can become "neither mediated nor internalized."[171] Idealist philosophy is therefore always in a rush to

---

167. Plato, *Timaeus*, 52e.
168. A term coined by Samuel Taylor Coleridge and modeled on Schelling's own neologism *Ineinsbildung* (*Biographia Literaria*, Ch. 10).
169. Kant, *Critique of Judgment*, 59.
170. Marder, *Plant-Thinking*, 126.
171. Marder, *Plant-Thinking*, 126.

> [unchain] the flower from its organic connection to the
> soil and [put] it on the edge of culture as a symbol of love,
> religious devotion, mourning, friendship, or whatever else
> might motivate the culling.[172]

The end result of modern idealist rationality's "thorough cultivation" and "biotechnological transformation" of plant-life is "a field of ruins."[173]

The "economic-teleological" principle guiding modern rationality—whereby, for example, "trees in and of themselves have no worth save when turned into furniture"[174]—is related to Kant's failure to grasp the *life* of Nature as more than a merely *regulative* judgment. While he found it acceptable for human subjects to *think* the internal possibility of nature as organic, he refused to grant that Life could be understood as constitutive of Nature itself and that humans could *know* the Life of Nature. "It is absurd," Kant writes, "to hope that another Newton will arise in the future who would explain to us how even a mere blade of grass is produced."[175] It followed that the only avenue open to Reason in its untamable desire to know Nature was by way of the "economic-teleological" principle, whereby the philosopher of Nature, in order to know his object, "must first manufacture it."[176] Modern rationality, in its techno-capitalist phase, has succeeded in reducing the entire planet to an "externality" for our economic system: Earth is raw material on one end of the cycle of consumption, and on the other, a garbage disposal for toxic waste. In order to avoid the deleterious ecological effects of such a system, is necessary to return to and to heal

---

172. Marder, *Plant-Thinking*, 123.
173. Marder, *Plant-Thinking*, 128.
174. Schelling, *Werke*, 1/7, 18; excerpted and translated by Matthews, *Schelling's Organic Form*, 4.
175. Kant, *Critique of Judgment*, Section 75.
176. Kant, *Opus Postumum*, 240.

Chapter 4: Etheric Imagination in Naturphilosophie

the vegetal repression and sensorial alienation from which it stems.[177]

The repression of vegetal existence, according to Marder, began as early as Aristotle, who was willing to grant of plants, due to their lack of both locomotion and perception, only that they "*seem* to live."[178] The "seeming" life of plants presents a taxonomic problem for Aristotle, whose formal logic forces a clear decision: either plants are ensouled, or they are not. But for the polar logic of imagination (no longer constrained by the principle of non-contradiction or the law of the excluded middle), the "seeming" life of plants reveals precisely what has been repressed by so much of Western metaphysics: that it is towards the ambiguous ontology of plant-life that philosophy must return to if it hopes to reconcile with sensory experience. Aristotle does finally grant a kind of life to plants by pointing to their nutritive capacity (*to threptikon*), which in animal life is homologous to the haptic sense (i.e., touch).[179] Touch is the basis of all *aesthesis*, only subsequently becoming differentiated into the other specialized senses.[180] In light of the vegetal origins of sensation, Marder is lead to wonder

> whether the sensory and cognitive capacities of the psyche, which in human beings have been superadded to the vegetal soul, are anything but an outgrowth, an excrescence, or a variation of the latter. The sensitivity of the roots seeking moisture in the dark of the soil [or leaves seeking light in the brightness of the sky] . . . and human ideas or representations we project, casting them in front of ourselves, are not as dissimilar from one another as we tend to think.[181]

---

177. Marder, *Plant-Thinking*, 22.
178. Aristotle, *De anima*, 410b23. Italics added.
179. Aristotle, *De anima*, 413b1–10.
180. Marder, *Plant-Thinking*, 38.
181. Marder, *Plant-Thinking*, 27.

Whereas Kant argued that "real metaphysics" must be "devoid of all mixture with the sensual,"[182] Marder suggests that the idealist reduction of plant-life to dead linear crystals "[survives] in human thought in the shape of Kantian immutable categories and forms of intuition to which all novel experiences must in one way or another conform."[183] Instead of forcing lived experience to obey the crystalline categories of thought, Marder's plant-thinking, akin to the logic of etheric imagination guiding this book, "destroys the Procrustean bed of formal logic and transcendental *a priori* structures—those ideal standards to which no living being can measure up fully."[184]

The plant-thinking of etheric imagination breaks through the crystalline molds of "dead thought"—what Bergson called "the logic of solids"[185]—to bring forth instead a *fluid* or *plastic* logic, a way of *thinking-with* the creative life of Nature, rather than attempting to flee from or master it.[186] Whereas in a crystalline logic of solids, thought "has only to follow its natural [intrinsic] movement, after the lightest possible contact with experience, in order to go from discovery to discovery, sure that experience is following behind it and will justify it invariably,"[187] in a fluid logic of plastics, thought becomes etheric, overflowing the sense-bound understanding's *a priori* categorical antinomies and pre-determined forms of intuition to participate directly in the imaginal life of cosmogenesis. "A theory of life that is not accompanied by a criticism of knowledge," according to Bergson,

---

182. Kant, *De mundi sensibilis*; translated by Matthews, *Schelling's Organic Form*, 4.
183. Marder, *Plant-Thinking*, 163; Hegel also considered plant growth to be linear, like crystals, whereas proper animals are elliptical in their movements (ibid., 119).
184. Marder, *Plant-Thinking*, 164.
185. Bergson, *Creative Evolution*, xvii.
186. Marder, *Plant-Thinking*, 166.
187. Bergson, *Creative Evolution*, xviii.

is obliged to accept, as they stand, the concepts which the understanding puts at its disposal: it can but enclose the facts, willing or not, in preexisting frames which it regards as ultimate.[188]

The plasticity of etheric imagination, on the other hand, preserves the unprethinkability of the creative advance of Nature by remaining "faithful to the obscurity of vegetal life," protecting it from the searing clarity of crystallized rationality.[189]

It is important to reiterate that Marder's plant-thinking, like Schelling and Whitehead's polar logic of etheric imagination, "rejects the principle of non-contradiction in its content and its form,"[190] at least for the purposes of speculative metaphysics.[191] It also rejects the corollary law of identity. A plant-like, polar logic of etheric imagination forces concepts to grow together with percepts and identities to become infused with difference. Both Schelling and Whitehead affirm Plato's argument in *Sophist* that "not-being" is a kind of being.[192] "Every kind," Plato writes, "has a plurality of Being and an infinity of Not-being."[193] This is to say that every actuality, every reality, includes within it both what it *is* and what it *is not*. Actualities are composed of being *and* becoming. Each actuality, though it at first appears to be merely a finite particular act appearing here and now, also carries within it a deep history of evolutionary facts and a divine lure toward a future of open

---

188. Bergson, *Creative Evolution*, xx.

189. Marder, *Plant-Thinking*, 173.

190. Marder, *Plant-Thinking*, 164.

191. To be clear, Whitehead's rejection is qualified, as the principle of non-contradiction still applies to analysis of the physical pole of concrescence. The conceptual pole, however, in that it feels a variety of contradictory potentials, is not subject to such a logic (*Process and Reality*, 348).

192. Whitehead, *Adventures of Ideas*, 222, 228; Schelling, *The Ages of the World*, 14–15.

193. Plato, *Sophist*, 256d–e. Excerpted and translated by Grant, *After Schelling*, 44.

possibilities. Actual occasions are both "here-now" in the present *and* "there-then" in the past and the future (and each in different ways). On paper, strict adherence to the logical principles of identity and non-contradiction may prevent the mind from making simple errors. But if reality is an ecology of living processes rather than a pile of dead things—if, as Plato has Timaeus say, the Universe is such that "living creatures keep passing into one another . . . as they undergo transformation"[194]—then adhering to these principles too strictly ends up blinding the mind to the creative advance of Nature. Thinking Nature otherwise requires reimagining the disincarnate logos driving so much Western philosophy. An *incarnate logos* attuned to the etheric imagination not only thinks Nature, it becomes *Nature thinking*. "The human who thinks like a plant," Marder continues, "literally becomes a plant, since the destruction of classical *logos* annihilates the thing that distinguishes us from other living beings."[195] Unlike modern rationality, which is said to be self-grounding, plant-life is open to otherness, dependent on something other than itself (i.e., other organisms, as well as earth, water, air, and light). In the same way, etheric imagination receives its power from the elemental life of Nature. It is no longer "I" who thinks Nature; rather, "*it thinks in me*."[196] As Frederick Beiser wrote of Schelling's intellectual intuition, through it "I do not see myself acting but all of nature acting through me."[197] Or as Schelling himself put it, the philosopher who is etherically attuned to Nature becomes "nature itself philosophizing (*autophusis philosophia*)."[198]

---

194. Plato, *Timaeus*, 92b–c. Excerpted and translated by Grant, *After Schelling*, 53.
195. Marder, *Plant-Thinking*, 164.
196. Schelling, *Modern Philosophy*, 48.
197. Beiser, *German Idealism*, 583.
198. Quoted in Grant, *After Schelling*, 188.

Epilogue

Incarnational Process Philosophy in the Worldly Religion of Schelling, Whitehead, and Deleuze

[The cosmotheanthropic aspiration] does not discard anything, does not put anything aside, nor despise or eliminate any portion of the real. [It] does not take refuge in the highest by neglecting the lowest; it does not make a separation by favoring the spiritual and ignoring the material; it does not search out eternity at the expense of temporality.

—Panikkar[1]

Permeating everything there is but one and the same life, the same ontological power, the same ideal bond. In nature there is nothing purely corporeal, but everywhere the same soul symbolically transmuted into flesh.

—Schelling[2]

[A]ctual entities, of course, do not add up to God . . . . [But] it is . . . the case that the pan-experientialism of process *ontology* comes enmeshed in the panentheism of process *theology*. For once one glimpses the mindful animation of minimal creatures, the plenum of creation itself comes alive. And then how do we name that life?"

—Keller[3]

JUST PRIOR TO THE ABOVE EXCERPT from Panikkar's Gifford Lectures (later published as *The Rhythm of Being*), he refers to the need to discover a "sacred secularity" as a "novelty for our times."[4] In his own Gifford Lectures sixty-two years later (published as *Process and Reality*), Whitehead attempted to articulate a novel cosmological scheme that, among other things, is responsive to contemporary civilization's need for

1. Panikkar, *The Rhythm of Being*, 36.
2. Quoted in Kelly, *Coming Home*, 63.
3. Keller, *Cloud of the Impossible*, 163–64.
4. Panikkar, *The Rhythm of Being*, 36.

the "secularization of the concept of God's functions in the world."[5] He was referring not only to the need to secularize and concretize the anthropic God of mystical feeling and religious worship (related, I argue, to what Whitehead calls God's consequent nature), but also to the need to understand God's more-than-human cosmic function as an original impulse granting relevant value to actual occasions of every grade (i.e., God's primordial nature). Schelling, for his part, seeks to overturn the traditional hierarchy that places theology at the crown of all the sciences with philosophy as its handmaiden. As Jason Wirth describes it, Schelling's search for a truly *philosophical religion* and his reversal of the traditional hierarchy between philosophy and theology (wherein a primary faith seeks understanding secondarily) requires that "we are first philosophical."[6] While Kant's philosophical approach to religion emphasizes the limits of what the understanding can know about the idea of God (*nothing*, because God is not a possible object of experience), Schelling's philosophy, like Whitehead's, approaches God as a *reality* enfolded within actual experience. His philosophical religion searches for the wisdom of God—not in the heights of clear and distinct reflection—but in the depths of darkness where the divine fire transforms all things into itself. Only through experience of this divine darkness does "[thinking discover] that it has a religious dimension."[7] With no less sense of urgency, Deleuze and Guattari argued in *What Is Philosophy?* that, in an age when "we have so many reasons not to believe in the human world," philosophy's most pressing task is to "give birth to new modes of existence, closer to animals and rocks," modes

---

5. Whitehead, *Process and Reality*, 207.
6. Wirth, *Schelling's Practice of the Wild*, 38.
7. Wirth, *Schelling's Practice of the Wild*, 38; See also Schelling's discussion of the divine fire that flares up in the human will's encounter with its own abyssal creativity in *Human Freedom*, 55–56.

of existence which renew "[belief] in this world, in this life."[8] Like Whitehead—whose speculative philosophical flights are bounded by that "essence to the universe which forbids relationship beyond itself, as a violation of its rationality"[9]— Deleuze emphasizes *immanence* as opposed to transcendence, *this world* as opposed to the next. "What singles out the philosopher [from the theologian]," Deleuze and Guattari write, "is the part played by immanence or fire."[10]

In the epilogue to follow, I draw on Schelling, Whitehead, Deleuze, and their contemporary interpreters in the hopes of taking a few steps closer to a viable philosophical religion. I emphasize the appropriation by these thinkers of several under-appreciated dimensions of both Platonic philosophy and Christian spirituality, not in order to defend some parochial point of view, but only to explore the related questions of what an immanent God might be, and what, with such a God, humanity can become. I thus attempt to transmute the cosmotheanthropic process philosophy articulated in the prior chapters into religious liturgy. Writing becomes a liturgical activity, according to Panikkar, when its sayings are sincere and its sacred re-enactments novel, when rather than repeat the dogmas of the past, it re-creates their meanings so they resonate in the present. "Liturgical time is not historical," writes Panikkar, since through it "the past irrupts into the present" and "the present transforms the future."[11]

For Schelling, Whitehead, and Deleuze alike, speculative philosophy, unlike dogmatic religion or hubristic science, does

---

8. Deleuze and Guattari, *What Is Philosophy?*, 74.
9. Whitehead, *Process and Reality*, 4.
10. Deleuze and Guattari, *What Is Philosophy?*, 45. While the need to emphasize God's immanence is evident in Schelling and Whitehead's process theology, they do not share Deleuze's outright rejection of all forms of transcendence. Rather, as we will see, they reimagine the traditional meaning of transcendence such that it enlivens our appreciation of this world rather than deadening it in favor of another.
11. Panikkar, *The Cosmotheandric Experience*, 98.

not paint the firmament on an umbrella, as if such human artifice might hold the torrent of chaosmogenesis at bay. Rather, genuine philosophical thinking "tears open the firmament and plunges into the chaos."[12] I must add, however, that the philosopher's task is not only to descend into the darkness of the groundless depths of Creativity. The worldly philosopher must also return to the surface to share the good news with others in the light of common day. New prayers, rituals, myths, festivals, and liturgies must be enacted, otherwise the creative Life of reality remains secret and unexpressed and so cannot renew the spirit of the human community.

This world-renewing incarnational task is especially difficult in that all three thinkers generated concepts in response to encounters with *non-ordinary* problematics, which is to say that the solutions distilled by their concepts problematize naïve egoic subjectivity by acting as alchemical catalysts that alter not only the contents of conscious thoughts, but the normally taken for granted imaginative background of thought itself. The concepts their philosophizing creates reposition thought on new, as yet undetected planes of immanence. They are *hermetic* thinkers whose philosophizing is in service not only to theoretical explanation, but to worldly renewal by way of the intensification of the hermeneutical depths of experience. Intensifying the hermeneutical depths of experience involves raising the groundlessness of Creativity to the level of conscious activity, thereby exploding the representational mirror constitutive of Cartesian-Kantian reflection and opening human experience to participation in the ongoing work of God in an unfinished world-in-process.

It is important in the context of Schelling, Whitehead, and Deleuze's efforts to creatively disrupt and dissolve the experiential rigidities of modern consciousness to also strive to forge connections between such disruptive tactics and

---

12. Deleuze and Guattari, *What Is Philosophy?*, 202.

the ameliorative and world-building projects of establishing coherent social values and politically just institutions. Schelling remarks that the intention of philosophy in relation to humanity is

> not to add anything but to remove from him, as thoroughly as possible, the accidentals that the body, the world of appearances, and the sensate life have added and to lead him back to the originary state [Ursprüngliche].[13]

This work of alchemical dissolution of modern humanity's habitual forms of thought and perception is an essential ingredient in Whitehead and Schelling's process philosophy.[14] But neither go quite as far as Deleuze, whose philosophy has been criticized as "little more than [a] utopian distraction" by Peter Hallward due to its otherworldliness.[15] Isabelle Stengers also criticizes Deleuze's tendency to celebrate the adventures of solitary heroic creators who fearlessly dive into chaos while at the same time downplaying the conditions of creativity provided by their habitat and their inevitable need for social recuperation upon returning to consensual reality.[16] Stengers contrasts Deleuze's celebration of unhinged creation with Whitehead's tremendous respect for the lessons of history and continual emphasis upon the importance of acquiring

---

13. Schelling, *Philosophy and Religion*, 15.

14. Whitehead would probably detect a resonance between Schelling's sense for the originality of the human soul and the "initial aim" of God's primordial nature that generates each moment of our experience immediately from eternity. But to be led back to the "originary state" is not to step behind or beyond the flow appearance so as to attain static eternity; rather, it is to re-connect with the process of aesthetic genesis itself. "Originary state" may be an unhelpful translation of Schelling's term *Ursprüngliche*, since it misleadingly freezes the fluidity of originality (i.e., "Creativity" in Whitehead's terms) by describing an event as through it were a "state."

15. Hallward, *Out of This World*, 162. See also Sherman's theological response to Hallward, "No Werewolves in Theology?" in *Modern Theology*.

16. Stengers, *Thinking With Whitehead*, 272. A similar criticism might be leveled against Nietzsche.

new habits in a way that is sensitive to the habitat those habits depend upon. "Each task of creation," writes Whitehead, "is a social effort, employing the whole universe."[17] While Hallward's concerns may be justified, Stengers' Whiteheadian corrective to Deleuze's penchant for skinny-dipping in the Acheron allows us to receive inspiration from Deleuze without forgetting Whitehead's pertinent imperative regarding the worldly responsibility of the philosopher:

> "[to] seek the evidence for that conception of the universe which is the justification for the ideals characterizing the civilized phases of human society."[18]

As we have seen in earlier chapters, while Schelling and Whitehead upset many modern norms, the goal of their philosophizing is not the production of esoteric concepts but the imaginative renewal of humanity's *communis sensus*, our common sense.

When it comes to the influence of the mainline religious and theological traditions of the West upon philosophy, Schelling, Whitehead, and Deleuze are equally pointed in their criticisms. Schelling rejects traditional theology's abstract conception of God as "the most unlimited being (*ens illimitatissimum*)." Reducing the divine to such a concept makes it nothing more than an "empty infinite" since it neglects the possibility of self-imposed finitude to God.[19] Schelling's "radically incarnational"[20] *Naturphilosophie* seeks to reverse the traditional preference for the heavenly and eternal over the earthly and historical by tying "even the development of divine life . . . to the old age of the physical."[21] Whitehead's ire

---

17. Whitehead, *Process and Reality*, 275.
18. Whitehead, *Modes of Thought*, 105.
19. Schelling, *The Ages of the World*, 7.
20. Wirth, *Schelling's Practice of the Wild*, 65.
21. Schelling, *The Ages of the World*, xxxix.

is directed at the idolatrous habit of conceiving of God along the lines of an all-powerful imperial ruler or distant unmoved mover.[22] "Religion," writes Whitehead, "has emerged into human experience mixed with the crudest fancies of barbaric imagination."[23] Deleuze also mocks the idea of a "great despot" or "imperial State in the sky or on earth" so typical of monotheistic common sense.[24] While this particular habit of religious thought is deemed dispensable, Whitehead is unwilling to jettison religious values outright, despite calls by the modern-minded to found civilization instead upon the abstractions of mechanistic science:

> Unfortunately for this smug endeavor to view the universe as the incarnation of the commonplace, the impact of aesthetic, religious, and moral notions is inescapable. They are the disrupting and the energizing forces of civilization.[25]

Whitehead points to the "Galilean origin of Christianity" as an example of a non-despotic religious persona, Jesus Christ, who "neither rules, nor is unmoved," but "dwells upon the tender elements in the world, which slowly and in quietness operate by love."[26] Deleuze also singles out Christian philosophy, both for praise and for disparagement. Those early modern Christian philosophers such as Nicholas of Cusa, Meister Eckhart, Giordano Bruno, and Jakob Böhme, though bold enough to risk their lives by challenging church authority and injecting a dose of immanence into Physis and Nous, nonetheless still refused to "compromise the transcendence of a God to which immanence must be attributed only

---

22. Whitehead, *Process and Reality*, 343.

23. Whitehead, *Science and the Modern World*, 192. The contemplative conception of God as unmoved mover is obviously not as crude. What it lacks is the emotional and moral intensity required to engender a religious vision.

24. Deleuze and Guattari, *What Is Philosophy?*, 43.

25. Whitehead, *Modes of Thought*, 19.

26. Whitehead, *Process and Reality*, 343.

secondarily."[27] Late modern Christian philosophers such as Blaise Pascal and Søren Kierkegaard, though they were still men of faith, created concepts that recharged, rather than diminished, immanence. They were "concerned no longer with the transcendent existence of God but only with the infinite immanent possibilities brought by the one who believes that God exists."[28] Deleuze suggests that, in the modern period, *belief* replaces *knowledge* as the dominant image of thought.[29] The "will to truth" that had guided philosophy for so long lost its viability, as with the new technical power of modernity came also a crippling epistemic skepticism, an inability to grasp truth outright. In the same vein, Schelling is forced to admit in the course of writing the first draft of his unfinished work *The Ages of the World* (1811) that he is much closer than most people probably conceive

> to this growing silent of knowledge which we must necessarily encounter when we know how infinitely far everything that is personal reaches such that it is impossible actually to know anything at all.[30]

Thus, no longer can the productivity of thought be "guaranteed in advance by the inherent connection between the good and the true"; rather, Deleuze believes that philosophical thought in the modern period requires "trespass and violence," treating the thinker of thought not just as a trustworthy friend, but also as a potential enemy.[31] Truth in the modern period can only be *inferred*, tracked with suspicion but without certainty. The new plane of belief is not simply destructive or crippling, however: it is also the necessary condition for the actualization of new mental and physical

---

27. Deleuze and Guattari, *What Is Philosophy?*, 45.
28. Deleuze and Guattari, *What Is Philosophy?*, 74.
29. Deleuze and Guattari, *What Is Philosophy?*, 53.
30. Quoted and translated by Wirth, *Schelling's Practice of the Wild*, 70.
31. Deleuze, *Difference and Repetition*, 139.

experiences. As with the Christian thinkers of immanence, Deleuze emphasizes the "unforeseeable directions of thought and practice" that belief makes possible, directions to be judged not based on the *object* of a belief, but on a belief's *effect*.[32] A related feature of modern philosophy for Deleuze results from thought's encounter and struggle with the unrepresentable natural forces underlying perceptual and affective experience, forces which paradoxically "*must* but *cannot* be thought."[33] For Schelling, as we have seen in earlier chapters, these natural forces "[crush] everything that may derive from thought," leaving the reflective mind silent and even Reason prostrate before it.[34] Given modern thought's sublime confrontation with the infinite forces of cosmogenesis, its concepts can no longer be understood to represent a stable reality or to mirror a static cosmos. Instead, as Deleuze scholar Joshua Ramey argues, "what matters . . . in an idea is . . . the range of experimental possibility it opens onto."[35]

Whitehead and Schelling share with Deleuze a sense for the importance of pragmatic, experimental thinking. While some process theologians may disagree, I believe that, in the context of religious experimentation, asking whether or not God really exists is largely irrelevant.[36] What becomes pragmatically important, instead, are the sort of thoughts and practices that *belief* in God makes possible for the believer, and for the society to which the believer belongs. Thinking

---

32. Ramey, *The Hermetic Deleuze*, 13.
33. Ramey, *The Hermetic Deleuze*, 16.
34. Schelling, , 2/3, 161; quoted and translated by Matthews, *Positive Philosophy*, 48.
35. Ramey, *The Hermetic Deleuze*, 16–17.
36. If I were to offer a Whiteheadian answer to the question concerning God's existence, I would suggest that God is not a particular existent thing (a finite actual occasion), but the universal experience running through all things (the infinite actuality). Given the general validity of Whitehead's cosmological scheme, that there exists an ordered, self-organizing universe is the only evidence of God we should expect to have.

with Schelling and Whitehead after Kant requires reimagining the power of philosophical concepts so that, rather than merely reflecting or representing the real, they allow us to participate in its becoming.[37] "The power of God," writes Whitehead, "is the worship He inspires." He continues:

> The fact of the religious vision and its history of persistent expansion, is our one ground for optimism. Apart from it, human life is a flash of occasional enjoyments lighting up a mass of pain and misery, a bagatelle of transient experience.[38]

The "religious vision," as Whitehead understands it, "gives meaning to all that passes, and yet eludes apprehension," providing life with "something which is the ultimate ideal, and the hopeless quest."[39] The religious vision, though aesthetically and emotionally ultimate, cannot be monopolized by the limited doctrines of any religion in particular. What can be said is that the rising or falling tide of each religious tradition through the ages depends upon the ability of its concepts, symbols, rituals, myths, architecture, and significant personalities to inspire worship in such a way that the human soul's intuition of God is called forth naturally from spiritual resources deeper than the everyday reach of Reason.[40] As Whitehead understands it, the psychology of modern civilization has little patience for the traditional image of God as an omnipotent dictator. In this respect, such images are "fatal," since "religion collapses unless its main positions command immediacy of assent."[41]

More often than any religious image per say, Deleuze's target is the illusion of *transcendence* as such, which results whenever we "[interpret immanence] as immanent *to* Some-

---

37. Keller, *Cloud of the Impossible*, 174.
38. Whitehead, *Science and the Modern World*, 192–93.
39. Whitehead, *Science and the Modern World*, 191–92.
40. Stengers, *Thinking With Whitehead*, 133.
41. Whitehead, *Science and the Modern World*, 191.

thing."[42] The illusion of transcendence resonates with three other illusions, or "thought mirages": (1) *universality*, which results when the immanent planomenon (i.e., the plane of immanence as noumenon) is conceived as immanent "to" a concept, (2) *eternity*, which results when we forget that concepts must be created and are not waiting in the sky for thinkers to discover, and (3) *discursiveness*, which results when concepts are reduced to logical propositions.[43] These illusions become a thick fog obscuring the plane of immanence, condemning the philosophical and religious thinker alike to continually grasp after immanence as though it might be made immanent "to" something, whether it be "the great Object of contemplation [the neo-Platonic One], the Subject of reflection [the Kantian transcendental subject], or the Other subject of communication [the Husserlian intersubjective transcendental]."[44] The plane of immanence cannot itself be thought, since it provides the very condition for thought.[45] Whenever a thinker believes he has thought the plane, we can be sure he has only contemplated, reflected, or communicated an idol. Each of the three illusions described by Deleuze and Guattari resonate with Whitehead's "fallacy of misplaced concreteness." As for Schelling, he is equally suspicious of the concepts of transcendence and immanence alike: "When will it finally be understood with respect to [the philosophical religion] we teach [that] immanence and transcendence are equally empty words?" Schelling argues that his approach "invalidates this opposition" since "in it everything flows together to a god-filled world."[46] Schelling also denounces the idea that static propositions can somehow capture what is important in creative thinking:

42. Deleuze and Guattari, *What Is Philosophy?*, 45.
43. Deleuze and Guattari, *What Is Philosophy?*, 49–50.
44. Deleuze and Guattari, *What Is Philosophy?*, 51.
45. Deleuze and Guattari, *What Is Philosophy?*, 37.
46. Schelling, 2/377; excerpted and translated by Snow, *Schelling and the End of Idealism*, 86.

> [T]here are no authentic propositions . . . that would have . . . an unlimited and universal validity . . . apart from the movement through which they are produced. Movement is what is essential to knowledge. When this element of life is withdrawn, propositions die like fruit removed from the tree of life.[47]

The pure immanence of Deleuze and Guattari's philosophical planomenon can be likened to "the friend," *Wisdom*, She who provides one of the conditions for the possibility of philosophy.[48] The friend is perhaps the paradigmatic "conceptual persona" of philosophy. Conceptual personae, according to Deleuze, have a "somewhat mysterious . . . hazy existence halfway between concept and preconceptual plane, passing from one to the other."[49] Schelling prefigures Deleuze's notion of conceptual personae when he affirms that philosophical concepts "are not supposed to be merely general categories," but rather ought to be "endowed by the philosopher with actual and individual life" so as to become "poetic figures."[50] In the case of the friend, Wisdom, it must be asked what it could mean to become friendly if the friend had not once been, and could not become again, a stranger. On the philosophical planomenon, the friend and the stranger, the thought and her thinker, never engage in *discussion* with one another. Discussion is useless to philosophy, since discussions about thinking almost always mistake finished propositions for the creative conceptions underlying them, as if the latter are always easily and deliberately expressed in sentence form (i.e., the illusion of discursiveness).[51] Once the discursive mirage has captured a thinker,

---

47. Schelling, *The Ages of the World*, 4.
48. Deleuze and Guattari, *What Is Philosophy?*, 3.
49. Deleuze and Guattari, *What Is Philosophy?*, 61.
50. Schelling, *Philosophy of Mythology*, 38.
51. Deleuze and Guattari, *What Is Philosophy?*, 22–28.

thinking can only circle about itself in dialectical pursuit of a shallow truth extracted from the agonism of opinions.[52] The best dialectics end in aporia (e.g., Plato's aporietic dialogues and Kant's table of antinomies), or even better, in their own self-overcoming, or *aufhebung*, whereby opposed opinions are swallowed up into the Circle of circles as necessary moments in the historical unfolding of the absolute Concept (e.g., Hegel's *Phenomenology of Spirit*). Deleuze is not a dialectical thinker, since he denies that any exchange of philosophical opinions might finally resolve itself in absolute identity. Real differences always remain unaccounted for. There will always be a proliferating plurality of conceptual personae (not to mention the fact that every concept is itself already a multiplicity).[53] Hegel imagined that his dialectic had reached the end of philosophy, which is why he sometimes implied that he was no longer a philosopher (a lover of wisdom), but had become wise.[54] For Deleuze the friend and the stranger remain necessary illusions for philosophy. Philosophy, in other words, "requires this division of thought between [friend and stranger]."[55] The philosophical creator of concepts must remain divided against herself at the same time that she befriends the image of thought projected in the division. To cancel this division, as Hegel attempted, would be to dissolve the necessary condition of thinking. The vitality of philosophy depends upon a philosopher's willingness to dwell within (without becoming immanent "to") continual crises of agonism and reconciliation, meeting therein a proliferation of strange friends and friendly strangers. Deleuze and Guattari write:

---

52. Deleuze and Guattari, *What Is Philosophy?*, 79.
53. Deleuze and Guattari, *What Is Philosophy?*, 15.
54. Magee, *Hegel and the Hermetic Tradition*, 129.
55. Deleuze and Guattari, *What Is Philosophy?*, 69.

> It is as if the *struggle against chaos* does not take place without an affinity with the enemy, because another struggle develops and takes on more importance—*the struggle against opinion*, which claims to protect us from chaos itself.[56]

To dwell or feel at home in crisis is no easy task. But this is the task required of the philosopher in the aftermath of Kant and modern philosophy more generally, especially if he is a Christian philosopher who has accepted the risk of thinking God's incarnation. To secularize the concept of God, as Schelling, Whitehead, and Deleuze demand, is to uncover "thought's relationship with the earth,"[57] to dig up what has been buried beneath the foggy illusions of transcendence estranging humanity from its terrestrial home. To think with the Earth is undoubtedly a creative act; but it is also a matter of recovery, or *resurrection*, and of uncovering, or *apocalypse*.[58]

Christian philosophy's paradigmatic conceptual persona is Christ, "the Word" who "became flesh and dwelt among us" (John 1:14). At first blush, He may seem, like other conceptual personae, to possess a less than incarnate, hazy existence closer to the transcendence of spirit or heaven than the immanence of any earthly topos. John signals this confusion when he writes that "The Light shines in the darkness, and the darkness did not comprehend it" (John 1:5).[59] Indeed, traditional theology has all too often emphasized Christ's transcendence, making Him more divine than human (and making humanity more sinful than graced). Despite His initially ghostly outline, Christ's ideality is not in any way *abstract*: He is rather an *intercessor*, the *seed* of a

---

56. Deleuze and Guattari, *What Is Philosophy?*, 203.
57. Deleuze and Guattari, *What Is Philosophy?*, 69.
58. These Christological concepts resonate with Deleuze and Guattari's geophilosophical concepts of "reterritorialization" and "deterritorialization," respectively.
59. New American Standard Bible.

peculiarly Christian mode of thinking. "A particular conceptual persona," writes Deleuze, "who perhaps did not exist before us, thinks in us."[60] Of Christ it is said that He was both in the beginning before us and will be in the end after us. His omnipresence (*parousia*) lays out a uniquely immanent image of thought based on *incarnation*. The Christian plane of immanence demands a creation of concepts whose defining problematic, or spiritual ordeal, is *death*, and whose solution, should it be realized, is an earthly *resurrection*. The Christian planomenon is unique because it is founded upon the birth, death, and resurrection of God on Earth, which is to say it depends upon the possibility of the *becoming-immanent of transcendence itself*. Only by surviving the incarnational ordeal can the Christian philosopher become inhabited by *living* thinking. "My old self," writes Paul, "has been crucified with Christ. It is no longer I who live, but Christ lives in me" (Galatians 2:20).

Like the philosophical friend, Christ's teachings can appear strange. "I tell you," He said, "Love your enemies and pray for those who persecute you" (Matthew 5:44). How can an earthly human being—normatively tied to family, friend, race, and nation—possibly live up to such an impossible, indeed *infinite*, demand? It is a demand that does violence to normal opinion and good sense. Nonetheless, this demand provides the peculiarly Christian problematic, an ordeal whose resolution requires *becoming-incarnate*, and thereby participating in bringing about an as yet unrealized providential plan(e), "on earth, as it is in heaven" (Matthew 6:10). This is the strangeness of the "Galilean origin" of Christianity mentioned by Whitehead: it generates a religious imaginary in which the persuasive love of a worldly advocate replaces the coercive power of a transcendent dictator. While Whitehead did not believe it possible, or even desirable, to

---

60. Deleuze and Guattari, *What Is Philosophy?*, 69.

construct a doctrinal unity out of the world's diversity of religions, he argued:

> that it is possible, amid these differences, to reach a general agreement as to those elements, in intimate human experience and general history, which we select to exemplify that ultimate theme of the divine immanence, as a completion required by our cosmological outlook.[61]

In other words, while humanity will certainly continue to disagree as to the particular qualitative aspects of religious facts and their proper moral interpretations, some coordination of these facts along a single plane of immanence can at least be attempted. Whitehead's cosmological candidate for the ultimate religious theme is Divine Eros. His philosophical intervention into traditional theology aimed to transform the transcendent God of "coercive forces wielding the thunder"[62] into the creaturely God of persuasion, "which slowly and in quietness [operates] by love."[63] Schelling similarly remarks that the natural world "is not coerced but is rather voluntarily subjected" to divine inspiration.[64] Given humanity's recently seized, god-like powers of technology, sustaining our planetary civilization would seem to depend upon the realization of such a secular Earth ethos. Our civilization is in dire need of a world-renewing metaphysical consensus regarding both the nature of divinity and the divinity of Nature. If we are unable to attune our human beliefs and practices to the divinity of the world, we run the risk of destroying it. According to Whitehead, the spirit of religion, though it is from time to time "explained away, distorted, and buried," has never once entirely left us "since the travel

---

61. Whitehead, *Adventures of Ideas*, 161.
62. Whitehead, *Adventures of Ideas*, 166.
63. Whitehead, *Process and Reality*, 343.
64. Schelling, *The Ages of the World*, 46.

of mankind towards civilization."⁶⁵ It can be said, however, that whenever religion takes flight from worldly concerns, it is the surest sign of a world nearing its end.

Whitehead traces the gradual realization of the concept of divine immanence through a "threefold revelation" stretching over approximately twelve hundred years: (1) it begins in Athens with an intellectual innovation by Plato, (2) then passes into Jerusalem where the person of Jesus Christ exemplified the apocalyptic (ἀποκάλυψις, to "un-cover") power of Plato's concept, and (3) finally it culminates in a metaphysical interpretation of these events generated during the formative period of Christian theology.⁶⁶

1. Whitehead regularly praises Plato's depth of intuition. Just as often, he admits Plato's failure to achieve a coherent overall statement of his conceptual scheme: he was "the greatest metaphysician, the poorest systematic thinker."67 It is for one concept in particular, though, that Whitehead was led to crown Plato "the wisest of men": the idea that

   the divine persuasion [Eros] is the foundation of the order of the world, but that it could only produce such a measure of harmony as amid brute forces [Chaos] it was possible to accomplish.⁶⁸

2. It was this idea, conceived in principle by Plato, that the person of Jesus Christ was to reveal in actual deed. Though the historical records of His life are

---

65. Whitehead, *Adventures of Ideas*, 172.
66. Whitehead, *Adventures of Ideas*, 166. While contemporary historians of Christianity may dispute precisely what was at stake during the formative period of Christian thought, Whitehead's scheme at least offers a sound basis for philosophical construction.
67. Whitehead, *Adventures of Ideas*, 166.
68. Whitehead, *Adventures of Ideas*, 160.

scattered and inconsistent, "there can be no doubt," writes Whitehead, "as to what elements . . . have evoked a response from all that is best in human nature":

> The Mother, the Child, and the bare manger: the lowly man, homeless and self-forgetful, with his message of peace, love, and sympathy: the suffering, the agony, the tender words as life ebbed, the final despair: and the whole with the authority of supreme victory.[69]

3. Finally, it was the early Church fathers who made the first sustained effort to grope towards a coherent account of God's persuasive agency in the world.[70] The major fruit of their labor was the direct statement of the divine immanence in the world in the third person of the Trinity. Unfortunately, despite this theological statement, the Church fathers failed to attain adequate metaphysical generality because they still exempted an infinite God from the categories applicable to the finite actual occasions composing the spatiotemporal world.[71] Like Plato in many of his written dialogues, they were unable to disavow the notion of a derivative physical world poorly imitating the Ideas eternally realized in the mind of a disincarnate God.

Deleuze's reading of Plato's dialogues destroys the Platonic two-world theory of perfect Ideas poorly copied by sensory images, but he is allured by Plato's alternative conception of pure Difference. Where Aristotle reduces difference to the remainder derived from the comparison of similars, understanding Plato requires risking the sanity of one's ego in pursuit of the dark, difficult, and dangerous Idea of *Difference in itself*. Plato's is an ontology of singularity, where

---

69. Whitehead, *Adventures of Ideas*, 167.
70. Whitehead, *Adventures of Ideas*, 167–69.
71. Whitehead, *Adventures of Ideas*, 169.

knowing an individual (be it ideal or actual) requires directly intuiting its uniquely authentic line of descent, rather than representing, identifying, or abstracting its general form. As Ramey puts it, "Knowledge is not a matter of generalization but of participation." He continues:

> The claim to participation is not simply the claim to be identified as a member of a class or token of a type. It is a claim to have passed a test or to have a basis for one's claim . . . . It is the difference an "immediate fact" of participation makes . . . . It is the selection of an icon from within a prodigious field of idols, false images.[72]

The difference is *initiatory*, "acquired by each person on their own account."[73] That is, it has to do with undertaking the descent into the chaos of the underworld, crossing the threshold between life and death, and returning to the realm of the living to tell the tale. As many scholar-practitioners know, philosophy without initiatory experience quickly turns stale, becoming overly pedantic and increasingly irrelevant to actual life. Without ritually enacted stories to perform on infinite planes stretching across the relative horizons of common sense experience, a philosopher's concepts cannot catch fire and acquire the persuasive agency of divine personality. The philosopher's desire to incarnate divine Ideas kindles a creative activity, allowing the clear light of these Ideas to be imaginatively ingressed into the concrete colors of common appearance in the form of physically instantiated symbols. Said otherwise, after the Christian-Platonic initiation, the philosopher's world is transfigured into a problematic network of occult icons whose meaning is uncovered intuitively through talismanic thinking. To think talismanically is to think pragmatically, to create sensible concepts that vibrate

---

72. Ramey, *The Hermetic Deleuze*, 118.
73. Deleuze, "Mathesis, Science, and Philosophy," ix–xxiv.

into the world, enacting new erotic bonds and shared fields of feeling. Ideas are thus ingressed into appearances, becoming symbols, moments of discontinuity in extensive physical space-time out of which the intensive oddity of self-reference emerges.[74] We become like God, poets of the world. "Why do we say that the word 'tree'—spoken or written—is a symbol to us for trees?" asks Whitehead. He continues, offering the following example of talismanic thinking:

> Both the word itself and the trees themselves enter into our experience on equal terms; and it would be just as sensible . . . for trees to symbolize the word "tree" as for the word to symbolize trees . . . . For example, if you are a poet and wish to write a lyric on trees, you will walk into the forest in order that the trees may suggest the appropriate words. Thus for the poet in his ecstasy—or perhaps, agony—of composition the trees are the symbols and the words are the meaning.[75]

Recursive oddities like the poet's tree unfold themselves into the physical plane like the organs of a developing embryo, erupting as problematic forces requiring of the flesh-hewn ego attempting to know them not new representations of a supposedly extra-mental or extra-bodily world, but self-immolation through eternally recurring death and resurrection. "These are the forces of that inner life" that the philosophically religious person must intimate, Schelling tells us, and "not without terror." These forces are the creative source of Life's "eternal recommencement," whereby it "continually incinerates itself and again rejuvenates itself from the ash."[76] Such incarnational thinking is an ecstatic, even violent act, always killing the neurons which support it, "making the brain a set

---

74. Deleuze and Guattari, *What Is Philosophy?*, 21–22.
75. Whitehead, *Symbolism*, 11–12.
76. Schelling, *The Ages of the World*, 20.

of little deaths that puts constant death within us."[77]

Whitehead, Schelling, and Deleuze's immanent and incarnational readings of Christianity, along with their retrieval of Plato's participatory doctrines of Persuasion and Difference, provide crucial ingredients in the world-renewing medicinal brew that is sorely needed by the contemporary world. Their attempts to secularize the concept of God follow from their belief in divine immanence, and in the capacity of an initiated humanity to participate in the ongoing work of the divine in an unfinished cosmogenesis. "God," said Whitehead, near the end of his life,

> is in the world, or nowhere, creating continually in us and around us. This creative principle is everywhere, in animate and so-called inanimate matter, in the ether, water, earth, human hearts . . . . In so far as man partakes of this creative process does he partake of the divine, of God, and that participation is his immortality, reducing the question of whether his individuality survives death . . . to . . . irrelevancy. His true destiny as co-creator in the universe is his dignity and his grandeur.[78]

Schelling referred to this co-creative work as *theurgy*, the meaning and goal of which

> is nothing other than to draw the Godhead down to what is lower, to produce the guiding concatenation . . . through which the Godhead would be able to act in nature.[79]

Discovering, valuing, and becoming-with modes of existence beyond those narrowly defined by our biological species, *Homo sapiens*, will surely help us survive the impending ecological crisis. But remembering the community

---

77. Deleuze and Guattari, *What Is Philosophy?*, 216.
78. Price, *Dialogues*, 297.
79. Schelling, *The Ages of the World*, 72.

of creatures out of whom we are composed and with whom we will always continue to compose ourselves also entails taking responsibility for our archetypal potential as the *Anthropos*, "the combinatory point of the entire cosmos," as Schelling describes it.[80] If I were to hazard a single sentence to describe the essence of Schelling's *oeuvre*, I would say he strove to narrate the becoming of the universe as the birth of God in the human soul—*cosmogenesis* as *anthropogenesis*. Again, this is not to say that our particular species is the necessary telos of all things, the end toward which all Nature tends. Our species is merely one example, perhaps the most ingressed on our planet, of a general archetypal lure guiding all creatures in this cosmos toward a wiser and more loving expressions of creation. In Whitehead's terms, Anthropos is God's consequent nature (what God is *becoming*), while Cosmos is God's primordial nature (what God *is*).[81] Though it is not an absolute distinction, what sets our species apart from all other animals on Earth is our capacity for *conscious* devotion to divine ideals like truth, freedom, beauty, love, and wisdom. God's ongoing work in the world to realize these ideals can be accomplished *through us* only if we are willing to participate. That "God is dead" means only, in Keller's terms, that the "creative source is no longer conceivable as omnipotently producing a world and directing it to its End."[82] The God of coercive commandments is dead, murdered by the Man to whom (as the Biblical story goes) He gave the World. Today, as even the World itself is dying at the hands of men, I offer this book as a humble attempt to help set the philosophical stage for the resurrection of a God of loving persuasion, a God Keller asks us to imagine "as unfolding *in and through* [the] world, as in its own flesh . . . as

---

80. Schelling, *The Ages of the World*, 71–72.
81. Or, metaphorically speaking, what God *was*. In Schellingian terms, "*Urnatur*, what in nature is oldest in nature" (Wirth, *Schelling's Practice of the Wild*, 37).
82. Keller, *Cloud of the Impossible*, 164.

hospitable to the indeterminate emergence of finite bodies with creativities all their own."[83] It could be that the growth of this new God in conscious human hearts is granting us the eyes to see the whole creation, not as dead or dying, but as groaning and suffering the pains of childbirth together with us (Romans 8:22).

---

83. Keller, *Cloud of the Impossible*, 164–65.

References

Abram, David. 1996. *The Spell of the Sensuous: Perception and Language in a More-Than-Human World*. New York: Vintage Books.

Adams, George. 1965. *Physical and Ethereal Spaces*. London: Rudolf Steiner Press.

Adams, George, and Olive Whicher. 1982. *The Plant Between Sun and Earth*. London: Rudolf Steiner Press.

Apffel-Marglin, Frédérique. 2008. *Rhythms of Life: Enacting the World with the Goddesses of Orissa*. Oxford: Oxford University Press.

Aristotle. *De Anima*. 2009. Translated by J. A. Smith. Retrieved from http://classics.mit.edu/Aristotle/soul.html

Aurobindo, Sri. 1995. *Bhagavad Gita and Its Message*. Edited by Anibaran Roy. Pondicherry, India: Sri Aurobindo Ashram Trust.

Auxier, Randall, and Gary Herstein. 2015, December. "The Quantum of Explanation: Whitehead's Radical Empiricism" (unpublished manuscript).

Bachelard, Gaston. 2005. *On Poetic Imagination and Reverie*. Translated by Colette Gaudin. Putnam, CT: Spring Publications.

Barfield, Owen. 1980. "*Towards* Interviews Owen Barfield." *Towards* 1 (6): 6–10.

Beiser, Frederick. 2002. *German Idealism: The Struggle Against Subjectivism, 1781–1801*. Cambridge, MA: Harvard University Press.

———. 2014. *After Hegel: German Philosophy, 1840–1900*. Oxfordshire: Princeton University Press.

Bergson, Henri. 2005. *Creative Evolution*. Translation by Arthur Mitchell. NY: Barnes and Noble.

Bergson, Henri. 2007. *The Creative Mind: An Introduction to Metaphysics*. Translation by Mabelle L. Andison. Mineola, NY: Dover.

Blake, William. 1977. *The Portable William Blake*. London: Penguin Books.

Boehm, Omri. 2014. *Kant's Critique of Spinoza*. Oxford: Oxford University Press.

Bortoft, Henri. 1996. *The Wholeness of Nature: Goethe's Way Toward a Science of Conscious Participation in Nature*. Hudson, NY: Lindisfarne Press.

Braeckman, Antoon. 1985. "Whitehead and German Idealism: A Poetic Heritage." *Process Studies* 14 (4): 265–86.

Broad, C. D. 1930. *Fives Types of Ethical Theory*. London: Routledge and Kegan Paul.

Buhner, Harrod Stephen. 2014. *Plant Intelligence and the Imaginal Realm:*

Beyond the Doors of Perception into the Dreaming Earth. Rochester, VT: Bear & Company.

Čapek, Milič. 1971. *Bergson and Modern Physics: A Reinterpretation and Re-Evaluation.* Dordrecht, Holland: D. Reidel Publishing.

Coleridge, Samuel Taylor. 2013. *Biographia Literaria.* Last updated January 26. http://www.gutenberg.org/files/6081/6081-h/6081-h.htm

Connolly, William. 2013. *The Fragility of Things: Self-Organizing Processes, Neoliberal Fantasies, and Democratic Activism.* Durham: Duke University Press.

Crosby, Donald. 2007. "Two Perspectives on Metaphysical Perspectivism: Nietzsche and Whitehead." *The Pluralist* 2 (3): 57–76. Retrieved from http://www.jstor.org/stable/20708915

Deleuze, Gilles. 1978. "Kant seminar, Cours Vincennes" (Lecture, April 4). Translated by Melissa McMahon. Retrieved from http://www.webdeleuze.com/php/texte.php?cle=65&groupe=Kant&langue=2

———. 1994. *Difference and Repetition.* Translated by Paul Patton. NY: Columbia University Press.

———. 1996. *Kant's Critical Philosophy: The Doctrine of the Faculties.* Translated by Hugh Tomlinson and Barbara Habberjam. Minneapolis: University of Minnesota.

———. 2011. "Mathesis, Science, and Philosophy." Translated by Robin Mackay. *Collapse: Philosophical Research and Development* 3, 140–155.

Deleuze, Gilles, and Felix Guattari. 1987. *A Thousand Plateaus: Capitalism and Schizophrenia.* Translated by Brian Massumi. Minneapolis: University of Minnesota Press.

———. 1994. *What Is Philosophy?* Translated by Hugh Tomlinson and Graham Burchell. NY: Columbia University Press.

Descartes, René. 1916. *The Discourse on Method.* Translated by John Veitch. London: J. M. Dent and Sons.

———. 2008. *Meditations on First Philosophy.* Translated by Michael Moriarty. Oxford: Oxford University Press.

Desmet, Ronald. 2007. "The Rebirth of the Ether." In *Chromatikon III: Yearbook of Philosophy in Process/Annuaire de la philosophie en procès*, edited by Michel Weber and Pierfrancesco Basile, 69–93. Leuven, Belgium: Presses universitaires de Louvain.

———. November 2014."Poincaré and Whitehead on Intuition and Logic in Mathematics" (lecture, University of Liège). Retrieved from https://www.academia.edu/10889792/Poincar%C3%A9_and_Whitehead_on_Intuition_and_Logic_in_Mathematics

Desmet, Ronny, and Timothy Eastman. 2009. "Relativity Physics." In

Handbook of Whiteheadian Process Thought, Volume One, edited by Michel Weber and William Desmond, Jr., 236–60. Frankfurt: Ontos Verlag.

Döderlein, Johann Ludwig, ed. 1975. *Brief über den Tod Carolines vom 2. Oktober, 1809.* Stuttgart-Bad Cannstatt: Frommann-Holzboog.

Fawcett, Douglas. 1921. *Divine Imagining: An Essay on the First Principles of Philosophy.* London: Macmillan.

Förster, Eckart. 2000. *Kant's Final Synthesis.* Cambridge, MA: Harvard University Press.

———. 2012. *The Twenty-Five Years of Philosophy: A Systematic Reconstruction.* Cambridge, MA: Harvard University Press.

Galilei, Galileo. 1957. "The Assayer." In *Discoveries and Opinions of Galileo*, translated by Stillman Drake, 231–80. NY: Doubleday.

Gare, Arran. 2012. "The Roots of Postmodernism." In *Process and Difference: Between Cosmological and Poststructuralist Postmodernisms.* Edited by Catherine Keller and Anne Daniell. Albany: SUNY Press.

Grant, Iain Hamilton. 2004. "'Philosophy Become Genetic': The Physics of the World Soul." In *The New Schelling.* Edited by Judith Norman and Alistair Welchman. NY: Continuum.

———. 2008. *Philosophies of Nature After Schelling.* NY: Continuum.

Griffin, David Ray. 1998. *Unsnarling the World-Knot: Consciousness, Freedom, and the Mind-Body Problem.* Eugene, OR: Wipf and Stock.

Hallward, Peter. 2006. *Out of This World: Deleuze and the Philosophy of Creation.* London: Verso Books.

Hallyn, Fernand. 1987. *The Poetic Structure of the World: Copernicus and Galileo.* Translated by Donald M. Leslie. NY: Urzone.

Hamrick, William, and Jan Van Der Veken. 2011. *Nature and Logos: A Whiteheadian Key to Merleau-Ponty's Fundamental Thought.* Albany: SUNY Press.

Hartshorne, Charles and William L. Reese, eds. 2000. *Philosophers Speak of God.* Amherst, NY: Humanity Books.

Hartshorne, Charles, and Creighton Peden. 2010. *Whitehead's View of Reality.* Cambridge: Cambridge Scholars Publishing.

Hegel, Georg Wilhelm Friedrich. 1896. *Hegel's Philosophy of Right.* Translated by S. W. Dyde. London: George Bell and Sons.

———. 2004. *Encyclopedia of the Philosophical Sciences.* Translated by A.V. Miller. Oxford: The Clarendon Press.

———. (1896) 2016. *Lectures on the History of Philosophy: Section Three, Recent German Philosophy—D. Schelling.* Translated by E. S. Haldane. Accessed April 4. Retrieved from https://www.marxists.org/reference/archive/hegel/works/hp/hpschell.htm

Heidegger, Martin. 1973. *Kant and the Problem of Metaphysics*. Translated by Richard Taft. Indianapolis: Indiana University Press.

———. 1985. *Schelling's Treatise on the Essence of Human Freedom*. Translated by Joan Stambaugh. Athens: Ohio University Press.

Henry, Granville C. 1983. "Whitehead's Philosophical Response." In *Explorations in Whitehead's Philosophy*. Edited by Lewis Ford and George Kline. NY: Fordham University Press.

Hermes. *The Emerald Tablet*. Various Translations. Accessed 1/27/2016. http://www.sacred-texts.com/alc/emerald.htm

Homer. 1998. *The Odyssey*. Translated by Robert Fitzgerald. NY: Farrar, Straus, and Giroux.

Horace. (1835) 2016. *The Epistles*. Translated by Philip Francis. NY: Harper and Brothers. Retrieved from https://archive.org/details/horace01phaegoog

Howe, J. Thomas. 2003. *Faithful to the Earth: Nietzsche and Whitehead on God and the Meaning of Human Life*. Lanham, MD: Rowman and Littlefield.

Hume, David. 1874. *A Treatise on Human Nature: Being an Attempt to Introduce the Experimental Method of Reasoning into Moral Subjects* and *Dialogues on Natural Religion*. Edited by T. H. Green and T. H. Grose. London: Longmans, Green, and Co.

———. 2007. *An Enquiry Concerning Human Understanding: And Other Writings*. Edited by Stephen Buckle. Cambridge: Cambridge University Press.

Husserl, Edmund. 1981. *Husserl, Shorter Works*. Translated by Fred Kersten. Edited by Peter McCormick and Frederick A. Elliston. Indiana: University of Notre Dame Press.

Huxley, Aldous. 1962. *Island: A Novel*. NY: HarperCollins.

James, William. 1920. *A Pluralistic Universe*. NY: Longmans, Green, and Co.

———. 1996. *Some Problems in Philosophy*. Lincoln: University of Nebraska Press.

Jaspers, Karl. 1955. *Schelling: Grofie und Verhangnis*. Munich: R. Piper.

Kant, Immanuel. (1781) 1998. *Critique of Pure Reason*. Translated by Paul Gruyer and Allen Wood. Cambridge: Cambridge University Press.

———. (1783) 1997. *Prolegomena to Any Future Metaphysics*. Translated by Gary Hatfield. Cambridge: Cambridge University Press.

———. (1784) 2016. "Idea for a Universal History with a Cosmopolitan Purpose." Translated by Lewis White Beck. Accessed April 4. Retrieved from https://www.marxists.org/reference/subject/ethics/kant/universal-history.htm#n1.

———. (1785) 2012. *Groundwork of the Metaphysics of Morals*. Translated by Mary Gregor and Jens Timmermann. Cambridge: Cambridge University Press.

———. (1786) 2004. *Metaphysical Foundations of Natural Science*. Translated by Michael Friedman. Cambridge: Cambridge University Press.

———. (1788) 1997. *Critique of Practical Reason*. Translated by Mary J. Gregor. Cambridge: Cambridge University Press.

———. (1790) 2005. *Critique of Judgment*. Translated by J. H. Bernard. Mineola, NY: Dover.

———. (1798) 2006. *Anthropology From a Pragmatic Point of View*. Translated by Robert B. Louden. Cambridge: Cambridge University Press.

———. (1804) 1993. *Opus Postumum*. Edited and translated by Eckart Förster. Translated by Michael Rosen. Cambridge: Cambridge University Press.

Kaufmann, Walter. 1975. *Nietzsche: Philosopher, Psychologist, Antichrist*. Princeton: Princeton University Press.

Kauffman, Walter. 1980. *Discovering the Mind, Volume One: Goethe, Kant, and Hegel*. NY: McGraw-Hill.

Keller, Catherine. 1986. *From a Broken Web: Separation, Sexism, and Self*. Boston: Beacon Press.

———. 2003 *Face of the Deep: A Theology of Becoming*. London: Routledge.

———. 2015. *Cloud of the Impossible: Negative Theology and Planetary Entanglement*. NY: Columbia University Press.

Kelley, James. 2011. *Anatomyzing Divinity: Studies in Science, Esotericism and Political Theology*. Walterville, OR: Trine Day.

Kelly, Sean. 2010. *Coming Home: The Birth and Transformation of the Planetary Era*. Great Barrington, MA: Lindisfarne Books.

King, Martin Luther, Jr. 1994. *The Papers of Martin Luther King, Jr. Volume 2: Rediscovering Precious Values, July 1951–November 1955*. Edited by Clayborne Carson, Ralph Luker, Penny A. Russel, and Peter Hollorans. Berkeley: UC Press.

———. "Remaining Awake Through a Great Revolution" (transcript). Speech delivered at Oberlin College, June 1965. Accessed April 5. Retrieved from www.oberlin.edu/external/EOG/BlackHistoryMonth/MLK/CommAddress.html

Kline, Moris. 1967. *Mathematics for the Nonmathematician*. Toronto: General Publishing Company.

Latour, Bruno. 2004. "Whose Cosmos, Which Cosmopolitics?" *Common Knowledge* 10 (3): 450–462.

Lawrence, Joseph. 2005. "Philosophical Religion and the Quest for Authenicity." In *Schelling Now: Contemporary Readings*. Edited by Jason Wirth. Bloomington: Indiana University Press.

Lederman, Leon. 2006. *The God Particle: If the Universe is the Answer, What is the Question?* NY: Mariner.

Leibniz, Gottfried Wilhelm. 1989. *Philosophical Papers and Letters*. Translated by Leroy E. Loemker. Dordrecht: Kluwer Academic Publishers.

Lubbock, Richard. "Alfred North Whitehead: Philosopher for the Muddleheaded." Retrieved from http://www3.sympatico.ca/rlubbock/ANW.html

Lucas, Jr., George. 1989. *The Rehabilitation of Whitehead: An Analytic and Historical Assessment of Process Philosophy*. Albany: SUNY Press.

Magee, Glenn. 2001. *Hegel and the Hermetic Tradition*. London: Cornell University Press.

Marder, Michael. 2013. "The Philosopher's Plant 3.0: Plotinus' Anonymous 'Great Plant'" (blog post). *Project Syndicate*, January 4. Retrieved from http://www.project-syndicate.org/blog/the-philosopher-s-plant-3-0--plotinus--anonymous--great-plant

———. 2013. *Plant-Thinking: A Philosophy of Vegetal Life*. New York: Columbia University Press.

———. 2014. *The Philosopher's Plant: An Intellectual Herbarium*. New York: Columbia University Press.

Marquet, J. F. 1992. "Schelling." In *Encyclopédie Philosophique Universelle*, edited by A., Jacob, 2085–93. Paris: Presses Universitaires de France.

Matthews, Bruce. 2011. *Schelling's Organic Form of Philosophy: Life as the Schema of Freedom*. Albany: SUNY Press.

McGilchrist, Iain. 2021. *The Matter With Things: Our Brains, Our Delusions and the Unmaking of the World*. London: Perspectiva.

Merleau-Ponty, Maurice. 1994. *La Nature, Notes, Cours du College de France*. Edited by Dominique Seglard. Paris: Editions de Seuil.

———. 2003. *Nature: Course Notes from the Collège de France*. Evanston, IL: Northwestern University Press.

Miller, Elaine P. 2002. *The Vegetative Soul: From Philosophy of Nature to Subjectivity in the Feminine*. Albany: SUNY Press.

Murphy, Michael. 2015. "The Emergence of Evolutionary Panentheism." In *Beyond Physicalism: Toward a Reconciliation of Science and Spirituality*. Edited by Edward F.Kelly, Adam Crabtree, and Paul Marshall. Lanham, MD: Rowman and Littlefield.

Naragon, Steve. 2014. "Kant's Career in German Idealism," In *The Palgrave Handbook of German Idealism*. Edited by Altman, M. New

York: Palgrave Macmillian.

Nassar, Dalia. 2010. "From a Philosophy of Self to a Philosophy of Nature: Goethe and the Development of Schelling's Naturphilosophie." In *Archiv für Geschichte der Philosophie* 92 (3): 304–21.

New American Standard Bible. 1960. New York: Thomas Nelson.

Nietzsche, Friedrich. 1920. *The Anti-Christ*. Translated by H. L. Mencken. New York: Knopf.

———. 1968. *Werke: Kritische Gesamtausgabe*. Edited by Giorgio Colli and Mazzino Montinari. Berlin: Walter de Gruyter.

———. 1968. *The Will to Power*. Translated by Walter Kaufmann. New York: Random House.

———. 1974. *On the Genealogy of Morals and Ecce Homo*. Translated by Walter Kaufmann. New York: Vintage.

———. 1980. *The Portable Nietzsche*. Translated by Walter Kaufmann. New York: Random House.

———. 1986. *Human, All Too Human: A Book for Free Spirits*. Translated by R. J. Hollingdale. Cambridge: Cambridge University Press.

———. 2001. *The Gay Science: With a Prelude in German Rhymes and an Appendix of Songs*. Translated by Bernard Williams and Josefine Nauckhoff. Cambridge: Cambridge University Press.

———. 2006. *The Nietzsche Reader*. Edited by Keith Ansell Pearson and Duncan Large. Malden, MA: Blackwell.

Norman, Judith. 2004. "Schelling and Nietzsche: Willing and Time." In *The New Schelling*. Edited by Judith Norman and Alistair Welchman. New York: Continuum.

Panikkar, Raimon. 1993. *The Cosmotheandric Experience: Emerging Religious Consciousness*. Maryknoll, NY: Orbis.

———. 2004. *Christophany: The Fullness of Man*. Maryknoll, NY: Orbis.

———. 2006. *The Experience of God: Icons of the Mystery*. Minneapolis: Fortress Press.

———. 2010. *The Rhythm of Being*. Maryknoll, NY: Orbis.

Penrose, Roger. 2011. *Cycles of Time: An Extraordinary New View of the Universe*. New York: Knopf.

Pinkard, Terry. 2002. *German Philosophy, 1760–1860: The Legacy of Idealism*. Cambridge: Cambridge University Press.

Plato. 1997. *Complete Works*. Edited by John M. Cooper. Cambridge: Hackett.

Plotinus. 2009. *The Six Enneads*. Translated by Stephen Mackenna and B. S. Page. Retrieved from http://classics.mit.edu/Plotinus/enneads.html

Plutarch. 1936. *Moralia, Volume V: Isis and Osiris*. Translated by Frank

Cole Babbitt. Cambridge, MA: Harvard University Press.

Pred, Ralph. 2005. *Onflow: Dynamics of Consciousness and Experience*. Boston: MIT Press.

Price, Lucien. 1954. *Dialogues of Alfred North Whitehead*. New York: Mentor Books.

Radhakrishnan, Sarvepalli and Charles A. Moore. 1957. *A Sourcebook in Indian Philosophy*. Princeton: Princeton University Press.

Ramey, Joshua. 2012. *The Hermetic Deleuze: Philosophy and Spiritual Ordeal*. London: Duke University Press.

Sallis, John. 2000. *Force of Imagination: The Sense of the Elemental*. Indianapolis: Indiana University Press.

Schelling, Friedrich Wilhelm Joseph. (1797) 1988. *Ideas for a Philosophy of Nature*. Cambridge: Cambridge University Press.

———. 1798. *Von der Weltseele: eine Hypothese der höhern Physik zur Erklärung des allgemeinen Organismus*. Hamburg: F. Perthes.

———. (1798) 2010. *On the World-Soul*. Translated by Iain Hamilton Grant. *Collapse: Philosophical Research and Development* 6, 66–95.

———. (1799) 2004. *First Outline of a System of the Philosophy of Nature*. Albany: SUNY Press.

———. (1800). 1978. *System of Transcendental Idealism*. Charlottesville: University Press of Virginia.

———. (1804) 2010. *Philosophy and Religion*. Translated by Klaus Ottmann. Putnam, CT: Spring Publications.

———. (1809) 2006. *Philosophical Investigations into the Essence of Human Freedom*. Translated by Jeff Love and Johannes Schmidt. Albany: SUNY Press.

———. (1810) 2002. *Clara, Or on Nature's Connection to the Spirit World*. Albany: SUNY Press.

———. (1813) 1997. *Abyss of Freedom/Ages of the World*. Translated by Judith Norman. Ann Arbor: University of Michigan Press.

———. (1815) 2000. *The Ages of the World*. Translated by Jason Wirth. Albany: SUNY Press.

———. (1827) 1994. *On the History of Modern Philosophy*. Translated by Andrew Bowie. Cambridge: Cambridge University Press.

———. 1861. *Schellings sämmtliche Werke*. Stuttgart: Verlag.

———. (1972) 2007. *The Grounding of Positive Philosophy*. Translated by Bruce Matthews. Albany: SUNY Press.

———. 1990. *System der Weltalter: Münchener Vorlesung 1827–28 in einer Nachschrift von Ernst von Lasaulux*. Edited by Siegbert Peetz. Frankfurt am Main: Vittorio Klostermann.

———. 2007. *Historical-Critical Introduction to the Philosophy of Mythol-

ogy. Translated by Mason Richey and Markus Zisselberger. Albany: SUNY Press.

Schickler, Jonael. 2005. *Metaphysics as Christology: An Odyssey of the Self from Kant and Hegel to Steiner*. Hampshire, UK: Ashgate.

Schindler, D. C. 2012. *The Perfection of Freedom: Schiller, Schelling, and Hegel between the Ancients and the Moderns*. Eugene, OR: Cascade Books.

Schlutz, Alexander. 2009. *Mind's World: Imagination and Subjectivity from Descartes to Romanticism*. Seattle: University of Washington Press.

Shaviro, Steven. 2009. *Without Criteria: Kant, Whitehead, Deleuze, and Aesthetics*. Cambridge, MA: The MIT Press.

Segall, Matthew David. 2014. *The Re-Emergence of Schelling: Philosophy in a Time of Emergency*. Saarbrücken, Germany: Lambert Academic Publishing.

———. 2016. "Minding Time in an Archetypal Cosmos." *Archai: The Journal of Archetypal Cosmology* 5.

———. 2021. *Physics of the World-Soul: Whitehead's Adventure in Cosmology*. Grasmere, ID: SacraSage Press.

Sherman, Jacob Holsinger. 2009. "No Werewolves in Theology?: Transcendence, Immanence, and Becoming-Divine in Gilles Deleuze." In *Modern Theology* 25 (1): 1–20.

Snow, Dale. 1996. *Schelling and the End of Idealism*. Albany: SUNY Press.

Steiner, Rudolf. 1947. *Knowledge of the Higher Worlds and Its Attainment*. Translated by George Metaxa. Spring Valley, NY: Anthroposophic Press. Retrieved from http://wn.rsarchive.org/Books/GA010/English/RSPC1947/GA010_cover.html

———. 1984. *The Spirit in the Realm of Plants*. Translated by G. F. Karnow. Spring Valley, NY: Mercury Press. Retrieved from http://wn.rsarchive.org/Lectures/19101208p01.html

———. 1995. *Intuitive Thinking as a Spiritual Path: A Philosophy of Freedom*. Translated by Michael Lipson. Hudson, NY: Anthroposophic Press.

———. 2020. *Interdisciplinary Astronomy: Third Scientific Course* (CW 323 lectures delivered in 1921 in Dornach, Switzerland). Translated by Frederick Amrine. Hudson, NY: Steiner Books.

Stengers, Isabelle. 2011. *Thinking With Whitehead: A Free and Wild Creation of Concepts*. Cambridge, MA: Harvard University Press.

Stone, Alison. 2005. *Petrified Intelligence: Nature in Hegel's Philosophy*. Albany: SUNY Press.

Toulmin, Stephen. 1990. *Cosmopolis: The Hidden Agenda of Modernity*. Chicago: University of Chicago Press.

Vassányi, Miklós. 2011. *Anima Mundi: The Rise of the World Soul Theory in Modern German Philosophy*. Dordrecht: Springer.

Warnock, Mary. 1976. *Imagination*. Berkeley: UC Press.

Watts, Alan. (1966) 1989. *The Book On the Taboo Against Knowing Who You Are*. New York: Random House.

Weber, Michel. 2011. "On a Certain Blindness in Political Matters." In *Cosmos and History: The Journal of Natural and Social Philosophy* 7 (2): 204–35.

Whicher, Olive. 1977. George Adams: Interpreter of Rudolf Steiner: his life and a selection of his essays. Sussex: Henry Goulden Ltd.

Whitehead, Alfred North. 1898. *A Treatise on Universal Algebra, with Applications*. Cambridge: Cambridge University Press.

———. (1905) 1953. "On Mathematical Concepts of the Material World." In *Alfred North Whitehead, An Anthology*, edited by F. S. C. Northrop and Mason W. Gross, 7–82. NY: Macmillan.

———. 1919. *An Enquiry Concerning the Principles of Natural Knowledge*. London: Cambridge University Press.

———. 1920. *The Concept of Nature*. Cambridge: Cambridge University Press.

———. (1922) 2007. *The Principle of Relativity*. New York: Cosimo.

———. (1925) 1967. *Science and the Modern World*. New York: The Free Press.

———. 1927. *Symbolism: Its Meaning and Effect*. New York: Fordham University Press.

———. (1929) 1967. *The Aims of Education*. New York: The Free Press.

———. (1929) 1978. *Process and Reality: An Essay in Cosmology*. New York: The Free Press.

———. (1933) 1967. *Adventures of Ideas*. New York: The Free Press.

———. (1938) 1968. *Modes of Thought*. New York: The Free Press.

———. 1961. *Interpretation of Science*. Edited by A. H. Johnson. New York: The Bobbs-Merrill Company.

Whitman, Walt. 2004. *Leaves of Grass: First and "Death-Bed" Editions*. New York: Barnes and Noble Classics.

Wirth, Jason. 2003. *The Conspiracy of Life: Meditations on Schelling and His Time*. Albany: SUNY Press.

———. 2011 "Schelling's Contemporary Resurgence." *Philosophy Compass* 6 (9): 585–98.

———. 2014. "Nature of Imagination." In *The Palgrave Handbook of German Idealism*. Edited by Altman, M. NY: Palgrave Macmillian.

———. 2015. *Schelling's Practice of the Wild: Time, Art, Imagination*. Albany: SUNY Press.

Wolfson, Elliot. 2006. *Alef, Mem, Tau: Kabbalistic Musings on Time, Truth, and Death*. Berkeley: UC Press.

Wyman, Mary A. 1956. "Whitehead's Philosophy of Science in Light of Wordsworth's Poetry." In *Philosophy of Science* 23.

Zajonc, Arthur. 1993. *Catching the Light: The Entwined History of Light and Mind*. Oxford: Oxford University Press.

Zucker, Francis. 1977. "Three Counter Strategies to Reductionism in Science." In *Mind in Nature: The Interface of Science and Philosophy*, edited by John B. Cobb, Jr. and David R. Griffin, 43–59. Washington, DC: University Press of America.

Name Index

Abram, David, 194, 207
Adams, George, 195ff
Amrine, Frederick, 12
Aristotle, 43, 93, 173, 207, 221, 242, 24
Auxier, Randall, 29
Bachelard, Gaston, 217
Barfield, Owen, 201
Beiser, Frederick, 30, 81, 191ff, 224
Bergson, Henri, 90, 99, 142, 149, 175, 223ff
Berkeley, George, 28, 81ff, 91ff
Blake, William, 10, 127, 206ff
Bortoft, Henri, 201
Braeckman, Antoon, 33
Buhner, Stephen Harrod, 104
Čapek, Milič, 99
Coleridge, Samuel Taylor, 33, 219
Connolly, William, 125, 147ff
Copernicus, Nicolaus, 39ff, 66
Crosby, Donald, 148, 150
Deacon, Terrence, 155
Descartes, René, 14, 17ff, 28, 41, 43, 63-66, 70-71, 74, 82, 84, 86, 92, 114, 118, 149, 155, 187
Desmet, Ronald, 102, 181, 194ff
Deleuze, Gilles, 17ff, 26ff, 35, 48ff, 124ff, 131, 136ff, 165–75, 217, 225–39, 242ff
Eastman, Timothy, 181
Einstein, Albert, 96, 98, 193, 199
Euclid, 97ff, 102, 111, 177, 196ff
Fawcett, Douglas, 154
Fichte, Johann Gottlieb, 30ff, 35, 48, 54, 128, 132, 204
Förster, Eckart, 128, 182-190
Galilei, Galileo, 63ff, 70, 149, 182
Gare, Arran, 32
Goethe, Johann Wolfgang von, 31, 54, 68ff, 204
Grant, Iain Hamilton, 31ff, 47, 105, 170, 172, 179, 188, 191ff, 203, 223ff
Griffin, David Ray, 28
Guattari, Felix, 35, 131, 217, 226ff, 231–39, 244ff
Hallyn, Fernand, 40
Hamrick, William, 32ff, 193, 197, 199
Hartshorne, Charles, 36, 149
Hegel, Georg Wilhelm Friedrich, 30ff, 35, 48, 51ff, 58, 83, 122, 171, 173, 203ff, 207ff, 214, 222, 237
Heidegger, Martin, 30, 135ff, 194
Herstein, Gary, 29
Homer, 26, 216
Howe, Thomas J., 140, 144, 161
Hume, David, 28, 41ff, 53, 83, 93ff, 113ff, 118, 208, 211
James, William, 30, 67ff, 142ff, 149
Kant, Immanuel,
  Critique of Pure Reason, 17, 25ff, 34ff, 40ff, 80-89, 100, 109, 111ff, 135ff, 177, 181ff, 185, 189, 201
  Prolegomena, 23, 25, 27, 42, 81, 97, 178, 181
  Idea for a Universal History, 60
  Groundwork of the Metaphysics of Morals, 51
  Metaphysical Foundations of Natural Science, 181
  Critique of Practical Reason, 48, 50, 124, 135ff
  Critique of Judgment, 20, 29, 34, 37, 49, 54-62, 112, 136, 181ff, 219ff
  Anthropology, 134
  Opus Postumum, 20, 24, 129, 181–90, 220
Kaufmann, Walter, 126
Keller, Catherine, 47, 126, 146ff, 157ff, 225, 234, 246ff
Kelly, Sean, 12, 225
King, Jr., Martin Luther, 46

259

Latour, Bruno, 71, 148
Leibniz, Gottfried Wilhelm, 28, 65, 69, 76, 92, 127, 165ff, 179
Lucas, George, 23, 28ff, 32, 36, 64
Magee, Glenn, 58, 173, 237
Marder, Michael, 188, 207–11, 213, 216–24
Matthews, Bruce, 31, 132, 138, 169, 220, 222, 233
McDermott, Robert, 12
McGilchrist, Iain, 11, 18ff
Merleau-Ponty, Maurice, 33, 165ff, 192ff, 197, 199, 205
Miller, Elaine, 214
Murphy, Michael, 149
Nassar, Dalia, 31
Newton, Isaac, 20, 28, 50, 62ff, 64, 66, 70, 76, 80, 91, 130, 149, 179, 184, 186, 198ff, 220
Nietzsche, Friedrich, 20, 58, 124ff, 139–48, 150, 152ff, 159ff, 175
Norman, Judith, 140, 159ff
Panikkar, Raimon, 13ff, 20ff, 48, 159, 212, 225, 227
Penrose, Roger, 154
Pinkard, Terry, 30ff, 83, 87, 132
Plato, 24ff, 30, 40, 47ff, 69, 79, 125, 130, 139, 151, 157, 162, 210, 212, 217ff, 223ff, 227, 235, 237, 241ff, 245

Plotinus, 210ff, 215
Poincaré, Henri, 97ff, 102
Pred, Ralph, 156, 158
Ramey, Joshua, 233, 243
Russell, Bertrand, 30, 98ff, 101
Sallis, John, 20, 124ff, 162ff
Schelling, Caroline, 140
Schelling, Friedrich Wilhelm Joseph von,
Ideas for a Philosophy of Nature, 56, 105, 128, 186, 200
On the World-Soul, 130, 188, 191
First Outline of a System of the Philosophy of Nature, 47, 131, 137
System of Transcendental Idealism, 83, 136
Philosophy and Religion, 90, 132, 198, 229
Essence of Human Freedom, 14ff, 26, 31, 132, 137, 140, 145, 151, 160, 171, 226
Clara, 191
Ages of the World, 56, 67, 80, 104, 132, 139ff, 159, 172ff, 177, 213, 223, 230, 232, 236, 240, 244ff
On the History of Modern Philosophy, 27, 35, 129ff, 192
The Grounding of Positive Philosophy, 112, 131, 133, 169, 233
Philosophy of Mythology, 33, 67, 126, 159
Schickler, Jonael, 207ff
Spinoza, Baruch, 28, 65, 92, 127, 132, 150, 179
Sherman, Jacob H., 12, 229
Schultz, Alexander, 16ff, 85
Shaviro, Steven, 73, 173
Snow, Dale, 132, 235
Steiner, Rudolf, 19, 24, 40, 120, 123ff, 157, 196ff, 207, 214ff
Stengers, Isabelle, 65, 117, 148, 229ff, 234
Swimme, Brian, 12
Tarnas, Richard, 12, 14
Toulmin, Stephen, 66
Van Der Veken, Jan, 32, 193, 197, 199
Warnock, Mary, 60
Watts, Alan, 12
Weiss, Eric, 12
Weber, Michel, 153
Wolfson, Elliot R., 159
Whicher, Olive, 195, 201
Whitehead, Alfred North,
Universal Algebra, 101, 195
Mathematical Concepts of the Material World, 98, 195
Principles of Natural Knowledge, 154, 187, 194
The Concept of Nature, 32, 65, 67,

80, 96, 99, 169, 183
The Principle of Relativity, 99, 180, 194ff
Science and the Modern World, 15, 19, 32ff, 63ff, 66, 69ff, 72ff, 76, 78, 83ff, 90ff, 106, 115ff, 125ff, 133, 149, 187, 231, 234
Symbolism, 119, 202, 244
The Aims of Education, 99, 130
Process and Reality, 27ff, 34, 36, 41, 44, 47ff, 55, 67, 71-80, 88ff, 106ff, 112ff, 116ff, 121ff, 125, 134, 143ff, 150ff, 153, 156, 160, 170, 179ff, 198, 202, 205, 211ff, 223, 225ff, 230ff, 240
Adventures of Ideas, 112, 115ff, 163ff, 167, 170, 172ff, 175, 198ff, 223, 240ff
Modes of Thought, 13, 69, 89ff, 108ff, 120, 132, 143ff, 170, 174ff, 201, 204, 230ff
Interpretation of Science, 93ff, 101ff, 115
Whitman, Walt, 10
Wirth, Jason, 13, 31, 131ff, 140, 165, 203ff, 206, 226, 230, 232, 246
Wordsworth, William, 33
Wyman, Mary, 33
Zajonc, Arthur, 68

www.ingramcontent.com/pod-product-compliance
Lightning Source LLC
Chambersburg PA
CBHW060408130526
44592CB00046B/1020